Handbook of Oregon Birds

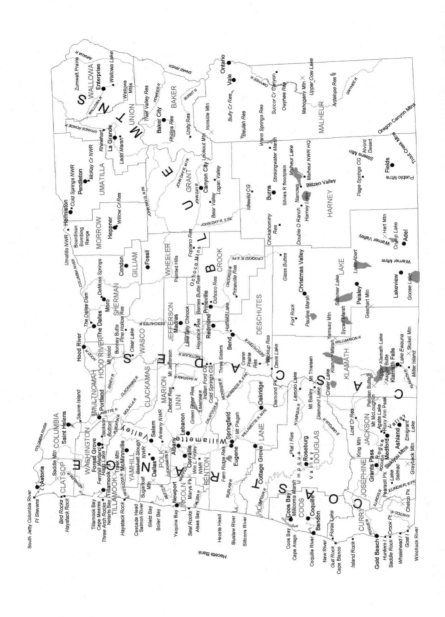

Handbook of Oregon Birds

A FIELD COMPANION TO *BIRDS OF OREGON*

Hendrik G. Herlyn and Alan L. Contreras

Illustrations by Ramiel Papish

Oregon State University Press
Corvallis

The paper in this book meets the guidelines for permanence and durability of the Committee on Production Guidelines for Book Longevity of the Council on Library Resources and the minimum requirements of the American National Standard for Permanence of Paper for Printed Library Materials Z39.48-1984.

Library of Congress Cataloging-in-Publication Data
Herlyn, Hendrik G.
  Handbook of Oregon birds : a field companion to birds of Oregon / Hendrik G. Herlyn and Alan L. Contreras.
    p. cm.
  Includes bibliographical references and index.
  ISBN 978-0-87071-571-6 (alk. paper)
  1. Birds--Oregon. 2. Birds--Oregon--Identification. I. Contreras, Alan, 1956- II. Title.

  QL684.O6H47 2009
  598.09795--dc22

                              2009011327

First published in 2009 by Oregon State University Press
Printed in the United States of America

Oregon State University Press
121 The Valley Library
Corvallis OR 97331-4501
541-737-3166 • fax 541-737-3170
http://oregonstate.edu/dept/press

Dedication

To Dave Marshall, with thanks for his lifetime dedicated to knowledge and conservation of Oregon birds

Contents

Introduction

The publication of *Birds of Oregon: A General Reference* (hereinafter *BOGR*, Marshall et al. 2003, reprinted with corrections 2006) provided an excellent modern reference to the state's birds. In particular, it provided a rich baseline of information about Oregon distribution, habitat, food, and population status. The book will be the primary source for most people interested in Oregon birds for many years to come. It is of special value to researchers because of the vast amount of detail that it offers and its comprehensive references.

The editors of *BOGR* had to make a number of decisions about content, based partly on an estimate of the audience for the book and partly on the mechanical limits on what can be put into a single volume. Except for the spectacular four-volume *Birds of British Columbia* (Campbell et al. 1997-2001), which serves as a shining if unreachable beacon for mere mortals writing bird books, state and regional books are today issued as single volumes. This was not always the case. Early bird books for Washington, New York, Colorado, and California were issued as multi-volume sets. However, the cost and market for such books today is generally considered prohibitive.

Plan of this book

Our intent in the present *Handbook* is to provide a "field-friendly" condensation of the status and distribution material from *BOGR*, plus additional detail on some aspects of Oregon ornithology that, while discussed in *BOGR*, are less emphasized and would benefit from some additional attention. We have also included some identification material that we think will be useful to Northwest observers because it focuses on issues that are not covered in sufficient detail in standard field guides. Our intent in this book is to cover in a manner useful to field observers the following aspects of Oregon ornithology.

Populations—By populations we mean subspecies and other geographically distinct groups that breed, move, or winter separately from other units of the same species. Examples of a population for purposes of this book include populations of Canada Geese, Hermit Thrushes, and Fox Sparrows. These are mapped when doing so will make understanding ranges easier.

Breeding density—*BOGR* provides an excellent overview of breeding distribution, but for reasons of space, density data from the Breeding Bird Survey and other such surveys were not used extensively. That information is used in greater detail as the basis for maps in this volume. Local observers commented on these maps and adjustments were made as needed.

Winter distribution—Most bird books focus on breeding-season distribution. Winter-distribution maps for many Oregon bird populations are included here.

Movements—The seasonal movements of populations are discussed in enough detail to allow the reader to know the origins and movement patterns of birds found at any location and season in Oregon. Much is not known about these movements, of course. Average spring arrival dates are shown for many species in the following format:

COOS	CLAT	LANE	BENT	PORT	CENT	MALH
5 Mar		2 Mar	12 Mar	21 Feb	18 Mar	28 Feb

The average arrival dates, usually based on at least ten years of data, are shown for Coos Co. (courtesy Tim Rodenkirk), Clatsop Co. (Mike Patterson), central Lane Co. (Tom Mickel), Benton Co. and adjacent valley areas (Alan McGie), metro Portland (Adrian and Christopher Hinkle), central Oregon (Craig Miller), and Malheur National Wildlife Refuge (refuge data). The Portland-area data were compiled and produced for the first time for this book; other compilations represent long-standing local collections. These dates provide a sense of the movement of many species in spring.

Identification—It is said that there can't be too many identification guides. It is also said that most such books could be dispensed with. Our intent in this book is to discuss only identification problems that seem too lightly touched on by the principal field guides, or for which Northwest observers have a practical need for information presented in a particular way. These sections will not attempt to replicate work in the most detailed references, though it may refer readers to those references for additional detail. Certain issues that are of special interest to Oregon observers (e.g., gulls and *Catharus* thrushes) are discussed in more detail.

Vagrants—BOGR included a brief summary of the status of vagrant birds in Oregon. This book provides a more detailed look at the more unusual birds to occur in Oregon, including a discussion of when, where, and under what conditions they occur. OBRC data are updated through the end of 2008, with selected additional records noted. Species that are currently on the OBRC review list are indicated by either a single (*) or double (**) asterisk preceding the species name. A single asterisk means that there is at least one record verified by photograph, specimen, video, or sound recording. A double asterisk indicates unverified species for which there is a sight record only. New sightings of any review species in Oregon should be carefully documented, and a written report along with any supporting evidence should be submitted to the OBRC.

This book does not discuss habitat, food, or status outside Oregon, or conservation issues except insofar as such issues make a natural cameo appearance within the discussion of one of our core subjects, for example the role of population changes elsewhere as a likely source of Oregon's records of Glossy Ibis or the role of forest practices in expansion of the range of Wrentit.

Citations—Few citations have been included in this volume for reasons of space. Readers in search of references should consult *BOGR*, which is designed to be a reference volume. In a few cases, a new reference has been added to the present volume. Taxonomy follows that in *BOGR*, plus any subsequent changes adopted by the American Ornithological Union.

Distribution maps—For most species, either a winter or a breeding range map is provided. In some cases where the winter range differs markedly from the summer distribution, two maps are shown. For a few species a migration route map is included. Unless otherwise noted, the map is of breeding range. Most maps show differing densities as two shades of gray. Common species that use essentially all plausible habitat in the state, e.g., American Robin or Mallard, are not mapped.

Vagrant occurrence maps and graphs—Each OBRC species with at least five records has a record map and seasonal graph, in order to provide another way of looking at the patterns of occurrence. The map shows single records as a small dot and multiple records as a large dot. In addition, some species no longer on the OBRC review list have dot maps showing accepted records in order to provide observers with an idea of occurrence. Likewise, split-month seasonality graphs are provided for most vagrants in order to provide observers with a guide to what to expect (or look for) at a particular time of year.

Illustrations—We chose to commission illustrations for this book based on what we thought Oregon field observers needed. In general, this meant species that are either not well illustrated in the standard field guides (e.g., juv. sparrows and overhead swallows), or those that provide regular challenges to Oregon observers owing to unique conditions in the Northwest (e.g., flying alcids).

The editors recommended a package of illustrations to the birding community via Oregon Birders On Line and we made a number of changes and additions to our list based on the responses received. We chose Oregon artist Ramiel Papish to produce the original art. Photographs from a number of photographers were used when we thought that photos would accomplish our purposes better than original art would.

Abbreviations

BOGR	*Birds of Oregon: A General Reference*
c.	central
Cal.	California
CBC	Christmas Bird Count
CG	Campground
Co.	County
Cr.	Creek
e.	east(ern)
fm	fathoms
ft	feet
HQ	Headquarters
Hwy	Highway
I.	Island
imm.	immature
juv.	juvenile
L.	Lake
mi	mi.
mtn(s).	mountain(s)
n.	north(ern)
Nat. Ant. Ref.	National Antelope Refuge
NF	National Forest
NP	National Park
NWR	National Wildlife Refuge
OBBA	Oregon Breeding Bird Atlas
OBRC	Oregon Bird Records Committee
Ore.	Oregon
R.	River
Res.	Reservoir
s.	south(ern)
SP	State Park
Sta.	State
U.	University
USFS	USDA Forest Service
V.	Valley
w.	west(ern)
W. A.	Wildlife Area
Wash.	Washington
wk(s)	week(s)
W.M.A.	Wildlife Management Area
yr(s)	year(s)

Acknowledgments
The following people, in addition to the original authors of *BOGR* accounts, contributed to this Handbook. Thanks to Harry Nehls for current information from the Oregon Bird Records Committee. Special thanks is due to David Bailey, Range Bayer, Wayne and Patty Bowers, Mike Denny, John Fitchen, Chuck Gates, Greg Gillson, Rich Hoyer, Tim Janzen, Carol Karlen, Ron Ketchum, Donna Lusthoff, Ron Maertz, Alan McGie, Tom Mickel, Craig Miller, Don Munson, Mike Patterson, Tim Rodenkirk, Aaron Skirvin, Mary Anne Sohlstrom, Kevin Spencer, Paul Sullivan and Dennis Vroman for their detailed comments on drafts of range maps and/or phenology tables.

We hope that you enjoy this handbook.
Hendrik Herlyn
Alan Contreras
Editors
April, 2009

Order ANSERIFORMES
Family Anatidae
Subfamily Dendrocygninae

*Black-bellied Whistling-Duck *Dendrocygna autumnalis*
Vagrant. Breeds from sc. and s. Arizona and the Gulf coast through C. and S. America.

One accepted Ore. record of a single bird photographed near Grants Pass, Josephine. Co., sometime in 1988.

*Fulvous Whistling-Duck *Dendrocygna bicolor*
Vagrant. Breeds from the southernmost U.S. through C. and S. America; also in tropical Africa and Asia.

One accepted Ore. record of a flock of 11 photographed at the N. Spit in Coos Bay, Coos Co., 14-24 Feb 1970. One of the birds was collected; the mounted specimen is now at the Audubon Society in Portland.

In addition, 1 was reported without details from Haystack Res., Jefferson Co., on 24 May 1965.

Subfamily Anserinae

Greater White-fronted Goose *Anser albifrons*
Taxonomy is complex; see *BOGR*. Migrates through Ore. Concentrates in major basins e. of the Cascades, especially Klamath. Lesser numbers stop along the lower Columbia R. and coast. Least frequent in migration along the s. Ore. coast, particularly in spring. Low densities winter in the Willamette V. and Klamath Basin. White-fronts are the first geese to migrate south; begin arriving in Summer L. and Klamath basins in late Aug. In the Klamath Basin numbers peak in late Oct and early Nov. Small numbers winter in w. Ore., the Klamath Basin, and sometimes Malheur NWR. Spring migrants are most common at Malheur NWR 15-25 Mar. Large movements over nw Ore. are typically the last wk of Apr.

> I.D. Notes: "Tule Geese" (*A. a. elgasi*) are noticeably larger than *A. a. frontalis* with proportionately larger bills and darker necks and heads. They tend to be in small groups, fly lower with a slower wing beat than the more common *frontalis*, and segregate from *frontalis*.

Emperor Goose *Chen canagica*
Rare but regular visitor in Ore. during migration and winter. Most commonly found on the coast, less often in the Willamette V. E. of the Cascades, recorded from Harney Co., the Klamath Basin, and Hart Mtn. Observed Oct - Apr. In rare cases has remained yr-round.

Snow Goose *Chen caerulescens*

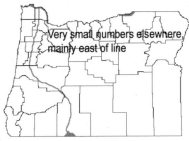

Very small numbers elsewhere, mainly east of line

winter distribution

Predominantly a spring and fall migrant, especially abundant in the large wetland and agricultural complexes of se. Ore. lake basins. In e. Ore., arrives in late Sep, becoming abundant in Oct. In w. Ore., seen as early as Sep, but most are observed beginning late Oct. Spring migration and arrival are dependent on weather conditions, but usually begin in early to mid-Feb. Usually common in Mar at major staging areas. Winters primarily along the lower Columbia R.; small flocks can sometimes be found in the Columbia Basin near the confluence of the Umatilla R. with the Columbia R. Individuals or small flocks are casual (nw) to rare (sw) in winter. Occasionally winters in the Klamath Basin, especially when weather conditions are mild. Departure from Ore. usually complete by early to mid-Apr, although a few may linger into summer.

Ross's Goose *Chen rossii*

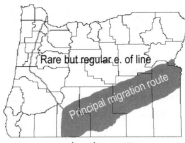

Rare but regular e. of line

Principal migration route

migration route

Common spring and fall migrant through the Klamath and Harney basins with records from most of Ore., usually singles or very small flocks. Most birds use a relatively narrow migration route across se. Ore. A few occasionally remain in the Klamath Basin through winter. Flocks arrive at Malheur NWR in very late Oct and (mostly) early Nov. During spring migration, move into the Klamath Basin in late Feb and Mar; most have departed by May.

Brant *Branta bernicla*
Two distinct subspecies in Ore., sometimes treated as separate species (see *BOGR* for taxonomic discussion). "Black" Brant (*Branta bernicla orientalis*) comprise the vast majority of brant occurring in Ore. Uncommon coastal migrant; winters in small numbers locally, mostly

at Yaquina Bay and the large bays of Tillamook Co. Rare inland. Arrivals in Ore. bays, probably of imms., sometimes as early as late Aug. Larger numbers of all ages arrive in late Oct or early Nov. The onset of northward movement in Ore. is often not clearly delineated and may vary from yr to yr, starting as early as Jan but usually from mid-Apr through mid-Jun to as late as mid-Jul. Northward flight along the coast is commonly observed in Mar and Apr. A few summer in Ore.

The pale-bellied "Atlantic" Brant (*B.b. bernicla*) occurs as a vagrant to Ore., usually found in flocks of "Black" Brant. Most reports are from the coast, but two were on Sauvie I. in Oct and Nov 1984. A brant observed at Yaquina Bay, Lincoln Co., during summer and fall of 1973 and another recovered at Coos Bay were characterized as pale-bellied, with nearly complete white neck markings; the identity of these birds cannot be confirmed. Since the AOU currently treats this form as conspecific with the "Black" Brant, the OBRC has not reviewed any of the past records. Any future sightings should be submitted to the OBRC.

I.D. Notes: The Cackling/Canada Goose Complex
The Willamette V./lower Columbia R. area has the most complex wintering aggregation of geese in N. America. The "white-cheeked" geese represent a very complex pattern in terms of subspecies and populations, which include both residents and long-distance migrants. Identification of these 2 recently split species is complicated by the fact that the medium-sized forms of both species (*B. c. parvipes* and *B. h. taverneri*) approach each other in size and coloration and cannot always be safely told apart in the field. The following subspecies occur in Ore.:

"Western" Canada Goose (*B. c. moffitti*): The largest of the Canada Geese, long-necked and pale-breasted.

"Dusky" Canada Goose (*B. c. occidentalis*): Similar to Western, but slightly smaller, with dark chocolate-brown breast.

"Vancouver" Canada Goose (*B. c. fulva*): Very similar to Dusky, slightly larger and darker.

"Lesser" Canada Goose (*B. c. parvipes*): Medium-sized, shorter-necked than Western, pale-breasted.

"Taverner's" Cackling Goose (*B. h. taverneri*): Very similar to Lesser, but with slightly rounder head, shorter neck, and darker breast.

"Ridgways" Cackling Goose (*B. h. minima*): Smallest of the "white-cheeked" geese, short-necked and compact, with a tiny bill. Breast variable, but usually rather dark brown. Sometimes with partial (rarely complete) neck ring.

> "Aleutian" Cackling Goose (*B. h. leucopareia*): Similar to Cackling, but slightly larger and lighter-breasted. Squarish head with reduced white cheek-patch, usually with a complete white ring at base of neck.

See *BOGR* for more detailed discussion of identification and movements of subspecies.

Cackling Goose *Branta hutchinsii*
A common winter resident in the Willamette V. and lower Columbia R. (subspecies *minima* and *taverneri*). Transient during migration on the coast, Klamath and other e. Ore. basins. Leave Ore. in late Apr. Non-breeders may not leave wintering grounds until early to mid-May. "Aleutian" subspecies primarily coastal in small numbers, occasionally in the Willamette V.

Canada Goose *Branta canadensis*
The "Western" Canada Goose is a widespread breeding resident throughout Ore., with the exception of mountainous and desert areas lacking reservoirs, lakes, or large rivers. Concentrations of wintering and breeding occur wherever agriculture and other human developments provide food and bodies of water provide sanctuary. Nesting begins in Mar in most areas; a few may start as early as Feb or as late as Apr. Migrant "Dusky," "Vancouver," and "Lesser" Canada Geese winter in Ore., Duskies almost exclusively in the Willamette V., Lessers more widespread throughout the state, especially as transients. "Vancouver" Canada Geese winter in small numbers in nw. Ore. The earliest fall migrants arrive in late Sep, but the first large influx usually occurs in early Nov. Most migrants arrive by Dec, but in the Ore. portion of the upper Columbia R. Basin, peak numbers may not occur until Jan.

Trumpeter Swan *Cygnus buccinator*

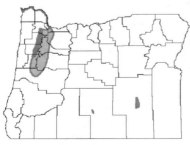

winter distribution

Locally uncommon breeder e. of the Cascades, most notably at Malheur NWR. Pinioned birds have been released on the Deschutes R. in Bend. Local elsewhere in c. and sc. Ore., mainly as single pairs. Most Malheur NWR birds remain for the winter, although some have traveled elsewhere in the e. portion of the state including Summer L. W.A., and to Cal. and Nevada. W. of the Cascades, wintering birds are most consistently noted in w. Polk Co. and Sauvie I., also along n. coast, lower Columbia R., Forest Grove, and Trojan Nuclear Power Plant. Rare s. of Polk Co. Migrants usually arrive on the coast in Dec, but sometimes as early as late Oct, leave Feb-Mar.

Tundra Swan *Cygnus columbianus*
Two subspecies; both have occurred in Ore. *C. c. columbianus* is a fairly common transient throughout the state but most abundant at large bodies of water and wetland complexes e. of the Cascades. Arrives early to mid-Oct e. of the Cascades and in early Nov on the w. side. Winters locally in large numbers,

winter distribution

with large flocks in the nw. interior, lower Columbia and locally in e. Ore. and smaller groups in sw. Ore. and on the outer coast. Spring migration numbers in the Klamath Basin and Malheur peak in mid-Feb, late Feb at Sauvie I. Lone birds occasionally summer in Ore. and sometimes associate with Trumpeter Swans.

The Eurasian subspecies, "Bewick's" Swan (*C. c. bewickii*), occurs as a very rare visitor with fewer than 10 records, usually found in flocks of Tundra Swans.

*****Whooper Swan** *Cygnus cygnus*
Vagrant. Eurasian species, rare but regular winter visitor to Alaska.
   Three accepted Ore. records:
1. One adult was photographed at Summer L. W.A., Lake Co., 11-21 Nov 1994.
2. One adult was photographed with a flock of Tundra and Trumpeter Swans near Airlie, Polk Co., 27 Nov –1 Dec 1997.
3. One was at Lower Klamath NWR, Klamath Co., on 24 Jan 1998.
In addition, there are several unreviewed records. Since the fall of 1991, up to 5 individuals have been reported wintering in the Klamath Basin along the Ore./Cal. border, and an adult with three possibly hybrid young was there 1-6 Nov 2000. During the fall of 1991, up to 3 Whooper Swans were observed at Summer L. W.A., Lake Co.

Some of these records may be of questionable origin. There is evidence that recent sightings near Airlie, Polk Co., pertain to escaped birds from a local waterfowl breeder, which may shed doubt on the origin of the 1997 record from that area. The Klamath and Summer L. birds are generally considered to be of wild origin by both the Ore. and Cal. records committees.

ID Notes: Care should be taken to separate this species from the similar "Bewick's" Swan (*Cygnus columbianus bewickii*), the Eurasian subspecies of the Tundra Swan. Bewick's Swan is smaller, with a shorter neck, and the yellow is restricted to the base of the bill.

Subfamily Anatinae

Wood Duck *Aix sponsa*
Regular breeder in the Willamette V., along slow reaches and backwaters of Cascade and Coast Range rivers, lakes, and ponds, and along the Columbia R. and coastal counties. Breeds locally in e. Ore. where wooded areas are available adjacent to slow-moving water. During spring and fall migration the species can appear almost anywhere that some habitat is available. Winters in small numbers throughout lowland w. Ore., local. Winters locally in e. Ore.; a significant concentration of hundreds is typically present at McNary NWR. Migrants begin moving n. from their wintering areas by Mar.

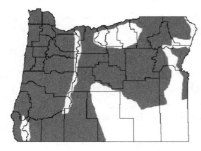 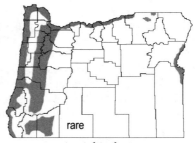

winter distribution

Gadwall *Anas strepera*
Abundant breeder locally in e. Ore., uncommon breeder in w. Ore. Common to abundant spring and fall migrant in e. Ore., common migrant in w. Ore. Least common and local in interior sw. Ore. As a winter visitant, Gadwalls are occasional in ne. Ore., uncommon but widespread elsewhere in the state. Winter numbers vary widely in the w. interior

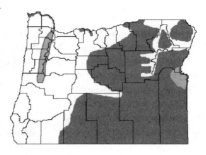

valleys and along most of the coast. Fall movements out of e. Ore. breeding areas begin in late Aug and early Sep. By late Sep migrants from more n. areas arrive and peak in mid- to late Oct. Most Gadwall depart higher-elevation areas of e. Ore. by mid-Nov. Spring movement is mainly in Apr.

*Falcated Duck *Anas falcata*

Vagrant. Breeds in e. Asia; rare visitor to the Aleutian Is. and w. Alaska.

Four accepted Ore. records, most or all of which may pertain to one returning individual:

1. One adult male was photographed at Kirk Pond, Lane Co., 14 Feb – 6 Mar 2004.
2. One adult male was photographed at Coburg, Lane Co., 16 Jan – Apr 2005.
3. One adult male was photographed at Eugene, Lane Co., on 14 Mar 2006.
4. One adult male was photographed at Coburg and Eugene, Lane Co., 13 Nov 2006 – 18 Jan 2007.

Eurasian Wigeon *Anas penelope*

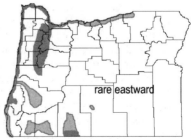

winter distribution

Rare to uncommon winter visitant e. of the Cascades. Annual in small numbers along the Columbia R. in Umatilla and Morrow cos., progressively less regular to the se. Uncommon but regular among American Wigeon flocks in w. interior valleys and on the coast. Eurasian Wigeon have been observed in fall as early as 16 Sep, but mid-Oct is a normal arrival date. Spring departure dates typically mid-Apr to mid-May, rarely to mid-June.

> I.D. Notes: Most female and imm. male American Wigeon
> show a thin dark line around the base of the bill. Eurasian
> Wigeon is not known to show this mark in any plumage. See
> Cox and Barry (2005) for additional useful distinctions.

American Wigeon *Anas americana*

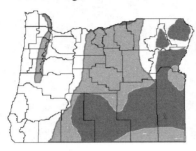

Rare to locally common breeder in e. Ore. (most common in s. half), rare in summer in w. Ore. Common to abundant migrant and wintering bird statewide. Rare summer resident in the Columbia R. estuary and very rare in the Willamette V. and coast. Migrating American Wigeon leave the state in early Apr, with most gone by very early May. Although adult males arrive at Malheur NWR in late Jul to molt, first fall migrants arrive in Aug with good-sized flocks along the coast in Sep and Oct. Statewide, wigeon numbers peak in Nov and Dec.

*American Black Duck *Anas rubripes*
Vagrant. The e. counterpart of the Mallard, with which it frequently interbreeds. Common but declining breeder in much of e. U.S. Status in Ore. is somewhat unclear, complicated by occasional introduction and the possibility of escapees.

Only 2 Ore. records have been accepted as wild birds:
1. One bird was collected by a hunter at Summer L., Lake Co., on 12 Nov 1950. The specimen is now at OSU.
2. One pure adult male was photographed and remained at Hood R., Hood R. Co., 4 Jan – mid-Dec 2000.

Several additional records have not been reviewed by the OBRC. The species was noted as an Ore. bird as early as 1887. An adult male was banded at Malheur NWR, Harney Co., on 14 Nov 1930. Another was seen there on 5 May 1977. One was banded near Ontario, Malheur Co., on 5 Mar 1951. One was observed on Sauvie I., Multnomah Co., on 26 Dec 1971, where at least 4 had been identified in hunters' bags up to that time, and 1 was at Eugene, Lane Co., on 25 Dec 1984.

Mallard *Anas platyrhynchos*
Common transient and summer and winter resident throughout the state. Large numbers breed in the marshes of se. and sc. Ore. Nesting is known in every co. Largest concentrations winter in the Klamath and Columbia basins. Other significant wintering areas include the Willamette V. and lower Columbia R. region from Portland to Astoria. Winter flocks are sometimes segregated by sex. Free-ranging domestic birds are also common in municipal parks. In w. Ore., pairs begin establishing territories by early Feb with first nesting attempts occurring late Feb, and nesting continuing through early Jun.

Blue-winged Teal *Anas discors*

COOS	CLAT	LANE	BENT	PORT	CENT	MALH
1-May		29 Apr	5 May	30 Apr	3 May	10 Apr

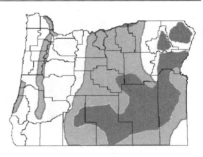

One of Ore.'s least common ducks. Uncommon summer resident in e. Ore., where it breeds in very small numbers throughout. Breeding in the Willamette V. is rare. Least regular in the sw. interior valleys. Rare irregular breeder s. to coastal Coos Co. Common spring and fall migrant in ne. Ore. and Malheur Co.; progressively less common further w.; uncommon to rare on the coast, varies yr to yr. Spring arrivals vary by region, some outriders often appear well before the main movements, rarely as early as late Feb. Fall movements are poorly known, in part owing to the difficulty of distinguishing them from Cinnamon Teal in formative or "eclipse" plumage. Based on movements of Cinnamons, numbers peak in the last half of Aug and most migrate by mid-Oct.

Cinnamon Teal *Anas cyanoptera*

COOS	CLAT	LANE	BENT	PORT	CENT	MALH
5 Mar		2 Mar	12 Mar	21 Feb	18 Mar	28 Feb

Common to fairly common breeder throughout the state, more local (major marshes) in w., uncommon to rare in sw. Ore. and high Cascades. Greatest numbers at Malheur NWR, Summer L. W.A., and Klamath Basin. Irregular local breeder along coast. Most depart e. Ore. breeding areas during Aug. Uncommon to rare in winter in w. Ore.,

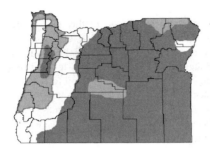

with small concentrations in favored areas not clearly related to geography, climate, or other obvious factors. Highest winter numbers often in lower Columbia R. V. Usually migrates nocturnally, and fairly early in spring, with arrival in mid-Feb and significant movement in Mar.

Northern Shoveler *Anas clypeata*

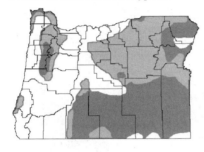

Locally common breeder in e. Ore., uncommon and sparse local breeder in w. Ore. Common spring and fall migrant statewide, rare to locally abundant winterer in e. Ore., uncommon to common in winter in w. Ore. At Malheur NWR, first birds arrive in late Feb or early Mar with the peak mid- to late Apr. Fall migrants begin arriving at Malheur NWR mid- to late Aug and peak in early Sep. Arrives on the coast as early as early Aug; widespread in small numbers by Sep.

Northern Pintail *Anas acuta*

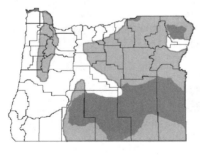

Uncommon to common breeder and abundant migrant e. of the Cascades; rare breeder but abundant migrant and winter visitant w. of the Cascades except in sw. interior. Tends to concentrate in winter, with most birds usually on Sauvie I., in the Klamath Basin, and Columbia R. below Portland. Numbers highly variable and flocks mobile s. into the Willamette V. to Fern Ridge Res. Migrates n. from wintering grounds in Feb and Mar. First migrants arrive in e. Ore. at ice breakup in mid-Feb; numbers peak in mid-Mar. N. migrants and dispersing young show up in early Aug, and by mid-Aug have become common. Fall migration peaks 25 Aug-10 Sep at Malheur. One of the earliest ducks to arrive along the outer coast with southbound birds appearing as singles and small flocks throughout Aug, common by early Sep. Often seen southbound over the near ocean during this period, sometimes accompanied by Green-winged Teal or tucked into early scoter flocks.

*Garganey *Anas querquedula*
Vagrant. Widespread in Eurasia, winters in c. and s. Africa and s. Asia. Rare but regular visitor to the outer Aleutian Is.
   Four accepted Ore. records:
1. A male in full eclipse plumage was photographed at the Nehalem sewage ponds, Tillamook Co., 17–19 Sep 1988.
2. An adult male in alternate plumage was photographed at the Bay City sewage ponds, Tillamook Co., 9–13 May 1992.
3. A male in eclipse plumage was at Fernhill Wetlands, Wash. Co., 22 Oct 2000.
4. An adult male was photographed at the Tangent sewage ponds, Linn Co., 14–17 May 2005.

While the male in alternate plumage is unmistakable, females and "eclipse" males closely resemble other species of teal and can be very difficult to identify. Males hold their dull formative plumage into winter, much longer than most ducks.

*Baikal Teal *Anas formosa*
Vagrant. Breeds from e. Siberia to Kamchatka, winters in e. Asia. Casual visitor to Alaska.
   Two accepted Ore. records:
1. An adult male was shot by a hunter e. of Finley NWR, Benton Co., on 12 Jan 1974. The mounted specimen is now at OSU.
2. An adult male was taken by a hunter on the s. side of Fern Ridge Res., Lane Co., on 31 Dec 2007.

Green-winged Teal *Anas crecca*
Two distinct subspecies, sometimes treated as separate species (see *BOGR* for taxonomic discussion). The common subspecies in N. America is the Green-winged Teal (*Anas crecca carolinensis*). In Ore., it occurs mainly as a migrant and winter visitor. Uncommon summer resident and breeder e. of Cascades and at montane lakes. Rare summer resident and very rare breeder w. of the Cascades. A common wintering bird in most of w. Ore. Birds begin moving n. from wintering areas in Feb. Most depart wintering areas by mid-Apr, but a few linger through May. Fall arrivals

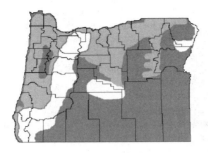

have been as early as mid-Jul, but the main migration on the coast begins in Aug with substantial numbers in Ore. coastal bays and estuaries (often lands on the open ocean, unlike most puddle ducks) in Sep. Numbers peak at Malheur NWR 1-15 Oct and most have departed by mid-Dec. In w. Ore., large numbers remain through the winter.

The Eurasian subspecies *A. c. crecca*, also known as "Common" Teal, is a rare but regular winter resident from mid-Nov to mid-Apr with an average of 2-5 reported each yr. Most reports come in mid- to late winter. Only the adult male can be separated in the field from the Green-winged Teal. There are also many reports of *A. c. crecca* X *A. c. carolinensis* hybrids.

> ID Note: In late summer and early fall, many birds can show a more heavily striped and spotted face than is illustrated in many field guides. This can give an impression similar to that of a female Garganey or Baikal Teal.

Canvasback *Aythya valisineria*
Uncommon but widespread breeder in e. Ore., mainly at larger marshes. Occasional summer resident w. of the Cascades with no known nesting records. Migrates statewide in small numbers; most common in e. Ore. and along the Columbia, uncommon in the Willamette V. and irregular in sw. interior valleys. Concentrates in winter, with most on the Columbia R. and small concentrations at Yaquina Bay and Siltcoos L. At Malheur NWR, it arrives in late Feb, numbers peak in mid-Apr, and most migrants are gone by early May. Fall movements are not noticed until Sep, with most arriving during late Oct and Nov.

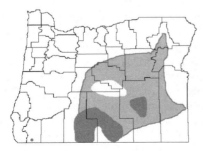

Local elsewhere if water open

winter distribution

Redhead *Aythya americana*
An uncommon summer resident in most of e. Ore.; locally common as a breeder at Malheur NWR and at other large marshes. In w. Ore., known to breed only at Fern Ridge Res. A common wintering species on the Columbia R. and the Umatilla NWR complex in Umatilla and Morrow cos., it

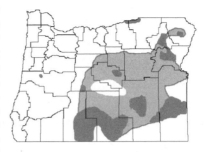

is uncommon and local in winter in the rest of e. Ore., except for many birds in the Klamath Basin in some winters. In w. Ore., very few winter inland. Uncommon in the Columbia R. estuary; local and irregular on coastal bays. At Malheur NWR, Redheads usually begin arriving in late Feb with numbers building until nesting begins in May. Fall migration begins in Aug and most birds leave the refuge by late Oct. Fall migrants may arrive relatively late on the coast, sometimes not until Nov.

Ring-necked Duck *Aythya collaris*
Breeds locally in small numbers throughout e. Ore. Breeding in w. Ore. is more patchy and has been confirmed s. to Lane and Coos cos. Fairly common in winter along the Columbia-Snake system where protected waters are available. Elsewhere in e. Ore. winters in small

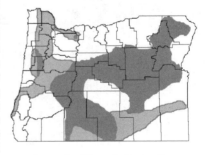

numbers as open water allows, regular in the Klamath Basin. Common to locally abundant in w. Ore. in winter, with large numbers sometimes present on protected waters away from the ocean.

Uncommon spring and fall migrant statewide, with concentrations possible on any sizable body of water during migration. Moves fairly early in spring, with significant numbers in Feb and Mar. Fall migration is protracted in e. Ore. with outriders in mid-Sep, greater numbers in Oct, a peak in Nov, and most non-wintering birds gone by early Dec. In w. Ore., most birds arrive from late Oct through Nov.

Tufted Duck *Aythya fuligula*

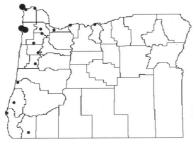

vagrant occurrence

Annual in Ore., but usually no more than a couple of birds per yr. All Ore. records have fallen between mid-Oct and early May, with most during Jan and Feb. Most are from the coastal lowlands or the Willamette V.; only 4 records e. of the Cascades.

Closely related to the scaups and often associated with them. Although Tufted superficially resembles Ring-necked Duck, more Ore. records have been with scaup than with Ring-necks. There are several Ore. records of Tufted Duck X scaup hybrids.

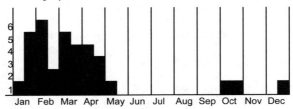

23 records (through 2001)

Greater Scaup *Aythya marila*

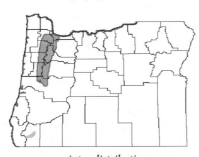

winter distribution

Abundant migrant and winter visitant in the Columbia R. estuary and common to abundant on coastal bays and lower river segments. On the coast, tends to concentrate on larger rivers. Rare and irregular in summer; does not breed. Rare to uncommon migrant and winterer in inland areas w. of the Cascades, but locally common on a few lakes and reservoirs. Regular on the Columbia R. upstream to Umatilla Co., where it is locally common. Occasional to rare migrant and winter visitant elsewhere in e. Ore. Large numbers pass along the coast with Lesser Scaup from late Mar through early May. Fall migration begins in Sep, but most move to major wintering grounds in Oct and Nov.

Lesser Scaup *Aythya affinis*
Uncommon local breeder in most e. Ore. cos. with suitable habitat. Occurs regularly on the c. Cascade lakes, although evidence of nesting is lacking. Fairly common migrant statewide on larger lakes and rivers; sometimes found in concentrations of thousands. Some birds linger s. of their breeding grounds

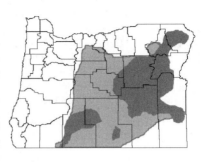

until mid-May or later. At Malheur NWR, spring migrants arrive mid- to late Feb, peak in mid-Apr, and most are gone by mid-May. Arrives very late in fall. Winters statewide where open water is available; least regular in ne. Ore. except on the Snake R., where common.

*Steller's Eider *Polysticta stelleri*
Vagrant. Breeds in arctic Siberia and on the coast of w. and n. Alaska.

One accepted Ore. record of an adult male photographed at the n. jetty of Coos Bay, Coos Co., where it remained 10-18 Feb 1992.

In addition, a well-described female was seen at Bray's Point n. of Florence, Lane Co., on 3 Feb 2007. This record has not yet been reviewed by the OBRC.

*King Eider *Somateria spectabilis*
Vagrant. Breeds circumpolar on arctic coasts. Rare but regular winter vagrant on the Pacific coast of the U.S.

Eight accepted Ore. records. All have been females or subadult males found on the ocean from rocky headlands, jetties, or in lower bays.

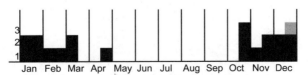

■ *King Eider: 8 records, 9 individuals*
▨ *King/Common Eider: 1 record*

1. A female was at Garibaldi Flats, Tillamook Co., on 10 and 11 Mar 1976.
2. A female was found dead at Cape Arago, Coos Co., on 18 Nov 1980. The specimen is now at the Ore. Institute of Marine Biology.
3. Two subadult males were photographed at Tillamook Head, Seaside, Clatsop Co., where they remained 16 Feb – Mar 1981.
4. A female was photographed at Bandon, Coos Co., where it remained 17 Oct 1991 – 21 Jan 1992.
5. A female was photographed at the s. jetty of the Siuslaw R., Lane Co., on 22 Oct 1993.
6. A female was photographed at Yaquina Bay, Lincoln Co., where it remained 8 Dec 1996 – 15 Feb 1997.
7. A female was photographed at Coos Bay, Coos Co., on 29 Apr 1999.
8. A female was at Seal Rock SP, Lincoln Co., on 17 Oct 1999.

In addition, a female eider at Sea Lion Caves, Lane Co., on 20 Dec 2000 was accepted as either a King or a Common Eider (*Somateria mollissima*). The latter species has never been recorded in Ore. A number of additional reports of King Eider have not yet been submitted to the OBRC or are still under review.

Harlequin Duck *Histrionicus histrionicus*

Rare local breeder in the n. Coast Range (Tillamook Co.), n. half of the Cascades (confirmed s. to Lane Co), and probably in the Wallowa Mtns. in very small numbers. Winters in small numbers along the rocky parts of the coast, where occasional non-breeding birds may summer. Migration is apparently directly to and from breeding grounds. Pairs are seen on breeding streams in greatest numbers between the second wk of Apr and the end of May, though a few pairs can be found through Jun. On the Ore. coast, numbers increase in Oct and diminish by Jun.

Surf Scoter *Melanitta perspicillata*

Abundant on salt water along the coast from fall through spring and uncommon during summer. Uncommon on fresh water near the coast. Inland, several are recorded from w. of the Cascades and a few from e. Ore. most yrs, usually in fall on large lakes and reservoirs. Arrival in nw. coastal wintering areas begins in late Aug, and numbers peak in Nov. Females begin northward migration in late Mar, but most coastal movement is from mid-Apr to mid-May. Most have left Ore. by early May. Many imms. remain in coastal wintering areas during summer.

White-winged Scoter *Melanitta fusca*
Abundant along the coast from fall through spring. Uncommon during summer on the ocean and inshore marine waters. Especially during migration peaks, they congregate farther seaward than Surf Scoters. Inland, casual to rare migrant on large water bodies on both sides of the Cascade crest, mostly Oct-Nov. They arrive as early as the first wk of July on coastal waters, and larger numbers appear from late Jul to early Sep. Most southward migration begins in Sep and extends through early Nov. A northward coastal shift begins in Mar, and most leave the coast by mid-May. Non-breeders less common off Ore. than are Surf Scoters, but small numbers may remain through the summer.

Black Scoter *Melanitta nigra*
Uncommon to locally common along the coast fall through spring, usually on the ocean; abundance is highest in n. Lincoln, Tillamook, and s. Clatsop cos. The least likely scoter to oversummer along the Ore. coast, and by far the rarest inland. A few arrive in mid-Aug; numbers peak in Oct-Dec. Most inland records are Oct-Dec. A northward coastal shift begins in Mar; breeders depart through the first half of May. A few remain off Ore. through May. Small numbers, probably yearlings, summer along the nw. coast.

Long-tailed Duck *Clangula hyemalis*
Rare to uncommon winter visitor along the coast and rare inland on the Columbia R. and on lakes throughout the state. Typically occur singly or in pairs, but small flocks have been observed along the coast. Rare but regular inland, including many e. Ore. lakes and reservoirs. Moves late in fall, most arrivals in Nov. Usually observed in Ore. from Oct through Apr, most frequently in Nov inland both w. and e. of the Cascades, and in Mar along the coast. The earliest fall record for e. Ore. is 28 Sep; the earliest fall inland w. Ore. record is 24 Oct. The latest e. Ore. record is 24 Apr, and the latest w. Ore. inland record is 1 Mar. Scattered coastal observations have occurred from May through Sep.

Note: Long-tailed Duck may be missed in quick scans of scoter flocks due to long dive times. Can be very hard to pick out against rough water owing to the "camouflage" effect of patchy plumage.

Bufflehead *Bucephala albeola*

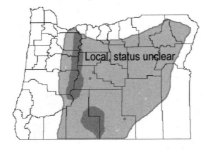

Local, uncommon breeder from c. and s. Cascades to c. Deschutes Co.; multiple summer records at lakes and reservoirs e. to Malheur Co. suggest possible breeding. Winters throughout Ore. At larger water bodies, it can be abundant, especially at coastal locations, esp. Coos Bay. Often found on very small bodies of water as well as on large lakes and rivers. Common migrant throughout the state in both spring and fall. Peak of spring migration is mid-Mar through late Apr, with a few migrants lingering into May. Small numbers of fall migrants begin arriving in Ore. in late Sep, generally peaking in late Oct or early Nov; in some yrs the first birds do not reach the outer coast until late October. Peak migration into the Klamath Basin is in late Nov and early Dec.

Common Goldeneye *Bucephala clangula*

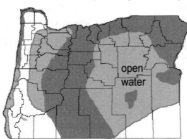

winter distribution

Rare irregular breeder in extreme ne. Umatilla Co. Very rare in summer elsewhere in ne. Ore. and in Malheur, Harney, and Klamath cos. Common in winter on larger bodies of open water in e. Ore., including the Columbia and Snake rivers. Progressively less common to w. Ore., with most birds along the Columbia R. and at the largest estuaries s. to Coos Bay. Local in small numbers at Cascade lakes and in the Willamette V.; irregular to the sw. interior valleys and s. coast. A common spring and fall migrant in most of e. Ore.; much less common in the w. They migrate early in spring; migrants at Malheur peak in Mar and early Apr and most are gone from w. Ore. by late Apr; a few stragglers may persist until mid-May. Can appear in fall in late Sep, but usually not seen until late Oct or Nov, with peak numbers in early Dec.

Barrow's Goldeneye *Bucephala islandica*

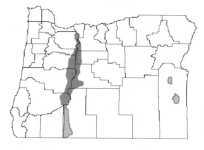
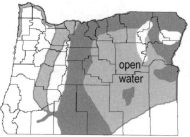

winter distribution

Uncommon from the Cascades eastward yr-round, but may concentrate in winter at certain favored spots. Breeds in small numbers at numerous montane lakes in the Cascades s. to s. Douglas Co. Rare local irregular breeder in the Blue and Wallowa mtns. and in sc. Malheur Co. Winters mainly on Cascade lakes and streams (uses smaller streams more often than does Common Goldeneye) and throughout c. and e. Ore. Largest numbers are typically found on the Columbia-Snake system w. to the Columbia R. Gorge. It is a rare winter visitant and transient w. of the Cascades, mainly nw., and is casual to rare to the sw. interior valleys and on the coast south of Lincoln Co. Wintering birds depart for breeding areas in mid-Apr.

*Smew *Mergellus albellus*
Vagrant. Breeds across n. Eurasia. Rare but regular migrant in the w. Aleutians, casual in w. Alaska.

Three Ore. records have been accepted as wild birds:
1. An adult male was photographed on both sides of the Columbia R. around Stevenson, Wash., and Cascade Locks, Hood R. Co., Ore., where it remained 26 Jan – 1 Apr 1991.
2. An adult male, likely the same bird, was in the same area 2 Jan – 16 Feb 1992.
3. An adult male was photographed at Malheur NWR HQ, 26 – 28 Feb 2001.

There are a few additional reports that may pertain to escaped birds.

Hooded Merganser *Lophodytes cucullatus*
The breeding range in Ore. is not entirely clear, but they breed locally throughout the Willamette V. w. to the coast and s. to Coos Co. Also breeds locally in the n. and c. Cascades and in e. Ore. Irregular local

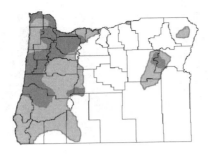

breeder in sw. Ore. During migration, widespread though uncommon across Ore., usually in sheltered areas of lakes and ponds and much less commonly on lower estuaries. Winters statewide on sheltered open water; often found on flooded pastureland. Migrants in Ore. begin arriving in Feb and peak in Mar, adding to the winter population. Apparently move n. after the end of the breeding season. Arrive on wintering grounds in early Oct and numbers usually peak by late Nov.

Common Merganser *Mergus merganser*

Widespread breeder, sometimes on surprisingly small streams, mainly in upland areas, less common on valley floors. Nearly absent as a breeder in the Columbia Basin and the Great Basin, where open water is scarce. Although they avoid lower estuaries during most months, large estuarine flocks of basic-plumage birds form following breeding. Such flocks often appear overnight in late Sep or early Oct along the Ore. coast. A common migrant and winter resident where open water remains. Migrants arrive in Ore. beginning in Feb, adding to the wintering population. Pairs and small flocks form prior to the May departure of migrants to breeding areas in Ore. or to the n. Pairs are often observed on rivers in the Cascades during Mar and Apr. Fall migrants provide the highest concentrations of the yr, peaking Oct through late Nov; many leave by mid-Dec.

Red-breasted Merganser *Mergus serrator*

Winter resident. Fairly common from fall through spring, mostly in coastal bays and estuaries but occasionally on the open ocean. Rare but regular inland migrant (statewide), especially in fall, and a few may winter on the Columbia R. Migration timing on the Ore. coast is poorly known. A few have been reported along the coast as early as Aug, but most arrive in Oct or Nov. A few have also been reported inland by late Aug, but they are most commonly seen from Nov through Jan. Northward migration from mid-Mar to early May peaks in Apr. Red-breasted Mergansers observed in Ore. during the summer are non-breeders.

Ruddy Duck *Oxyura jamaicensis*
Locally common e of the Cascades in summer, particularly in freshwater marsh complexes in sc. and se. Ore. Uncommon summer resident in ne. Ore.; nests sporadically and very locally. Irregular breeder at scattered sites in nw. Ore., s. to Lane and montane Douglas cos. Moves into w. interior valleys

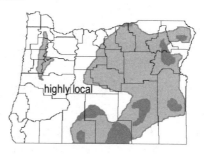

and coastal estuaries to winter, with many migrants using Upper Klamath L. and Malheur NWR en route. Concentrates in winter, with hundreds using one site and none at nearby areas. Spring migration w. of the Cascades from Feb through early Apr, though individuals may remain along the coast into early May. First appear at Malheur NWR in late Feb, with numbers peaking in late Apr or early May. Fall migration begins in Sep and continues into Dec when numbers peak at coastal locations. Many remain at open water in e. Ore. until late fall.

Order GALLIFORMES
Family Phasianidae
Subfamily Phasianinae

Chukar *Alectoris chukar*

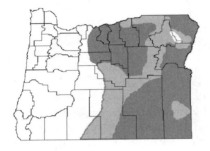

Common permanent introduced resident of e. Ore. Populations are distributed in rocky steppe habitats. Summer distribution is closely linked to water availability. During winter Chukars use snow-free slopes or lower-elevation valleys.

Gray Partridge *Perdix perdix*

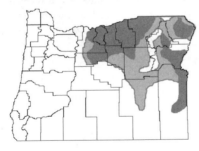

Introduced species, currently thrives mainly in the valleys of the ne. and Columbia Basin cos. A few still occur in the Malheur-Harney lakes basin and in the n. half of Malheur Co. Resident throughout the yr. Relatively sedentary, coveys seldom travel more than a quarter of a mile.

Ring-necked Pheasant *Phasianus colchicus*

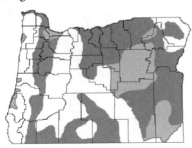

Introduced and somewhat local, with numbers fluctuating and augmented by additional introductions. Most abundant in the agricultural regions of e. Ore. Local in the Willamette V., probably sustainable only by reintroductions. Most common in the agricultural areas of n. Malheur and Harney cos., the "wheat belt" cos. along the Columbia R. in c. Ore., and the foothill regions of the Blue Mtns. Generally rare and local along the coast, often only in dune grass.

Subfamily Tetraoninae

Ruffed Grouse *Bonasa umbellus*

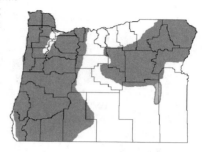

Common but retiring resident throughout most forested regions of the state. See *BOGR* for taxonomy. Two color morphs occur, with some intermediates. Most in w. Ore. are red, those in e. Ore. are gray; however, both morphs occur in mixed broods on both sides of the state. It is not present in riparian or aspen stands of se. Ore. desert regions.

Greater Sage-Grouse *Centrocercus urophasianus*

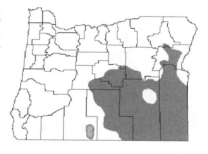

The northernmost Ore. population is in the Baker V. Most common in the se. desert regions; generally limited to sagebrush habitats. Males begin attending leks in late Feb. Hens attend leks later, peaking in late Mar. Peak lek attendance by males is in mid-Apr. Sage-grouse move to wet meadows, lakebeds, or irrigated fields in late summer. Timing of these movements depends on weather, which influences forb availability. During winter, sage-grouse concentrate in large flocks where sagebrush is available, not buried by snow.

Spruce Grouse *Falcipennis canadensis*

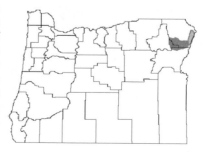

Typically uncommon in conifer forest above 5,000 ft in the Wallowa Mtns. of Baker, Union, and Wallowa cos. They may still inhabit the Hat Point area on the rim of Hells Canyon, but have not been seen there in recent yrs. The subspecies present in Ore. is *F. c. franklinii*. Spruce Grouse are occasionally reported from the n. Blue Mtns. outside the Wallowas, but no reports have been confirmed. They are most frequently seen in summer in Engelmann spruce, lodgepole pine, and subalpine fir forests.

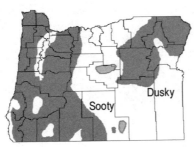

breeding range map for both Dusky Grouse and Sooty Grouse

Dusky Grouse
Dendragapus obscurus
Dusky Grouse is resident in the Blue and Wallowa Mtns. and is reported occasionally west to the Ochocos. It is a bird of dense evergreen forests and has no significant migratory movements.

Sooty Grouse
Dendragapus fuliginosus
Sooty Grouse is a fairly common resident in coniferous forests from the Cascade crest to the coast, with broad areas of absence around low-elevation urban and unforested valley areas. Male breeding behavior usually increases in Mar and peaks in Apr. Travel toward winter range begins in early summer; females with broods have limited mobility and delay travel until mid- or late summer.

Sharp-tailed Grouse *Tympanuchus phasianellus*
Sharp-tailed Grouse were considered extirpated from the state by the 1970s, but recent reintroduction programs have had some success in ne. Ore. The subspecies in Ore., Columbian Sharp-tailed Grouse (*T. p. columbianus*) is the palest and grayest of six. A small breeding population has been established n. of Enterprise in the Parsnip Cr. drainage of Wallowa Co. since 1994. Sharp-tails have also been reported near Findley Buttes on the Zumwalt Prairie and on Tick Hill n. of Wallowa, but these sightings have not been confirmed. In the 1990s, several unconfirmed sightings were reported in Baker Co. near Little Lookout Mtn. It is possible birds could be reoccupying historic range from small populations or reintroductions in w. Idaho that are within 20 mi of Baker Co.

Subfamily Meleagridinae

Wild Turkey *Meleagris gallopavo*
Introduced. Densities are highest in forests and interspersed open habitats at low to mid-elevation in the Klamath, Ochoco, Blue, and Wallowa mtns., w. Cascades, Umpqua V., Willamette V., and ne. Cascades. Local in the Coast Range, e. Columbia Basin, High Lava Plains, and se. Cascades.

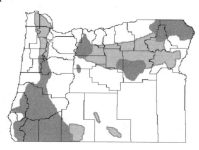

Family Odontophoridae

Mountain Quail *Oreortyx pictus*
In w. Ore., found in most forested mountainous areas, generally above 1,600 ft., but may move to valley bottoms in winter, and occasionally visits backyard bird feeders. Low numbers are found in nw. Ore. Casual along the outer coast, where it is usually found at lower elevations along the beachgrass-forest

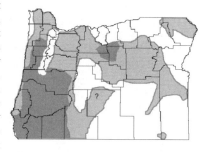

ecotone or in the edge between forest and towns, sometimes at feeders. In e. Ore., uncommon and local in c. and ne. Ore., rare s. to Malheur and Harney cos., rare in Lake and e. Klamath cos., uncommon in sw. Klamath Co.

California Quail *Callipepla californica*
It is resident statewide except for most forests of the n. Coast Range and w. Cascades; it is generally absent from the coastal plain n. of Coos Bay and is absent from high-elevation areas of the Cascade range and e. Ore. mtns. It has recently expanded up many drainages on the w. face of the Blue Mtns. to elevations of 3,500 ft in summer. It extends into the Cascades and Coast Range via lowland river valleys primarily where there are dispersed farms and residences. Common resident in rural and even some suburban areas, particularly in e. Ore. where many coveys gather at feeding stations during winter.

[**Northern Bobwhite** *Colinus virginianus*]
Introduced to Ore. The last remnants of these populations are believed to have been extirpated from Umatilla and Malheur cos. in the 1990s. The species is today considered absent from Ore. except to the extent that some birds escape from breeders or are locally released for hunting.

Order GAVIIFORMES
Family Gaviidae

Red-throated Loon *Gavia stellata*
Abundant nearshore transient and uncommon to locally common in winter, mostly within 0.5 mi from shore, along the coast, and in the lower Columbia R. estuary. It is progressively less frequent farther from the coast up the Columbia R. at least to Portland, and on lakes and large rivers. Very rare in e. Ore., with a few wintering. Imms. remain on the ocean throughout the yr, but are rare in summer at most Ore. wintering areas.

Northward flight during Mar-Jun peaks in Mar-Apr but peaks may vary by yr and even by location of observation points. Southbound movement is extended and peak dates vary yr to yr. Occurs from late Aug through Oct, peaking in early Sep; a second wave peaks from late Oct through mid-Nov, but is sometimes extended through mid-Dec. Rare in Nov at large bodies of water e. of the Cascade crest.

*Arctic Loon *Gavia arctica*
Vagrant. Formerly considered conspecific with the Pacific Loon, this species breeds across n. Eurasia and locally in w. Alaska.

Two accepted Ore. records:
1. A basic-plumaged individual was well seen and photographed at Yaquina Bay, Lincoln Co., where it remained 16 May – 7 Jun 1998.
2. One basic-plumaged bird was photographed at Brownsmead, Clatsop Co., 9 Dec 2007 – 9 Feb 2008.

In addition, there are a number of unsubmitted records of this difficult to identify species.

> ID Notes: The Arctic Loon in basic plumage can be told from the very similar Pacific Loon by its slightly larger size, obvious white flank patches that are usually visible in swimming birds, its larger bill, a flat, squarish head (reminiscent of Common Loon), an unmarked white throat without the dark "necklace" of Pacific, whiter cheeks, and a darker nape.

Pacific Loon *Gavia pacifica*
The flight of Pacific Loons by the thousands along the coast each spring and fall is one of Ore.'s most dramatic bird migrations. This is the most abundant loon off the Ore. coast (though not in estuaries), especially in Apr and May and possibly in Oct. Occasional inland in fall throughout state; regular in small numbers in Cascade lakes. Migration timing varies between yrs. Spring migration off Ore. appears more compressed than fall

but the actual timing of the movement varies from yr to yr. Northward migration begins from early to mid-Mar and extends as late as early Jun; spring peak is normally during mid-April but sometimes much later.

Promontory censuses indicate a fall peak from mid-Oct to mid-Nov. Changes in weather can result in a holdup or sudden release of thousands of birds; highest numbers have followed weather fronts in the Gulf of Alaska. Inland records pick up in Oct and Nov and extend through winter. Uncommon along the coast through most of winter, but may form rafts in late winter and spring.

> I.D. Notes: The straight bill, distinguishing Pacific from Red-throated and Yellow-billed, is less robust than that of Common Loons; Pacific's head is larger and its neck thicker than those of the Red-throated. In flight, Pacific's wing-beats are faster than those of Common. The feet appear larger, the forecrown is rounder, and the hindcrown more sloped than those of Red-throated. Fall transitional plumage extends through late Oct.

Common Loon *Gavia immer*
Common to abundant transient along coast; uncommon to locally common on large freshwater bodies; less frequent e. of the Cascades. Numbers and frequency decrease progressively upstream in Columbia R.; occasional on the Columbia R. throughout the yr from the coast to McNary Dam, Umatilla Co.

Oregon's only breeding record was on Lower Eddeeleo L., in the Waldo L. Wilderness Area, Lane Co. An adult and immature were in the Bull Run watershed nw. of Mt. Hood and two adults were on Waldo L., e. Lane Co. in summer, 1988. Jun and Jul records also come from Diamond L. Two adults with 2 well-developed juv. or imm. birds were on Waldo L. in 1948. Loon L. in Douglas Co. is named for a supposed nest of this species; the eggs were collected but their whereabouts are unknown.

Flight during migration extends to 20-25 mi from land along the coast and over a broad front inland. Common Loons are the most widespread loon in winter, occurring on both salt and fresh water and regularly on the Columbia R. to e. Ore.; this is the only loon regular on inland fresh water. In summer, most remaining imms. stay on coastal salt water. Spring migration off Ore. and Wash. peaks in Apr and May. Inland, spring flocks sometimes exceeding 400 peak in mid-Apr at Wickiup Res., Deschutes Co., while smaller numbers may be found on many sizeable inland lakes and reservoirs. Fall numbers are usually highest in Oct or Nov.

Yellow-billed Loon *Gavia adamsii*

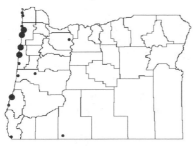

vagrant occurrence

Rare annual visitor, almost all records coastal. The majority of Ore. records are of transient birds found between early Nov and early Jun. Individuals are occasionally found from early Jul to late Sep that appear to be non-breeding, mostly subadult, summer transients. Five inland records, as far e. as Wallowa L. Often uses fairly shallow water for a loon.

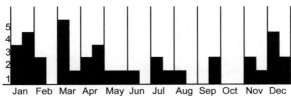

30 records (through 2000)

Order PODICIPEDIFORMES
Family Podicipedidae

Pied-billed Grebe *Podilymbus podiceps*

A common breeder in Klamath, Lake, Malheur, and Harney cos. and an uncommon local breeder in most of the rest of the state. Most winter on coastal lakes (locally very common) and in the w. interior valleys. Widespread in winter e. of the Cascades at lower elevations where open water allows. Migratory movements are not often reported, but usually most abundant e. of the Cascades when spring arrivals peak early Mar to Apr. At Malheur NWR, average arrival 11 Mar and begin leaving in mid-Aug, peak migration in Sep, and most are gone by Oct. On the coast first fall arrivals are usually in early Aug. At Upper Klamath L. numbers peak in Oct and drop sharply by Nov.

Horned Grebe *Podiceps auritus*

COOS	CLAT	LANE	BENT	PORT	CENT	MALH
			27 Feb		6 Apr	20 Apr

Rare breeder e. of the Cascades. Malheur NWR averages 4-5 pairs per summer, but nests are not found there each yr. Has also nested at Downy L., Wallowa Co., Sycan Marsh, Lake Co., and near Riley, Harney Co. Present late Jun at Upper Klamath L. where up to 10 birds have been observed. Rare along coast (non-breeders) in summer.

Uncommon spring and fall transient on lakes, reservoirs, and large rivers in and w. of the Cascades, and uncommon to common e. of the Cascades. In winter, common along coast in estuaries and near-shore ocean, uncommon in the Willamette and Umpqua valleys, and rare e. of the Cascades. Numbers increase in early spring along coast, with a peak in early Apr. Most have departed w. Ore. by early May. Transients are fairly common during Apr in high Cascade and e. Ore. lakes and reservoirs. At Malheur NWR, earliest arrival is 8 Apr, mean 20 Apr. At Malheur NWR, breeders depart Aug-Sep. During Oct-Nov, small flocks are common at many montane and Great Basin lakes. Earliest fall arrival at Diamond L. 9 Oct, maximum 20 on 16 Oct 1989, latest fall departure 21 Nov. They reach the outer coast by late Aug to early Sep. Most depart e. Ore. by early Dec.

Red-necked Grebe *Podiceps grisegena*

This is the least common grebe in Ore. in all seasons. Five to 20 birds at Rocky Pt., Upper Klamath L. form the only consistent breeding population in Ore. Breeding records away from Upper Klamath L. include Howard Prairie Res., Jackson Co. (twice), and 1 breeding record each at Malheur NWR, Indian L., Umatilla Co., Big Lava L., Deschutes

Co. and Klamath Marsh. There are a small number of summer records not involving known breeding.

The Red-necked Grebe reaches its greatest numbers during winter along the coast, esp. in Lincoln Co. Extremely rare in winter away from the coast. During peak fall and spring migration can be locally uncommon on larger waterways in the Willamette V. Rare and local e. of the Cascades in winter. Migration to inland breeding areas occurs Mar to early May while coastal numbers decrease. Arrive in breeding areas by mid-Apr. By early Sep most depart breeding areas and numbers increase coastally Aug to Nov, with a peak in Oct.

Eared Grebe *Podiceps nigricollis*

COOS	CLAT	LANE	BENT	PORT	CENT	MALH
					5 Apr	30 Mar

This species has been reported breeding in nearly every e. Ore. co., but principal breeding areas are in Klamath, Lake, and Harney cos. Local in Wallowa, Union, and Grant cos. Not known to summer or breed near coast. In winter, very uncommon on coastal bays and in the

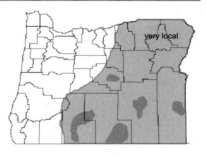

Willamette and Rogue valleys; in some yrs none can be found in some areas. Very rare in winter most yrs in e. Ore.; greater numbers winter e. of the Cascades with mild temperatures. Numbers decrease on coast in Feb. Mean spring migrant arrival 30 Mar at Malheur NWR; mid-Mar in Klamath Co. Migrates mid-Aug in e. Ore.; peaks at Malheur NWR Sep to early Oct. In Aug and Sep, it is abundant at L. Abert, uncommon in the Cascades, rare to uncommon in the Willamette and Rogue valleys, and rare on the coast.

Western Grebe *Aechmophorus occidentalis*

Common breeder in e. Ore., especially at large lakes and marshes having open water in Klamath, Harney, Goose L., and Warner basins. Also breeds at numerous smaller water bodies. W. of the Cascades it first bred at Fern Ridge Res., Lane Co., in the 1990s; it is now a regular breeder there in significant numbers. In winter, most common in coastal bays, on the ocean near shore, and in the Columbia R. estuary. Small numbers winter in the Willamette V. and even fewer e. of the Cascades,

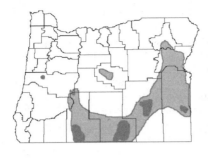

though small flocks winter locally. During spring and fall, concentrations appear on Cascade mountain lakes and the Columbia R. Earliest arrival is 10 Mar in Klamath Co.; average arrival is 20 Mar at Malheur NWR. Begin departure from breeding areas in Aug; peaking Sep-Oct. Most depart from Malheur NWR by Nov.

Clark's Grebe *Aechmophorus clarkii*

COOS	CLAT	LANE	BENT	PORT	CENT	MALH
					12 May	4 May

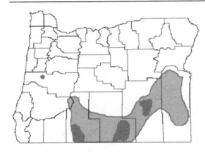

Breeding range in Ore. overlaps that of Western Grebe, but Clark's is not as common. Upper Klamath L. and Goose L. in Lake Co. and Cal.'s Modoc Co. support the largest known concentrations of this species within its range. Clark's Grebe has been present during summer on Fern Ridge Res., Lane Co., in recent yrs and has bred in increasing numbers since 1998. It is unclear what proportion of *Aechmophorus* grebes that spend spring and fall in high Cascade lakes are Clark's. In winter, this species occurs in w. Ore., mostly along the coast in very low numbers. Earliest arrival in the Klamath Basin is 10 Mar 1985. No data on departure dates from breeding areas, but assumed to be similar to Western Grebe; see that species for additional details.

Order PROCELLARIIFORMES
Family Diomedeidae

*Shy Albatross *Thalassarche cauta*
Vagrant. Extremely rare offshore visitor from the s. hemisphere; vagrants have been recorded off Wash. (twice) and Cal. (3 times).
   Two accepted Ore. records:
1. A subadult was photographed at Heceta Bank, Lincoln Co., on 5 Oct 1996.
2. One bird was photographed at Heceta Bank, Lincoln Co., on 7 Oct 2001.

*Wandering Albatross *Diomedea exulans*
Vagrant. Extremely rare offshore visitor from s. hemisphere.
   One accepted Ore. record of a bird well photographed off Newport, Lincoln Co., on 13 Sep 2008.
   There is only 1 previous record for N. America, a bird found on land in Cal. in 1967 (AOU 1998). A bird seen off Cal. in fall 2008 is thought to be the same as the Ore. bird.

Laysan Albatross *Phoebastria immutabilis*
Uncommon winter visitor and rare at other seasons far offshore. In 30 at-sea observations where distance was recorded, sightings ranged from 12 to 529 mi offshore; median 30 mi. We are only aware of 4 sightings from shore. Primarily found seaward of the continental shelf near areas of strong upwelling and along boundaries between different water masses. The Laysan Albatross appears off the W. Coast mainly in fall and winter. Ore. records exist for every month with most for Dec-Mar and Aug-Oct; the latter is the season of the majority of historical oceanic birding trips. Record number of birds seen was 15 in Jan 1963, 43 on 13-14 Dec 1998, and 94 on 13 Dec 1999, all from cruise or research vessels.

Black-footed Albatross *Phoebastria nigripes*
Regular visitant spring through fall offshore; irregular in winter. Greatest abundance occurs at shelf break and upper slope in water depth over 100 fm. Local concentrations occur around fishing vessels. Locations with higher than average numbers off Ore. are Astoria Canyon off the Columbia R., off Cape Blanco, and around the margins of Heceta and Stonewall banks off the c. coast. It is rare within 15 mi of shore or in less than 75 fm of water. Occurs in low numbers off the continental shelf. Arrives in good numbers off the Ore. coast in Apr, which may correspond to the arrival of failed and non-breeding birds from nesting colonies. Numbers off Ore. and Wash. remain remarkably consistent

Apr-Sep. Numbers drop significantly by late Oct. Few, usually all-dark juvs., occur offshore in winter.

*Short-tailed **Albatross** Phoebastria albatrus*

vagrant occurrence

Vagrant. Breeds on islands off Japan and Taiwan. During the first half of the 20th century, it had come close to extinction, but recently the population is increasing again, leading to increased sightings in the ne. Pacific.

Nine accepted Ore. records:

1. An imm. was observed on a pelagic trip 32 mi. w. of Yachats, Lincoln Co., on 11 Dec 1961.
2. An imm. was seen 20 mi. sw. of the Columbia R. Bar, Clatsop Co., in Jun 1978.
3. A juv. bird was 44 nautical mi. w. of Cape Falcon, Clatsop Co., on 9 Nov 1996.
4. A juv. in first basic plumage was 21 nautical mi. w. of Sisters Rock, Curry Co., on 13 Dec 1999.
5. A juv. bird was 32 nautical mi. w. of Yachats, Lincoln Co., on 21 Oct 2000.
6. A juv. was photographed at Heceta Bank, Lincoln Co., on 24 Mar 2001.
7. A subadult was at Heceta Bank, Lincoln Co., on 12 July 2005.
8. A juv. was found dead on the beach at Seven Devils Wayside, Coos Co., on 3 Sep 2005.
9. A juv. was photographed at Perpetua Bank, Lincoln Co., on 18 Mar 2006.

In addition, there is an unsubstantiated sight record 20 mi. w. of Depoe Bay, Lincoln Co., on 19 Sep 1989. This record has not been reviewed by the OBRC.

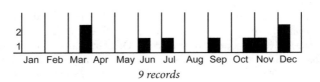

9 records

Family Procellariidae

Northern Fulmar *Fulmarus glacialis*

Irregularly common to abundant winter visitor, especially beyond 5 mi from shore. Highest concentrations are along the shelf break; but widely dispersed from inshore to deep waters beyond the continental shelf. One inland record: 9 Feb 1983 at Steamboat, Douglas Co. Variably common Jul-Mar; typically rare Apr-Jun when most of the population is near breeding colonies in Alaska. However, some of the highest densities have been in mid-summer. Peak numbers in Oct. Variable in abundance, periodically invading in large numbers in cold-water winters and remaining the following summer. May be driven inshore by strong westerly winds and seen from low headlands.

The majority of birds (8:1) off Ore. in most yrs are medium or dark colored, not light, evidently originating from the breeding colonies on the Aleutian Is. and s. Alaska. However, in some yrs, e.g., fall 2007, many light-phase birds are seen.

*Murphy's Petrel *Pterodroma ultima*

Vagrant. Breeds on islands in the sc. Pacific and disperses to Hawaii and the ne. Pacific far offshore.

Four accepted Ore. records, including 3 specimens:
1. One found dead on the beach 5 mi. s. of Newport, Lincoln Co., on 15 Jun 1981 (specimen at Smithsonian Museum of Natural History).
2. A female was found live at Horsfall Beach, Coos Co., on 6 Mar 1987. The bird died later (specimen at Los Angeles Natural History Museum).
3. A female was found dead on the beach 2 mi. s. of Cape Blanco, Curry Co., on 27 Mar 1988 (specimen at Los Angeles Natural History Museum).
4. Eleven birds were observed and photographed between 44 to 173 nautical mi. offshore between Lincoln and Curry cos., 31 Oct – 2 Nov 2005.

Several recent reports have not yet been reviewed by the OBRC. In addition, there are a number of reports of unidentified dark *Pterodroma* petrels that could not safely be separated from the very similar Solander's Petrel (*P. solandri*) or the "Dark-rumped Petrel" species pair.

Mottled Petrel *Pterodroma inexpectata*

This species breeds around s. New Zealand and the subantarctic islands and disperses to the n. Pacific and the Bering Sea. It is a rare but regular migrant far offshore from Alaska to Cal. In Ore., it occurs as a casual

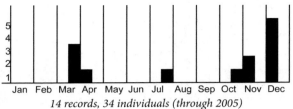

14 records, 34 individuals (through 2005)

Plus 21 deepwater records
in fall, 2005

vagrant occurrence

visitor, mainly from Nov to Apr. The majority of live observations have occurred far from shore, but there is at least one sighting from a coastal viewpoint at Boiler Bay, Lincoln Co., on 10 Dec 1987.

Most Ore. records were of single birds, but 9 were observed 60 mi. w. of Waldport, Lincoln Co., on 31 Mar 1981; a total of 62 were recorded off the s. Wash. and n. Ore. coast, of which 28 were about 97 mi. off the Ore. coast, on 19 Apr 1985; 3 were 45 mi. w. of Tillamook and Lincoln cos. on 11 Dec 1990, and 12 were found during a seabird survey 20-215 mi. off the Ore. coast 20 Oct – 2 Nov 2001.

**Juan Fernandez Petrel *Pterodroma externa*
Vagrant. Breeds on the Juan Fernandez Is. off Chile. Outside the breeding season, ranges in the e. Pacific n. to Hawaii and Middle America. Very rare vagrant to N. American waters.

One accepted sight record in Ore. of a well-described bird 51 mi. w. of Brookings on 7 Jun 2002.

**Hawaiian/Galapagos Petrel *Pterodroma phaeopygia/sandwichensis*
Vagrant. Until recently, these two closely related species were considered conspecific under the name Dark-rumped Petrel (*P. phaeopygya*). They breed in the Hawaiian and Galapagos archipelagos, respectively. Outside the breeding season, Hawaiian Petrel ranges in the e. Pacific ne. of the Hawaiian Is., and Galapagos Petrel has been recorded n. to Clipperton Atoll off C. America. Vagrants have reached Cal. waters 13 times, all believed to have been Hawaiian Petrels, although none of the records could be safely assigned to either species, as the two forms are currently considered to be inseparable in the field.

There are two accepted sight records of this species pair in Ore.:
1. One was observed 45 nautical mi. w. of Port Orford, Curry Co., on 8 Aug 2002.
2. One was observed 45 nautical mi. w. of Florence, Lane Co., on 10 Aug 2002.

In addition, a bird was reported off Yaquina Head, Lincoln Co., on 7 Aug 2008. This record has not yet been reviewed by the OBRC.

*Cook's Petrel *Pterodroma cookii*

Vagrant. Nests on islands off New Zealand; post-breeding birds disperse to the n. Pacific. Rare but regular visitor from May to Dec off Cal.

One accepted Ore. record: Two were photographed 92 mi. w. of Cape Sebastian, Curry Co., on 20 Oct 2005.

In addition, 2-3 "Cookilaria"-type petrels were seen 76 nautical mi. w. of Florence, Lane Co., on 1 Aug 2002. The OBRC accepted this record as "species unresolved," since the very similar De Fillipi's Petrel (*P. defillipiana*) could not be ruled out, although there are no known records of that species in N. America.

**Streaked Shearwater *Calonectris leucomelas*

Vagrant. Breeds abundantly off Japan, Korea, and China; post-breeders disperse widely in the w. Pacific. Casual around Hawaii and in the e. Pacific.

One accepted sight record from Ore. of a single bird over Heceta Bank, 35.3 mi. w. off the coast of Lane Co., on 13 Sep 1996.

In addition, 1 was reported 50 mi. w. of Cape Lookout, Tillamook Co., on 17 Sep 2000. This record has not yet been reviewed by the OBRC.

Pink-footed Shearwater *Puffinus creatopus*

These are the common light-bellied shearwaters off Ore. in summer. Considered by some to be a light morph of Flesh-footed Shearwater, with which it shares behavior, flight-style, and soft-part coloration. Common summer visitor and very common fall transient offshore on shallow shelf waters. Usually seen seaward of 40 fm depth, approximately 5-10 mi off Ore.'s shores. Infrequently seen from shore. Arrive in low numbers in Feb-Mar; gradually build in numbers becoming common Jul-Oct; depart in Nov. Absent Dec-Jan, or very rare in warm-water winters.

Flesh-footed Shearwater *Puffinus carneipes*

One of the rarest of the seabirds to occur annually in Ore. Single birds are sometimes found in flocks of other shearwaters. Rare late-fall transient offshore at the w. edge and slopes of the continental shelf. Rare or irregular at other times of yr. For 29 birds observed at sea where distance was recorded, sightings ranged from 5 to 60 mi from land; median 29 mi. Four sightings from shore. Most records fall between 27 Aug and 31 Oct; otherwise 1 or 2 records each in Feb, Mar, Apr, May, Jul, and Dec. Record high number in Ore. in a single day is 6 birds 7 Oct 2001 on Perpetua Bank.

*Greater Shearwater *Puffinus gravis*

Vagrant. Breeds in the s. Atlantic. Regular visitor to the Atlantic coast of the U.S., extremely rare in the Pacific.

One accepted Ore. record of a bird photographed off Newport, Lincoln Co., on 8 Aug 2008.

*Wedge-tailed Shearwater *Puffinus pacificus*

Vagrant. Breeds widely across the tropical Pacific and Indian Ocean. There are two color morphs.

Two accepted Ore. records:

1. A dark-morph bird was found dead on Nye Beach at Newport, Lincoln Co., on 26 Mar 1999.
2. A dark-morph bird was observed in flight 25 mi. w. of Depoe Bay, Lincoln Co., on 2 Oct 1999.

Buller's Shearwater *Puffinus bulleri*

Common regular late-fall transient offshore on shelf and slope waters. Most are found over 5 mi from shore. Rarely seen from shore but in some yrs a few are seen, usually in very small loose flocks. Single early birds sometimes arrive in late Jul; variably common Aug-Nov, peak late Sep-mid-Oct; rare to Dec.

Sooty Shearwater *Puffinus griseus*

This seabird, the most abundant in Ore., has recently suffered severe declines or significant population shifts in the e. N. Pacific. Still an abundant summer visitor and transient offshore on the inner shelf. Most numerous 3-6 mi offshore. Frequently viewed from shore, especially from elevated viewpoints, sometimes in huge numbers. Also occur regularly within the mouth of the Columbia R., rarely upriver to Hammond. Begin arriving in Ore. in Mar, peak in Jul; southward migration begins Aug, abundant to Oct, most are gone by mid-Dec; rare in winter. Tens to hundreds of thousands of birds may be seen migrating past coastal points Jul-Sep.

Short-tailed Shearwater *Puffinus tenuirostris*
These very abundant seabirds are uncommon off Ore. in winter. Their arrival coincides with some of the Pacific Northwest's stormiest late-fall weather. Uncommon to fairly common late-fall and winter transient; irregular spring transient offshore. Occasionally seen from shore in early winter, sometimes in large flocks. Small numbers noted offshore beginning in Sep; variably common Nov-Jan; remaining in some yrs until May; very rare or absent in summer. May be the most numerous (often the only) shearwater offshore late Nov-Feb. Actual status difficult to ascertain because of similarity to abundant Sooty Shearwaters.

> I.D. Notes: Short-tailed looks very much like the abundant Sooty Shearwaters—all dark, but slightly smaller with shorter bill and tail. Some have a paler chin and throat area; some have a slightly dark-capped look when seen well. There are subtle differences in underwing pattern as well. See Gillson (2008) for additional identification discussion.

*Manx Shearwater *Puffinus puffinus*
Vagrant. Breeds in the n. Atlantic, winters to e. S. America. Virtually unknown from the W. Coast until the 1990s, this species is now a rare but increasing visitor along the Pacific coast from Alaska to Cal., with breeding suspected off British Columbia and s. Alaska.

vagrant occurrence

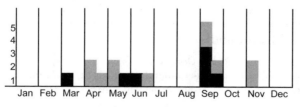

■ *Manx Shearwater (7 records)*

▨ *Manx-type Shearwater (11 records)*

Seven accepted Ore. records:
1. One was observed at Boiler Bay, Lincoln Co., on 1 Sep 2000.
2. One was observed at Boiler Bay, Lincoln Co., on 12 Sep 2000.
3. One was seen 51 mi. w. of Brookings, Curry Co., on 7 Jun 2002.
4. One was at Tierra Del Mar, Tillamook Co., on 7 Sep 2002.
5. One was seen 6 mi. w. of Newport, Lincoln Co., on 1 Mar 2003.
6. One was 1 mile w. of Newport, Lincoln Co., on 20 May 2003.
7. One was seen 2 mi. w. of Yaquina Bay, Lincoln Co., on 30 Sep 2006.

In addition, there are numerous reports of small black-and-white shearwaters not safely identifiable to species level. The OBRC has accepted a number of these "Manx-type" shearwaters as "species unresolved" (see below).

**Black-vented Shearwater *Puffinus opisthomelas*
Vagrant. Breeds off Baja Cal. and regularly disperses n. to c. Cal. Rare vagrant farther n.

Four accepted sight records for Ore.:
1. One was observed at Bandon, Coos Co., on 22 Nov 1992.
2. One was seen at Boiler Bay, Lincoln Co., 28-30 Aug 2000.
3. One was seen at Boiler Bay, Lincoln Co., on 11 Nov 2001.
4. One was at the s. jetty of the Columbia R., Clatsop Co., on 17 Nov 2002.

> Note: The Black-vented Shearwater is the "expected" species off the N. American Pacific coast. However, the Manx Shearwater has been verified from Ore., Wash., and Cal. There are many sight records of unidentified small black-and-white shearwaters from Ore., most seen between late Aug and early Nov and from mid-Apr to early May. While most have been at or just off the beaches, some have been found up to 16 mi. offshore. The OBRC has accepted 11 such reports as relating to "Manx-type" *Puffinus* shearwaters. All are from Apr, May, Sep, or Nov.

Family Hydrobatidae

**Wilson's Storm-Petrel *Oceanites oceanicus*
Vagrant. Abundant breeder around Antarctica. Outside the breeding season (Apr to Sep) disperses widely across s. oceans, rare to n. Pacific.

Two accepted Ore. records:
1. One was among a concentration of shearwaters and storm-petrels off the s. jetty of the Columbia R., Clatsop Co., on 31 May 1976.

2. A lone bird was observed from a research vessel about 80 mi. w. of Nestucca Bay, Tillamook Co., on 24 Jul 1996.

Fork-tailed Storm-Petrel *Oceanodroma furcata*
Breeds at Three Arch Rocks and Haystack Rock, Tillamook Co.; Island Rock, Hunters I., North Crook Point Rock, Saddle Rock, Whalehead I., and Goat I., Curry Co. It can be seen over the outer shelf, at the margins of offshore banks such as the Heceta-Stonewall complex, and along the margins of the Columbia plume. Highest numbers in Jun and Jul over the upper continental slope, where they were most common in waters on the warmer seaward side of the shelf break fronts. Occasionally observed from land singly or in small flocks of 20 or more. Unusually large numbers nearshore on occasion. Rarely seen near colonies, as they are nocturnal. Even offshore the likelihood of detection can be low as they are small birds and easily missed in the waves and swells unless close to a boat.

Leach's Storm-Petrel *Oceanodroma leucorhoa*
Nests on about 15 soil-covered offshore islands within the Ore. Is. NWR. Seven islands in Curry Co. account for the bulk of the population, with Goat I. and the islands off Crook Point accounting for most. Far fewer birds nest on the n. coast, where there are only three colonies of note: the two Haystack Rocks in Tillamook and Clatsop cos., and the Three Arch Rocks NWR complex, also Tillamook Co. Few are seen in Oregon's waters during the non-breeding season. During Nov and Jan none were seen offshore during aerial surveys and numbers were low in Mar and Sep. Occasionally forced close to shore by gales and on a few occasions blown inland where they have been observed in w. Ore. valleys and waterways. This most often happens in the autumn, but has occurred in spring.

*Black Storm-Petrel *Oceanodroma melania*
Vagrant. Breeds on islands off s. Cal., Baja Cal., and in the Gulf of Cal. Post-breeders regularly disperse n. to c. Cal.
    One accepted Ore. record: a flock of 10 was photographed at Seaside, Clatsop Co., on 8 Sep 1983.

Order PELECANIFORMES
Family Phaethontidae

*Red-billed Tropicbird *Phaethon aethereus*
Vagrant. Breeds on tropical is. in the Atlantic, e. Pacific, Indian Ocean and the Caribbean. Outside breeding season, ranges widely in tropical and subtropical oceans. Occasional visitor off the W. coast of N. America. A single accepted Ore. record of a bird well photographed 25 mi. off Florence, Lane Co., on 13 May 2008.

Family Sulidae

*Masked Booby *Sula dactylatra*
Vagrant. Ranges widely across tropical and subtropical oceans; rare vagrant to n. Pacific.
   One accepted Ore. record of a moribund bird collected and photographed at N. Portland, Multnomah Co., on 15 August 2006. The specimen is at the Slater Museum, Univ. Puget Sound.

*Blue-footed Booby *Sula nebouxii*
Vagrant. Breeds widely in the tropical e. Pacific and on islands in the Gulf of Cal. Casual visitor to the Pacific coast of s. Cal. and Salton Sea, vagrant farther n.
   One accepted Ore. record of a subadult photographed at Yaquina Head, Lincoln Co., where it remained 7-9 Sep 2002.

**Brown Booby *Sula leucogaster*
Vagrant. Breeds widely across tropical and subtropical oceans, n. to Gulf of Cal. Casual visitor to the s. Cal. coast and Salton Sea.
   One accepted sight record for Ore.: a juv. was seen by many observers on an offshore birding trip 15 mi. wsw. of Depoe Bay, Lincoln Co., on 3 Oct 1998.
   In addition, a freshly dead adult female was found at Cape Arago, Coos Co., in late Oct 2008. The specimen is at the Ore. Institute of Marine Biology. This record has not yet been reviewed by the OBRC.

Family Pelecanidae

American White Pelican *Pelecanus erythrorhynchos*
Breeds at a few interior sites with differing regularity, including Malheur, Lower Klamath, and Upper Klamath NWRs; Summer L. W.A.; Warner Basin; and on islands in the Columbia R. e. of Arlington. Post-breeding and non-breeding birds may occur anywhere in e. Ore. Small numbers occur occasionally in w. Ore., most regular at Fern Ridge Res., Lane

Co., where dozens have occurred in recent yrs. Summer numbers in the Portland area have increased since 2000. Rare on the outer coast. Very rare across the state in winter. Average arrival date at Malheur NWR is 24 Mar with first nearly a month earlier; average at Warner Basin is 2 Apr.

Brown Pelican *Pelecanus occidentalis*

Common spring, summer, and fall visitor along the coast. Starting in the late 1990s, large numbers began concentrating inside the Columbia R. mouth in and around E. Sand I. The possibility of breeding on E. Sand I. became evident in 2001 but has not been confirmed. Non-breeding adult and subadult birds begin to reach Ore. during Apr in most yrs. Post-breeding adults arrive during May and Jun, juvs. during Jul and Aug. Peak numbers, sometimes in the thousands at favored sites, occur during Aug and Sep. The main southward movement takes place during Nov most yrs, but during stormy, unsettled falls many leave during Oct.

In mild falls with good food supplies, many linger through Dec, sometimes in high numbers. In some yrs many attempt to overwinter, especially along the s. Ore. coast. Very rare to the Willamette V. and sw. interior valleys. On 13 Oct 1997, 1 was at McNary Dam; it or another was near the mouth of Deschutes R. on 19 Oct 1997.

Family Phalacrocoracidae

Brandt's Cormorant *Phalacrocorax penicillatus*

Brandt's Cormorants nest colonially on offshore islands and mainland cliffs and are the most common of the cormorants on the Ore. coast in summer. Present all yr. Birds first appear at breeding colonies in Mar. At the end of breeding season some movement into estuaries occurs, but this is the least-likely cormorant to be found upriver. Fall and winter movements of Ore. birds are unclear, although there is a northerly movement in Oct with a possibly related increase in numbers in Puget Sound and British Columbia. Winter numbers are distinctly lower than summer numbers in Ore. and it is usually the least-common cormorant in winter.

Double-crested Cormorant *Phalacrocorax auritus*

This is the most abundant and widespread of the three cormorant species found in Ore., occurring inland and on the coast. Common breeder in spring and summer at bays and estuaries, and on islands and cliffs along the coast and lower Columbia R. Smaller breeding populations are present in most available habitat in e. Ore. Migrant and wintering birds are uncommon to sometimes abundant along the coast, on larger

winter distribution

rivers, lakes, and reservoirs in w. Ore. A few winter e. of the Cascades on unfrozen water bodies, including the Snake R., but otherwise absent in winter from se. Ore.

Birds arrive as early as Feb at Malheur and Upper Klamath breeding grounds. There is some migration, beginning in Aug, to the Columbia R., n. Willamette R., freshwater sites w. of the Cascades, and marine locations extending from British Columbia to the Gulf of Cal. Departures peak mid-Sep to mid-Nov. From late Sep through Oct, large flocks of migrants can be seen moving s. along the coast.

Pelagic Cormorant *Phalacrocorax pelagicus*

Seemingly misnamed, Pelagic Cormorants are rarely seen far from land. Common yr-round along the entire coast; not found away from salt water, but sometimes travels surprisingly far up coastal rivers. Breeds where rocky cliffs with ledges are present; does not breed along the sandy coast from Coos Bay to Florence. This species is seen in estuaries during all months; no distinct migrations. Birds start to establish nest sites in late Mar. Breeding season can continue through Aug. Post-breeding local dispersal occurs and there is some movement into estuaries; there is little evidence of any seasonal migration.

Family Fregatidae

*Magnificent Frigatebird *Fregata magnificens*

Vagrant. Breeds in the tropical w. Atlantic (n. to Florida) and e. Pacific. Regularly disperses to s. U.S.; vagrant along the Pacific coast.

Seven accepted Ore. records:

1. One apparent imm. was collected at Tillamook Lighthouse, Clatsop Co., on 19 February 1935. The skeleton is now at the U.S. National Museum, the skin at the Natural History Museum in San Diego.
2. One was observed at Gold Beach, Curry Co., 1 on 24 July 1979.

■ *Magnificent Frigatebird (7 records)*

▨ *Magnificent/Greater Frigatebird (1 record)*

3. Single imm. birds were seen at Newport, Lincoln Co., and Florence, Lane Co., on 29 July 1983. These sightings were felt to most probably be of the same bird, seen within a few hours about 42 mi. apart.

vagrant occurrence

4. A juv. was photographed at Charleston, Coos Co., 7-11 March 1987.

5. An adult male was at Newport, Lincoln Co., on 18 August 1987.

6. An imm. was at Portland, Multnomah Co., on 4 June 1987. This bird was possibly ship-assisted.

7. A juv. was seen at Cape Arago, Coos Co., on 1 February 1992.

In addition, a record of a flying bird observed at Beverly Beach, Lincoln Co., on 17 March 2003 was accepted as either a Magnificent or a Great Frigatebird (*F. minor*). In 2008, single frigatebirds were reported from the Columbia R. near Multnomah Falls, Multnomah Co. on 12 Apr, and 63 mi. off Tillamook, Tillamook Co., on 8 Aug. These reports have not yet been reviewed by the OBRC.

Order CICONIIFORMES
Family Ardeidae

American Bittern *Botaurus lentiginosus*

winter distribution

Uncommon to fairly common breeder e. of the Cascades. In w. Ore., uncommon along the coast, at Sauvie I., and in the Willamette V.; local and irregular in the interior sw. Wintering birds found throughout the state except for Blue Mtns.; rare to uncommon on coast, and very rare e. of the Cascades in winter. Migratory movements poorly known. Average arrival date at Malheur NWR is 4 Apr, but noted as early as 22 Feb. Southbound migration starts in Jul, peaks in late Sep at Malheur.

Least Bittern *Ixobrychus exilis*
One of the least-known breeding birds of Ore., and one of the rarest. Rare spring and summer resident in larger freshwater marshes of se. Ore. Most reports from Upper Klamath L., Klamath Marsh NWR, Malheur NWR, Crump and Hart lakes. Scattered records in the Rogue and Willamette valleys. Recent breeding evidence in Ore. is scanty. Arrives in Ore. by late Apr and May. Young observed flying mid-Jul at Malheur L. Latest dates in Ore. are in Sep.

> Note: this species occurs in islands or edges of dense marsh vegetation of hardstem bulrush and cattail. At Crump and Hart lakes, Lake Co., it occurs in islands of cattails surrounded by deeper water, or at edges of marsh along shore with deeper water on at least one side of emergent vegetation.

Great Blue Heron *Ardea herodias*
The Great Blue Heron is a fairly common to common resident and breeder along estuaries, streams, marshes, and lakes throughout the state. However, ice in winter often precludes presence or causes reduction in numbers in e. Ore. and at high-elevation lakes. Most common yr-

round in riparian parts of the Coast Range, Willamette V., and along
the Columbia R. Also present at Cascade lakes and reservoirs spring
through fall. Sometimes found on the edge of the ocean feeding from
rocks or at cr. mouths. They gather at colonies during Feb (late Jan to
mid-Mar); larger colonies have earlier arrival dates. Few data available
for Ore. on dispersal of fledglings. Hatch-yr birds are frequently seen in
Cascade lakes and reservoirs Jul-Oct.

Great Egret *Ardea alba*

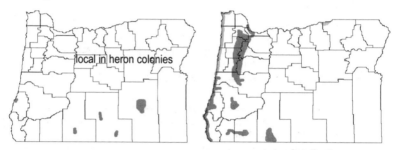

winter distribution

Most abundant spring-fall at major lakes and marshes e. of the Cascades.
Present yr-round in the Klamath Basin, but more common Apr-Nov.
Fairly common to abundant on the s. coast except during May/Jun when
uncommon to fairly common and concentrated at Coos Bay. In early
summer, it is rare w. of the Cascades, but is a regular local breeder around
Coos Bay. Average arrival date at Malheur NWR is 26 Mar, 12 Apr at Hart
Mt. Nat. Ant. Ref./Warner V. In fall, occurs statewide, especially in the
sc. and se. Willamette V. and s. coast. In winter, rare e. of the Cascades
and accidental at Malheur NWR, but locally common on coast and in
the Willamette V.; uncommon to fairly common in Umpqua V. Early
dispersants to interior sw. Ore. arrive in late Jul and are uncommon to
fairly common by late Oct through mid-Jan, after which they decline
in numbers and are casual by May. In the early 2000s, numbers in the
Portland area in late summer have increased significantly.

Snowy Egret *Egretta thula*

Breeds regularly but in varying numbers primarily in se. Ore. Uncommon
to fairly common spring through fall in the Klamath Basin, occasional
to uncommon in ne. Malheur Co., rare in the Rogue V. Rare in summer
and fall on the coast n. mainly to Coos Bay, casual to w. interior valleys.
Average arrival date at Malheur NWR is 18 Apr with earliest record over
a month earlier, at Hart Mt. Nat. Ant. Ref./Warner V. average date is 2

May. Most birds have left by Oct. A few winter at Coos Bay most yrs, otherwise very rare in winter.

*Little Blue Heron *Egretta caerulea*
Vagrant. Breeds in the se. U.S. and s. Cal., disperses widely after breeding.
Four accepted Ore. records:
1. A young adult in breeding plumage was photographed at the Willamette R. near the Buena Vista Ferry, Marion & Polk cos., 16-18 May 1985.
2. A bird in non-breeding plumage was at the Willamette R. near Milwaukie, Clackamas Co., on 18 Jun 1987.
3. A white imm. was photographed at Brownsmead, Clatsop Co., 20 Jan – 11 Mar 1990.
4. One adult was photographed at Tualatin R. NWR, Wash. Co., on 11 Jun 2006.
In 2008, imms. were reported and photographed at Bybee L., Multnomah Co, on 1 Sep; at Neskowin, Tillamook Co., on 11 Nov; and at Siletz Bay, Lincoln Co., from 23 Dec to late Feb 2009. These sightings may all pertain to the same bird and have not yet been reviewed by the OBRC.

In addition, there are a number of reports that were not accepted by the OBRC. Immature (white-plumaged) birds are easily confused with the similar Snowy Egret, and all sightings should be carefully documented.

*Tricolored Heron *Egretta tricolor*
Vagrant. Breeds in the se. U.S. and nw. Mexico. Casual visitor to s. Cal.
Two accepted Ore. records:
1. An adult in alternate plumage was photographed at Finley NWR, Benton Co., 12-31 May 1976.
2. An adult in basic plumage was photographed at Ona Beach SP, Lincoln Co., 11-13 Nov 1993.
In addition, 1 was collected at Malheur NWR, Harney Co., on 31 Oct 1945. This record has not been reviewed by the OBRC.

Cattle Egret *Bubulcus ibis*
Rare breeder in the Great Basin with only a few pairs occasionally nesting at Malheur NWR and elsewhere in the Harney Basin. Much less regular and in smaller numbers since the mid-1990s than it was in the 1970s-80s. Casual transient in spring in the Klamath Basin. Average arrival date at Malheur NWR is 6 May. Latest departure date from Malheur NWR is 10 Oct. In fall, it is uncommon e. of the Cascades including Malheur NWR with scattered records elsewhere. Uncommon to rare on coast

Oct-Apr, mostly in late fall and early winter; very rare in w. interior valleys fall through spring.

Green Heron *Butorides virescens*
Uncommon but regular migrant and summer resident throughout w. and sc. Ore. Rare and irregular in the Cascades and in e. Ore. In the e., most regular in s. Klamath Co.; also several records at Page Springs, Harney Co. Rare in winter with most in sw. Ore., especially on the coast. A 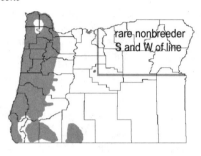 noticeable influx of migrants occurs in Ore. in mid-Apr. Fall movements are essentially unknown.

Black-crowned Night-Heron *Nycticorax nycticorax*
Fairly common summer resident e. of the Cascades where it breeds locally at large wetlands. Colony sites vary in response to changing water conditions. Some individuals arrive at nesting areas in late Mar, most by early to mid-Apr. Beginning in Jul and Aug, post-breeders and young are observed more often away from colonies as they begin dispersal. There are mid-Aug observations in the Cascades, probably representing birds dispersing from e. Ore. breeding areas. Numbers build at Malheur NWR in Sep and most are gone by early Nov, while birds are present yr-round in the Klamath Basin. About 100 birds usually winter in the Klamath Basin, Klamath Co., primarily along the Link R. in Klamath Falls. During some winters they remain at Malheur NWR, Summer L., and Umatilla NWR.

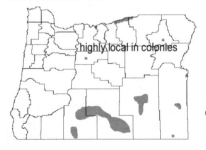

winter distribution

Occasionally observed during early summer in w. Ore., especially at Fern Ridge Res., and may nest, but nesting has not been documented since the early 1900s. From late summer through early spring, night-herons are rare to uncommon in w. Ore. Local roosts or regular sightings are known from lower Rogue and Chetco rivers, Coos Bay, near Tillamook, Medford, Grants Pass, Myrtle Point, Roseburg, and Portland. In c. Douglas Co., birds are usually found at roosts mid-Jul through mid-Apr. Migration routes and wintering areas of Ore. birds are not well documented.

Family Threskiornithidae
Subfamily Threskiornithinae

*White Ibis *Eudocimus albus*
Vagrant. Breeds along the Atlantic coast of the se. U.S.; also in C. and n. S. America.

One accepted Ore. record of an adult photographed at Newport, Lincoln Co., 15-16 Nov 2000.

*Glossy Ibis *Plegadis falcinellus*
Vagrant. Breeds along the Atlantic coast of the e. and s. U.S.; also in S. America, s. Eurasia, Africa, and Australia.

Only 1 accepted Ore. record to date: an adult was photographed at Malheur NWR, Harney Co., 20-28 May 2006.

Multiple reports from Malheur NWR in the spring of 2008 have not yet been reviewed by the OBRC. Very similar to White-faced Ibis; all subsequent records need to be carefully documented. This species should especially be looked for in ibis flocks in se. Ore.

White-faced Ibis *Plegadis chihi*

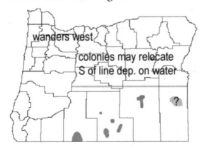

Breeds at Malheur NWR, at several wetland sites in Harney and Lake cos. and Swan L. and Wood R. wetlands in Klamath Co. Additionally, a new colony site recently appeared at Lower Klamath NWR, just s. of the Ore. border. E. of the Cascades, generally common from May through Sep near breeding areas. Rare wanderer elsewhere in e. Ore. W. of the Cascades its presence has recently become apparent on the coast and occasionally in the Willamette V. in spring. In winter, occasional to rare on the coast and at Sauvie I. and Malheur NWR.

Average arrival at Malheur NWR is 28 Apr; earliest 7 Apr. Exhibits nomadic behavior, regularly shifting nesting colonies between yrs in response to changing wetland conditions. Post-fledging, ibises wander widely during Aug and Sep; most depart the state by mid-Oct; occasional as late as early Nov.

Order FALCONIFORMES
Family Cathartidae

Turkey Vulture *Cathartes aura*

COOS	CLAT	LANE	BENT	PORT	CENT	MALH
15 Feb	25 Mar	22 Feb	17 Feb	4 Feb	7 Mar	15 Mar

The Turkey Vulture is a common to abundant transient throughout the state and an uncommon to common summer resident except in high mtns. It is most common at lower elevations. The first individuals are noted during Feb in most yrs; many arrive in Mar, with peak migration in mid-Apr. The bulk of fall passage in w. Ore. is in the second half of Sep to early Oct. At Malheur NWR, fall migration begins in Aug, peaks 1-15 Sep; most have left by Oct; latest is 20 Oct. Major flights are often seen in late Sep staging at the s. end of the Rogue V. to cross over the Siskiyous. Small numbers are regular in winter in sw. Ore., with a small winter roost (up to 20 birds) w. of Eugene in the 2000s.

Family Accipitridae
Subfamily Pandioninae

Osprey *Pandion haliaetus*

COOS	CLAT	LANE	BENT	PORT	CENT	MALH
15 Mar	30 Mar	13 Mar	22 Mar	16 Mar	23 Mar	15 Apr

Breeds statewide except in arid treeless regions of se. Ore. and Columbia Basin grasslands. Found commonly nesting along larger rivers, natural lakes and reservoirs, along the coast, and elsewhere. Nesting pairs e. of the Cascades forested zone are limited to some along the Columbia R. e. to Umatilla, and localized nesting in the Blue and Wallowa mtns., including the Snake R. In winter, rare but increasingly regular on the s. coast and in w. Ore. interior valleys. Casual elsewhere. Some Ospreys that breed in Ore. begin returning from the wintering grounds in late Feb and early Mar, but the large influx generally starts near the first day of spring and continues over the next several wks.

Subfamily Accipitrinae

White-tailed Kite *Elanus leucurus*
Rare to very rare breeder, probably permanent resident, in the w. interior valleys and along the coast. The highest concentration of known nest locations is in Jackson Co. The extent of the visitant population w. of the Cascades at any season is unknown, but kites are uncommon to locally common fall through winter. Origins of wintering birds are uncertain. Birds arrive at roosts as early as 6 Sep and leave as late as May, but some

may leave before the end of Feb or even Dec. E. of the Cascades, about one-third of visitants have appeared in Aug; the remainder occurred in other months, primarily s. of the Wallowa and Ochoco mtns.

Bald Eagle *Haliaeetus leucocephalus*

Breeds in most of Ore. except in the c. Columbia R. region and in Malheur Co. It is a fairly common breeder at Upper Klamath L., along the Columbia R. below Portland, and at Crane Prairie and Wickiup res., Deschutes Co., and an uncommon to very rare breeder elsewhere. Found throughout the state during the non-breeding season. Very common in winter and early spring in the Klamath and Harney basins, Columbia R. estuary, and L. Billy Chinook; common in winter and early spring at most sizable rivers and lakes with open water in e. and c. Ore., around Fern Ridge Res., and on the coast. Bald Eagles are most abundant in Ore. in late winter and early spring.

Northern Harrier *Circus cyaneus*

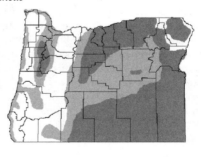

Common during summer and migration in open habitats e. of the Cascades, with numbers decreasing in most areas during winter, except at lower elevations and at major marshlands, where regular. W. of the Cascades, they occur in the interior valleys and along coastal lowlands as locally uncommon summer residents and common transients and winterers. Along the coast they are most common in winter. Casual transients above timberline and over forested habitats statewide. In late Feb numbers begin to increase across e. Ore. as abundance declines in coastal areas.

Note: First-yr birds of both sexes are reddish-brown; some are mistakenly identified as females.

Peak of migration at Malheur NWR occurs between mid-Mar and mid-Apr. Throughout the state, dispersal begins in late Jul and continues into Sep. Fall migration at Malheur NWR peaks from mid-Sep to mid-Oct and numbers begin to increase along the coast in Sep. Most near the coast are imms. or females.

Sharp-shinned Hawk *Accipiter striatus*
An uncommon breeder throughout Ore. in forested areas from sea level to timberline. It is least common in the breeding season in se. Ore. Uncommon transient and winter visitor across the state in wooded areas or semi-open country. During fall migration, many birds move through the state to wintering grounds farther s. Migrating birds often pass along higher ridges of the Cascades and Steens Mtn. in fall. Numbers begin increasing at Malheur NWR in late Feb, with peak spring migration occurring by mid-Apr. Arrive on nest sites in late Apr-early May. Southward migration begins in mid-Aug and peaks mid-Sep to mid-Oct.

Cooper's Hawk *Accipiter cooperii*
An uncommon breeder in forests and woods throughout state except in arid treeless areas of se. Ore. Nests in small numbers in wooded montane and riparian areas in se. Ore. An uncommon transient and winter visitor statewide, and may retreat from high elevations in winter. Earliest arrival at a nest site is reported to be 28 Mar (w. Ore.), while most pairs throughout Ore. were observed at or about their nest sites by mid-Apr. Although often thought of as permanent residents in Ore., the breeding population in the Blue and Wallowa mtns. of ne. Ore. is highly migratory. Migratory status of birds breeding in w. Ore. is unknown. Birds presumably breeding n. of Ore. are counted during fall migration at Bonney Butte, near Mt. Hood. Median passage date (during Sep-Oct monitoring period) averaged 25 Sep for 1994-98 (20 Sep for juvs., 30 Sep for adults), with a gradual decline to almost no birds in late Oct.

Northern Goshawk *Accipiter gentilis*

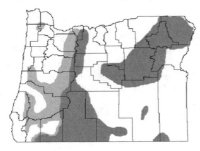

Uncommon to fairly common permanent resident in suitable habitat between 1,900 ft and 6,100 ft elevation in forested portions of the Cascade, Blue, and Klamath mtns. Highest densities are found e. of the Cascade crest. Rare local nester in the s. half of the Coast Range. Breed locally on Steens Mtn., Hart Mtn., and in the Ore. Canyon Mtns. Uncommon to rare transient and winter resident; can appear anywhere in the state in forested and unforested habitats. At the Bonney Butte Hawk Watch site, 80% of fall passage occurred 11 Sep-17 Oct.

Red-shouldered Hawk *Buteo lineatus*

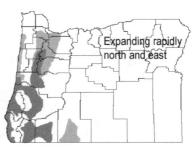

Locally uncommon breeder in most of w. Ore. Expanding rapidly; may have bred at Malheur NWR and in s. Klamath Co. in the 2000s. Uncommon from Lane Co. southward in winter, with concentrations in Coos Co. and around Fern Ridge Res. Rare but increasing in winter in the n. Willamette V. and along the n. coast. E. of the Cascades, most observations were in fall and winter until a spate of reports of juvs. in the mid-2000s. Very uncommon winter visitor in the Klamath Basin, n. rarely to Deschutes and Crook cos., where reports are increasing. Post-breeding dispersal into Klamath Basin and other wintering areas generally occurs late Aug-Mar. Seen at or near Malheur NWR regularly in Sep in the 2000s.

Note: *B. l. elegans* occurs in Ore., but an imm. bird seen at Frenchglen in fall 2007 appeared to be of the eastern subspecies *B. l. lineatus* (D. Farrar et al.), which has recently been documented as a rare fall migrant in sw. Idaho (Carlisle et al. 2007). It is not clear where any such birds have come from.

*Broad-winged Hawk *Buteo platypterus*

Vagrant. Common breeder in the e. U.S., w. to c. Alberta. Winters from Mexico to n. S. America.

Nine accepted Ore. records to date:
1. One was photographed at Malheur NWR, Harney Co., on 29 May 1983.

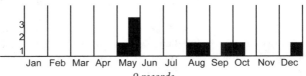

9 records

2. An imm. was at Malheur NWR, Harney Co., on 2 Oct 1983.
3. An imm. was seen at the e. edge of the Coast Range, Wash. Co., on 6 Aug 1983.
4. An imm. was at P-Ranch, Harney Co., on 26 May 1989.
5. An imm. was at Roaring Springs, Harney Co., on 23 May 1992.

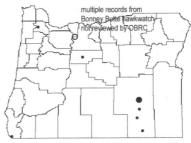

vagrant occurrence

6. An imm. was at Malheur NWR, Harney Co., on 19 Sep 1992.
7. One bird was at Fields, Harney Co., on 5 May 1996.
8. An imm. was at Brookings, Curry Co., on 16 Dec 1996.
9. One subadult was near Madras, Jefferson Co., on 17 Aug 1999.

There are numerous additional records that have not been reviewed by the OBRC. Migrant Broad-winged Hawks have been reported almost annually from the Bonney Butte Hawk Watch site, Hood R. Co., since its inception in 1994. On 29 Sep 1999 a kettle of 65 passed over the station. While kettles of this species are routine e. of the Rockies, such occurrences are virtually unknown on the W. Coast.

Swainson's Hawk *Buteo swainsoni*

COOS	CLAT	LANE	BENT	PORT	CENT	MALH
					20 Apr	5 Apr

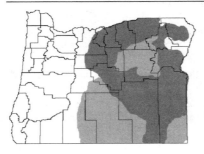

Breeds in the bunchgrass prairies e. of the Cascades with highest concentrations in the foothills of the Blue and Wallowa mtns. Local and uncommon in the se. quarter of the state, most often in the vicinity of irrigated hayfields. Rare in the Klamath Basin though common just across the Cal. border. There are a few records from w. of the Cascades during migration and 2 early-winter records in Lane Co. Mean arrival is 5 Apr at Malheur NWR, and 5-10 Apr in Wasco Co. Peak movement occurs during 10-25 Apr. Migratory flocks of non-breeding birds begin assembling in late Jun and grow in number until departure. Fall migration begins in Aug with peak movement 20 Aug-10 Sep.

Red-tailed Hawk *Buteo jamaicensis*
Fifteen subspecies are currently recognized; three have been recorded in Ore. Highly variable in appearance. *B. j. calurus* is a common permanent resident throughout the state, though local in colder areas at high elevations and e. of the Cascades in winter. Attains highest breeding densities along the northern foothills of the Blue and Wallowa mtns. where grasslands and forests meet, and in the Klamath Basin. The dark *B. j. harlani* and smaller *alascensis* that breed in Alaska are rare and unpredictable winter visitors.

Resident pairs begin defending territories in Jan on Sauvie I. and in the Willamette V. while migrants e. of the Cascades establish territories immediately upon their return about 20 Mar. The peak of the spring movement of returning breeding birds and transients occurs in Mar. The fall influx of northerly populations into the state occurs from late Aug to mid-Nov with the peak passage of adults in the last wk of Sep and the first 2 wks of Oct. Imms. tend to move a wk earlier than adults. Some red-tails remain on their territories yr-round; others, especially in colder areas where rodents are less available in winter, are more migratory.

Ferruginous Hawk *Buteo regalis*
Uncommon to rare resident in open landscapes e. of the Cascades. Most common in n. Malheur Co. and along the foothills of the Blue Mtns. from Zumwalt Prairie (Wallowa Co.) w. to the Columbia R. floodplain of Gilliam Co. Isolated breeding attempts have been recorded in Wasco Co. Although 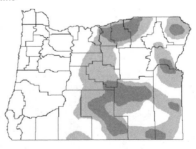 locally common in the Ft. Rock basin and Christmas V., they are less common in c. and sc. Ore. to rare in the Klamath Basin. Few remain in their Ore. breeding range during winter; most regular in the Klamath Basin and sc. Ore. The species is casual in winter in w. Ore. but has been seen annually in recent yrs. In the Rogue V. it is a regular but rare winter visitor. Typically arrive on their breeding territories in late Mar. Fall migration occurs from Sep through mid-Nov.

Rough-legged Hawk *Buteo lagopus*

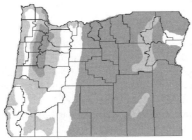

winter distribution

Uncommon to common in winter in open country throughout the state. Numbers vary markedly from yr to yr. Most common in open areas e. of the Cascades, where it can be common in some yrs. Generally uncommon w. of the Cascades in interior valleys, though can be locally common in some yrs. Least common on the coast and in sw. Ore.: in yrs of lower numbers may be absent from these areas altogether. In some yrs they are abundant e. of the Cascades but not on the w. side, perhaps because the prey base e. of the mtns. was so good that no further movement was necessary.

Usually begin arriving mid-Oct, with peak numbers in late Nov and early Dec. Some migrants pass through on their way farther s. Most start leaving the state late Mar to early Apr, but timing appears affected by weather. Peak numbers most often occur around mid-Apr. Exceptionally late birds have been recorded in May. Aberrant records exist for summer, including an imm. seen in late Jun and Jul 1998, and a bird in late Aug 1985.

Golden Eagle *Aquila chrysaetos*

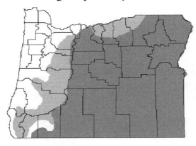

Common to uncommon yr-round resident in all counties e. of the Cascade Range. Has bred in Clackamas, Coos, Curry, Douglas, Jackson, Josephine, Lane and Linn cos. of w. Ore. Irregularly observed in winter in nw. Ore. and along the coast. Uncommon fall migrant along the Cascades summit. Courtship displays begin as early as mid-Feb at low-elevation sites. Most adult pairs in Ore. are resident yr-round and exhibit strong fidelity to nest territories. Young disperse in early fall. There is a small migratory movement of northern birds through the state in fall.

Family Falconidae
Subfamily Caracarinae

*Crested Caracara *Caracara cheriway*
Vagrant. Breeds in the southernmost U.S. (Arizona, Texas, Florida) and across Middle America to n. S. America.
Four accepted Ore. records:
1. One adult was observed 5 mi. e. of Gold Beach, Curry Co., 10 Feb – 21 Apr 1990.
2. One was photographed near Langlois, Coos Co., 25-29 Apr 2005.
3. One was photographed at the Corvallis Airport, Benton Co., 12-14 Apr 2006.
4. One was photographed at Myrtle Point, Coos Co., on 21 Apr 2007.
An additional report from Owyhee L., Malheur Co., on May 3, 1978 has not been submitted to the OBRC.

Subfamily Falconinae

American Kestrel *Falco sparverius*
The kestrel breeds statewide in open terrain from sea level to the alpine zone in the mtns. It winters throughout the breeding range except at high elevations. It is less common in winter in e. Ore. Numbers increase with the incursion of wintering birds at low elevations in w. Ore. At all seasons it is least common, even rare, on the outer coast.

Kestrel movements are significant and poorly known. A few resident pairs are on breeding territory in e. Ore. in January; this number is thought to be much higher in w. Ore. In spring, migrant kestrels arrive at Malheur NWR in late Mar and reach a peak in Apr, with most being transients. Kestrels drift s. in Sep with movements depending on local food and weather, but are gone by mid-month in c. Ore. At Bonney Butte, on the se. flanks of Mt. Hood, 95% of the passage occurred 31 Aug to 20 Oct. Peak counts at Malheur NWR occur 20 Aug to 15 Sep. At least 80 kestrels were seen along a single 20-mile stretch of road nw. of Enterprise, Wallowa Co., in mid-Aug 2007, suggesting that a migratory movement was occurring in the area (ALC, Trask Colby).

Merlin *Falco columbarius*
There are no confirmed breeding records for Ore., but regular reports of Merlins in summer almost annually since the 1970s suggest that occasional breeding is likely in montane areas from the c. Cascades n. and eastward. Merlins are regular in Ore. in migration and winter. In winter, can be found throughout the state in open or semi-open habitats, but most regular near major estuaries, lakes, reservoirs, and occasionally in cities where food supplies are reliable.

Two of the three subspecies that occur in N. America can regularly be found in Ore.; a third has been reported. *F. c. columbarius* is the most commonly reported form statewide and the state's few possible breeding records are thought to refer to this form. *F. c. suckleyi*, a very dark form that breeds in Alaska and w. Canada, is uncommon in winter, mainly on the outer coast but sometimes in the w. interior valleys. The palest, sky-blue toned *F. c. richardsonii* is reported occasionally in winter; rarely in w. Ore. Observers at the Dutchman Peak HawkWatch site in sw. Ore. tentatively identified the subspecies of 13 migrating Merlins as follows: 9 *F. c. columbarius*, 2 *F. c. suckleyi*, and 2 *F. c. richardsonii*. However, there are no specimens of *richardsonii* from Ore.

F. c. suckleyi is considered mostly sedentary, *F. c. columbarius* mostly migratory, but numbers of *suckleyi* appear every fall to winter in w. Ore. Spring migrants are typically gone by the end of Apr, but reports of birds through mid-May do occur. Fall migrants begin appearing in early Sep, rarely late Aug. Migrating Merlins at the Bonney Butte HawkWatch site se. of Mt. Hood were first observed 7 Sep and last observed 24 Oct with the bulk of passage between 20 Sept and 22 Oct. At Dutchman Peak HawkWatch site near Medford, Merlins were first observed 22 Sep and last observed 2 Nov, with bulk of passage between 30 Sep and 29 Oct.

Gyrfalcon *Falco rusticolus*

vagrant occurrence

Ore. is at the s. edge of its normal winter range. The majority of Gyrfalcons seen in Ore. are imms. or adults of the "gray" type, but there are several reports of "white" birds. The Gyrfalcon is a regular winter visitant to Ore., usually with fewer than 5 reports per yr. Reported from Ore. from late Sep to late Apr, usually as single individuals. The majority of sightings come from coastal and Willamette V. lowlands near waterfowl concentrations and from Wallowa Co.

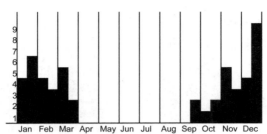

Gyrfalcon: 29 records, 30 individuals (through 2002)

Peregrine Falcon *Falco peregrinus*

The three subspecies occurring in Ore. are sometimes referred to by historic English or Latinate names. In Ore., peregrines occur as resident and migratory populations. *F. p. anatum* is a regular breeder and uncommon migrant. They nest on cliffs, usually within 1 mi of some form of water. The dark *F. p. pealei* is an uncommon but regular migrant and winter resident along the Ore. coast. It is difficult to determine the frequency at which *tundrius* moves through Ore. because *anatum* and *tundrius* are difficult to separate in the field.

Prairie Falcon *Falco mexicanus*

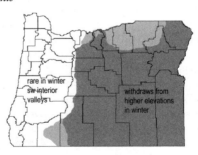

Breeds throughout the open country e. of the Cascades wherever cliffs and outcrops provide opportunities for nesting. W. of the Cascades, breeding has been documented at two locations in Jackson Co. May be found throughout their breeding range in winter though in reduced numbers. Rare but regular fall and winter visitors to open areas of interior w. Ore. For at least two decades, they have wintered almost annually in nc. Lane Co. and sc. Linn Co. In Jackson Co., more regular and are considered uncommon in winter. Casual on the coast. Prairie Falcons appear at their nesting sites in Ore. by late Mar. Begin departing from the breeding area as soon as prey becomes difficult to find; this usually coincides with the onset of aestivation of ground squirrels in Jul. At this time, Prairie Falcon numbers increase at higher elevations as they follow spring up into the mtns. They can sometimes be found hunting in meadows above timberline in the Cascades in late summer.

Order GRUIFORMES
Family Rallidae

Yellow Rail *Coturnicops noveboracensis*

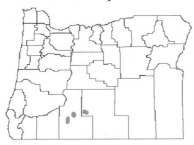

Rare local breeder in shallowly flooded sedge meadows in Klamath and Lake cos. Found at multiple sites in the Wood R. V. and at Klamath Marsh NWR. Also found at Sycan Marsh, Lake Co. Yellow Rails have been heard calling at Camas Prairie, 8 mi e. of Lakeview and have been reported irregularly at Big Marsh, in n. Klamath Co. and from the Sprague R. V. at several sites between Copperfield Draw and Beatty. First heard calling in late Apr, with peak calling 1 May to 9 Jun. Most rails are quiet by late Jul. Extremely rare migrant to w. Ore.; fewer than 10 reports. The secretive nature of this species leads one to speculate that its distribution may be more wide-ranging than currently known.

Virginia Rail *Rallus limicola*
This is a rare to locally abundant breeder. In w. Ore., breeds in freshwater and brackish marshes. In e. Ore., large marshes in Klamath, Lake, and Harney cos. host numerous breeders each yr, as do smaller wetland patches. It is also found in small marshes scattered in the midst of wooded areas, and occasionally in high-elevation marshes. Average spring arrival in Corvallis, Benton Co., is 26 Mar, although some may arrive much earlier. E. Ore. migrants begin to arrive in Mar; average arrival date at Malheur NWR is 20 Apr. Fall movements are poorly known, but outer coastal sites appear to have a significant increase in rails during October (ALC). Largest numbers winter in marshy areas on and near the coast, but may be found wintering in any marshy habitat that remains usable. It is absent from frozen areas in winter, but regularly present at local warmer sites. Far more common on the coast than inland in winter.

Sora *Porzana carolina*

COOS	CLAT	LANE	BENT	PORT	CENT	MALH
winters	winters	6 Apr	5 Apr		18 Apr	20 Apr

Rare to locally abundant breeder in freshwater marshes throughout Ore., including a few locations at fairly high elevations. The Sora chiefly winters where overnight freezing is rare. Winters annually in the Rogue

V., Jackson Co., and on the coast, becoming less common further n. Rare and irregular inland in winter n. of the Rogue V.; very rare e. of the Cascades. Regular spring and fall transient throughout the state in suitable habitat. Spring arrival begins with a trickle of individuals in Mar. Generally present at coastal sites by early Apr. Common in Mar in the Klamath Basin. At Malheur, fall migration begins in late Aug and peaks in the first half of Sep; most birds are gone by mid-Oct. Migration timing in w. Ore. is similar.

*Common Moorhen *Gallinula chloropus*

Vagrant. Cosmopolitan. In America, breeds in the e. U.S. and from c. Cal. s. through Middle and S. America.

Eight accepted Ore. records, the majority from Malheur NWR and all but 1 in May:

1. One adult was seen at Malheur NWR, Harney Co., on 20 May 1972.

vagrant occurrence

2. One was photographed at Garrison L., Port Orford, Curry Co., on 1 May 1976.
3. One was photographed at Malheur NWR, Harney Co., 22-24 May 1981.
4. One adult was at the Denman WA, Jackson Co., on 30 May 1982.
5. One adult was photographed at Malheur NWR, Harney Co., on 16 May 1982.
6. A male was collected at Winema Cr., Neskowin Beach, Tillamook Co., on 13 Feb 1983. The specimen is at Carnegie Museum of Natural History in Pittsburgh, PA.
7. A displaying pair was photographed at Krumbo Reservoir, Harney Co., 27-29 May 2001, but no nest or young were observed.

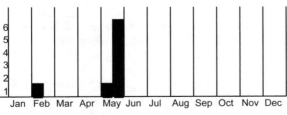

8 records, 9 individuals

8.   One bird was at Elk R., Curry Co., 16-17 May 2001.
In addition, there are unreviewed reports from Malheur NWR in May 1984, 2004, and 2005.

American Coot *Fulica americana*

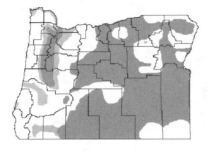

Found throughout most of Ore. in all seasons where open water is available, but breeding distribution is complex and not well understood. Some birds may be permanent residents. Very rare local breeder in coastal Lincoln, Lane, Douglas, and Coos cos. Locally very common breeder inland w. of the Cascades. Abundant breeder at large e. Ore. marshes; local away from such sites. Regular spring and fall transient and winter visitant statewide where water remains open. At Malheur NWR, spring arrivals begin in mid-Feb; peak numbers occur in mid-Apr; transients leave by mid-May. Throughout the state beginning in Sep, the coot gathers on larger lakes for autumn migration. Large flocks may remain at some lakes into Nov. Portions of these flocks may remain into Dec, or all winter if water remains open. More numerous on the coast in winter than at other times of yr. Coastal populations begin to increase to winter levels in Sep. In winter, hundreds to thousands are often found in coastal areas where little or no breeding occurs. They are largely gone from the coast by the first wk of May.

Family Gruidae
Subfamily Gruinae

Sandhill Crane *Grus canadensis*

COOS	CLAT	LANE	BENT	PORT	CENT	MALH
		20 Feb		24 Feb	19 Mar	17 Feb

See *BOGR* for discussion of subspecies movements. Breeds throughout se., sc., ne., and c. Ore. in large emergent marsh-meadow wetlands, as well as scattered smaller meadows among the Blue Mtns. A few pairs also nest in montane meadows in the w. Cascades. The largest breeding concentrations occur at Malheur NWR, Sycan Marsh, the Silvies R. floodplain near Burns, Chewaucan Marshes, Warner V., and Klamath Marsh NWR. A common spring and fall migrant in the Malheur-

Harney Basin and Klamath Basin, esp. in Mar and Apr. Migrants arrive in w. Ore. in late Feb or early Mar. Most leave Ore. by early Nov. Some winter on Sauvie I. and singles are sometimes found in the Willamette V. in winter.

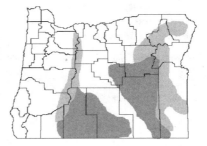

Order CHARADRIIFORMES
Family Charadriidae
Subfamily Charadriinae

Black-bellied Plover *Pluvialis squatarola*

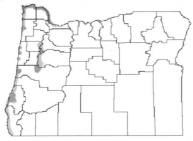

winter distribution

Fairly common to common transient on the coast; rare to locally uncommon transient in nw. interior valleys. Occasional in Apr and early May in the Rogue V. E. of the Cascades, an uncommon transient in the Klamath Basin and at Malheur NWR, otherwise rare to absent in e. Ore. Southbound adults begin arriving in Ore. in early Jul with a peak in Aug probably comprising adults, while imms. begin arriving in late Aug and probably comprise the bulk of the early Sep peak. Another peak occurs in Oct.

In winter it is a locally common resident on the coast, rare to locally uncommon in w. interior valleys (mainly c. and s. Willamette V.), and absent e. of the Cascades. Spring movements are obscured by the presence of a sizable wintering population on the coast, but there is obvious movement from mid-Apr through mid-May. Most birds are gone by late May. The few birds found in early Jun on the coast are probably non-breeders that summer locally.

A note on Golden-Plovers: The true status of American vs. Pacific Golden-Plover in Ore. is still unclear because many published sight records cannot be distinguished to species, as indeed some birds in the field cannot. See *BOGR* for details of specimen records and how unidentifiable records are handled.

American Golden-Plover *Pluvialis dominica*
Occasional to uncommon migrant in w. Ore. (mainly coastal) and locally rare, irregular migrant in e. Ore., with most reports at Malheur NWR, in the Klamath Basin, and in Umatilla Co. This is mainly a southbound migrant in Ore., with birds of known identity occurring primarily in Sep and early Oct, latest e. bird 4 Nov. Fall sight records are numerous, mainly from late Aug through Oct, but include some reports of adults in Jul, as well as birds in the first wk of Nov. Rare in the Willamette V. and at Sauvie I. Single birds and flocks of fewer than 10 are the norm;

peak fall counts of golden-plovers rarely exceed 15. Winter reports of golden-plovers are few and are discussed under Pacific Golden-Plover, to which they probably pertain. Far fewer birds thought to be of this species pass through Ore. in spring. The small number of sight records are mostly from May or the last few days of Apr.

Pacific Golden-Plover *Pluvialis fulva*
Rare to uncommon migrant; most birds occur on the outer coast. Very rare to rare in winter on the coast and in the Willamette V. Mainly a fall migrant, but spring reports have increased in recent yrs. Most sight records of southbound birds in w. Ore. range from 12 Jul to 24 Nov, with most reports in Sep. Peak fall counts thought to be of this species rarely exceed 5 to 7 birds. Very rare e. of the Cascades. A few winter reports of golden-plovers are probably of this species, based on its pattern of wintering in very small numbers on the Pacific coast. Most migrants have been reported from mid-Apr to late May, with most records in May. Spring reports usually involve 1 or at most 2 birds; peak is 9. There are very few inland reports in spring, all in May.

*Lesser Sand-Plover *Charadrius mongolus*
Vagrant. Breeds in c. and ne. Asia; rare but regular migrant in the Aleutian Is.
   Four accepted Ore. records, all of birds that stayed for several days:
1. An adult in basic plumage was photographed at Bayocean Spit, Tillamook Co., 11-17 Sep 1977.
2. An adult in prebasic molt was photographed at the s. jetty of the Columbia R., Clatsop Co., 16-21 Oct 1979.
3. One adult in breeding plumage was photographed at Bandon, Coos Co., 11 Jul-14 Aug 1986.
4. One adult was photographed at Seaside, Clatsop Co., 16-18 Jul 2005.
Until recently this species was called Mongolian Plover.

Snowy Plover *Charadrius alexandrinus*
E. of the Cascades, the Snowy Plover is a summer resident breeding on alkaline flats and salt pans found in Harney and Lake cos. It is reported intermittently from White L., Klamath Co. These interior summer residents winter along the Cal. coast and in Baja, and rarely if at all in Ore. Inland plovers return to breeding sites in Apr, and nesting begins late Apr, with peak nest initiation from mid-May to mid-Jun.
   On the Ore. coast this species is found yr-round between Heceta Head (Lane Co.) and Cape Blanco (Curry Co.), breeding locally. Nesting at Bayocean Spit, Tillamook Co., was last documented in 1995. Nesting was

documented at Necanicum R. mouth, Clatsop Co., in 2000. Incidental reports have come from several other places along the coast during the breeding season, e.g., Pistol R., Euchre Cr., and Sixes R. mouths in Curry Co., and 1 from Sand L., Tillamook Co., in May 1995. In winter, they are known from coastal breeding sites, with concentrations typically found at Bandon, Siltcoos, and Sutton beaches. A few wintering birds have also been found at Bayocean Spit, Tillamook Co., through 2000. On the coast, wintering plovers disperse to breeding sites in Mar. Late season broods may not fledge until mid-Sep on coast.

Wilson's Plover Charadrius wilsonia

Vagrant. Breeds along the Atlantic and Gulf coasts of the U.S. and from Middle America and the Caribbean to n. S. America. Along the Pacific coast in w. Mexico and most of Baja Cal.

One accepted Ore. record of a bird photographed at Bullards Beach SP, Coos Co., 9-17 September 1998.

Semipalmated Plover *Charadrius semipalmatus*

COOS	CLAT	LANE	BENT	PORT	CENT	MALH
24 Apr			24 Apr		29 Apr	

Uncommon to locally abundant migrant, with most birds at coastal estuaries and some concentrations in spring at larger lakes of se. Ore.; rare in fall in the Cascades. In winter, uncommon at larger estuaries, mainly on the s. coast; rare in w. interior valleys; essentially absent e. of the Cascades. Rare irregular local breeder in Harney and Coos cos. Southbound adults appear in Ore. by early Jul, with peak numbers in the hundreds through early Aug. Juvs. begin arriving in mid-Aug, with peak numbers in the hundreds dropping slowly throughout the fall; most depart by Nov. In the w. interior valleys, numbers are much lower, with peak flocks under 25 birds. Peak of spring passage is mid-Apr to mid-May. Generally absent from late May through early Jul, with rare summering and breeding birds.

**Piping Plover *Charadrius melodus*
Vagrant. This declining species breeds in the interior in sc. Canada and the nc. U.S. and on the Atlantic coast from S. Carolina to Newfoundland.

One accepted sight record for Ore. of a single bird observed on Neahkahnie Beach, Tillamook Co., 6-8 Sep 1986.

Killdeer *Charadrius vociferus*
Common spring and summer resident throughout the state with breeding records from every co., although absent or rare at higher elevations. During winter, Killdeer are uncommon to rare in e. Ore., but common to abundant w. of the Cascades. In particular, large numbers are found in the agricultural landscape of the Willamette V. Winter flocks as large as 1,000 birds are not uncommon in the c. and s. Willamette V. Small groups and solitary birds winter on the coast along beaches and in coastal fields. Coastal numbers increase during periods of cold weather at more northerly or inland areas. Killdeer initiate breeding activities earlier than most Ore. birds. In the Willamette V., eggs are found as early as mid-Mar, with peak laying dates from late Mar to Apr. Breeding dates are later e. of the Cascades. They retreat from the higher Cascades before Oct.

*Mountain Plover *Charadrius montanus*
Vagrant. Breeds in the interior prairies in sc. Canada and the nc. U.S. Winters from c. Cal. s. to Mexico.

vagrant occurrence

Ten accepted Ore. records, all in late fall or winter:

1. One was photographed at Bayocean Spit, Tillamook Co., 19-20 Nov 1977.
2. One was photographed at Siletz Bay, Lincoln Co., on 3 and 21-26 Feb 1983.
3. On bird in winter plumage was observed at the beach near Tahkenitch Cr., Douglas Co., on 23 Jan 1988.
4. Two adults were seen on the beach s. of Bandon, Coos Co., on 6 Dec 1989.
5. One bird was at Ankeny NWR, Marion Co., on 4 Dec 1995.
6. A winter-plumaged bird was s. of Corvallis, Benton Co., 19-21 Dec 1995.

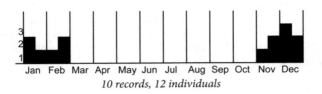

10 records, 12 individuals

7. One was near Floras L., Curry Co., on 7 Nov 1999.
8. A juv. was photographed at the Dunes Overlook, Douglas Co., and remained 16 Nov 1999 – 8 Jan 2000.
9. One was photographed at Brownsville, Linn Co., 2-3 Jan 2008.
10. One to two birds were photographed at New River, Curry Co., 17-20 Feb 2008.

A number of additional records have not been reviewed by the OBRC. Two birds appeared in a large flock of Killdeer near the Corvallis Airport, Benton Co.; 1 was collected and the other remained 2 Jan – 10 Mar 1967. Two birds were seen se. of Oakville, Linn Co., on 22 Dec 1981.

*Eurasian Dotterel *Charadrius morinellus*
Vagrant. Breeds across n. and c. Eurasia to n. Siberia, locally in n. and w. Alaska.
  One accepted Ore. record: an imm. was photographed near the s. jetty of the Siuslaw R., Lane Co., 24-26 Sep 2000.

Family Haematopodidae

Black Oystercatcher *Haematopus bachmani*
Uncommon to fairly common resident on rocky shores and sand/gravel beaches along entire coast. Along sandy c. coast, present only as occasional dispersing or wandering individual, typically on jetties. Egg laying takes place in May and early Jun. In non-breeding season they form groups of up to 30 (rarely 45) and use traditional feeding and roosting areas. Individuals will move into bays during rough weather on the outer coast.

Family Recurvirostridae

Black-necked Stilt *Himantopus mexicanus*

COOS	CLAT	LANE	BENT	PORT	CENT	MALH
					17 Apr	16 Apr

Locally uncommon to fairly common summer resident of Klamath, Lake, Harney, and Malheur cos. Local breeder in Umatilla, Morrow, and Union cos. Recently nested in the Willamette V. at Baskett Slough

NWR and at Fern Ridge Res. Regular spring and fall migrant through e. Ore. and irregular spring and casual fall migrants through w. Ore. Spring movements in small flocks and occasionally individually. Main movement during Apr and May with peak during mid-Apr. Earliest at Klamath NWR 19 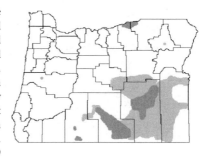 Mar 1979, and at Malheur NWR 20 Mar 1984. The peak of fall movement occurs during Aug with much lower numbers through Sep; latest at Malheur NWR 26 Oct and at Lower Klamath NWR 27 Oct. Very rare fall wanderer w. of Cascades.

American Avocet *Recurvirostra americana*

COOS	CLAT	LANE	BENT	PORT	CENT	MALH
					27 Apr	26 Mar

A common breeder e. of the Cascades at wetlands of sc. and se. Ore. Most breeders occur in Klamath, Lake, Harney, and Malheur cos. Smaller numbers also occur in adjacent areas and northeastern parts of the state where habitat is appropriate. In w. Ore., sightings in the Willamette 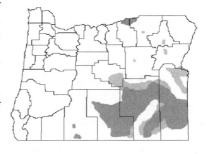 V. are rare, with records of migrants for wetland refuges such as William L. Finley NWR and the Fernhill Wetlands. On the coast, spring and fall migrants are uncommon with annual reports from Tillamook and Coos Bay. Wintering birds are rare, most records from Coos Bay. Birds arrive in the Great Basin from late Mar through Apr. In late summer and early fall, birds are common and locally abundant at various staging sites with greatest numbers found at L. Abert, Summer L., Goose L., and Malheur L. Birds depart for wintering grounds in Sep and Oct, although there are records of flocks lingering into Nov.

Family Scolopacidae
Subfamily Scolopacinae

Spotted Sandpiper *Actitis macularia*

winter distribution

A widespread transient and breeder throughout the state. Most birds depart by Oct, though a few remain w. of the Cascades. Winter occurrence in Ore. is seldom reported apart from a few on CBCs, mainly coastal and sw. interior, very rare e. of the w. Cascades. Northbound migrants begin to appear in early Apr; average arrival dates are 16-30 Apr for w. Ore., early May in the Cascades of e. Douglas Co., 28 Apr for c. Ore., and 2 May for Malheur NWR. Fall migration is not well known but peaks at Malheur NWR during Aug and in w. Ore. most birds are gone after Sep. Observations in fall suggest that local breeders leave by late Sep while the small number of local winter birds do not arrive until late Nov. Movements of this species are not well understood.

Solitary Sandpiper *Tringa solitaria*

Uncommon to rare migrant in fresh water or brackish habitats throughout Ore.; rarest along outer coast and in alkali habitats. Spring adults more common in w. interior valleys; fall juvs. are more common than adults in all regions and more common e. of the Cascades; occasional in extreme e. Ore. In migration, frequents muddy ponds and sewage lagoons as well as livestock wallows. Sometimes found in migration at high-elevation lakes. Most spring sightings are from the last wk of Apr through the first wk of May. Late spring record for w. Ore. from Seaside, 20 May 2000; late spring e. Ore. record from Fields, 30 May. The spring high count is 8 from Banks, Wash. Co., last wk of Apr 1984.

Two locations in the Ore. Cascades have hosted probable nesting of Solitary Sandpiper: Gold L. bog in the Willamette NF, Lane Co., and Olallie Meadows in the Mt. Hood NF, Marion Co. Possible breeding individuals have also occurred at Downy L., e. Wallowa Co., just outside Wallowa-Whitman NF. An early fall record was 2 Jul 1990 at Seaside, Clatsop Co.; the main movement begins late Jul. Fall adults arrive before juvs., but juvs. are more common and remain through late Sep. A late fall record w. of the Cascades at the n. spit Coos Bay was 22 Oct 1997. A fall high count was 6 at Malheur NWR, Harney Co., 17 Aug 1977.

Wandering Tattler *Tringa incana*
Fairly common migrant during spring and fall along the entire Ore. coast. Fall movement along the coast extends from early Jul through Oct with peak numbers noted from late Jul to mid-Aug. The latest departure date is 22 Nov, though there are a few winter reports. Very rare vagrant inland with fewer than a dozen reports, most from e. of the Cascades in fall. Rare and irregular in winter along the Ore. coast with sightings reported from mid-Dec through mid-Mar. Spring migration occurs from mid-Apr to early Jun with peak numbers moving through the state during early May.

*Spotted Redshank *Tringa erythropus*
Vagrant. Breeds across n. Eurasia to Siberia. Rare migrant in the w. Aleutians, casual elsewhere on the W. Coast.
    One accepted Ore. record: a bird in winter plumage was photographed at the s. jetty of the Columbia R., Clatsop Co., 21 Feb – 15 Mar 1981.

Greater Yellowlegs *Tringa melanoleuca*

COOS	CLAT	LANE	BENT	PORT	CENT	MALH
					7 Apr	17 Mar

Uncommon to locally common migrant on shorelines and open wet areas statewide. Winters on the coast and locally inland. Bred at Downy L. swamp, Wallowa Co., several times in the 1980s. Significant southbound movements begin early, with small flocks of adults usually appearing during the last few days of

winter distribution

Jun, increasing in Jul. Widespread after early Jul, with peak of juv. passage in Sep. Most birds are gone from e. Ore. by early Nov, but some linger in mild yrs. They winter along the entire coast, but most are at Coos Bay and only smaller flocks are scattered northward along the coast in most yrs. Small numbers winter locally in the Willamette V. They winter more rarely in the Umpqua and Rogue valleys. A few can also be found in the Klamath Basin and Umatilla Co. in winter, with scattered records elsewhere (especially along the Columbia R.) in mild yrs when open water with unfrozen edges is available for foraging.

Spring movements in w. Ore. are somewhat obscured by the presence of a significant wintering population on the s. coast, but a noticeable movement occurs in late Mar and especially Apr, with some birds present through early May and stragglers rarely to early Jun. Spring movement is more apparent e. of the Cascades. Average arrival at Malheur is 17 Mar and peak of passage is in the first half of Apr. A similar pattern holds true in the Klamath Basin.

Willet *Tringa semipalmata*

COOS	CLAT	LANE	BENT	PORT	CENT	MALH
1 Apr					20 Apr	10 Apr

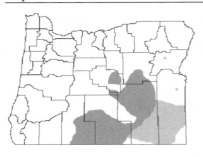

Western Willets (*T. s. inornatus*) breed at isolated and dispersed sites of the Great Basin. Willets are a common spring and summer resident e. of the Cascades in Klamath, Lake, Harney, Malheur, and Grant cos. Also confirmed in Crook Co. Willets appear at most Ore. breeding sites in mid-Apr, with an early date from Malheur NWR of 21 Mar. Following breeding activities, some Willets congregate at pre-migratory wetland staging sites for a relatively short period and depart for coastal wintering sites in Jun and early Jul. There are no winter records of Willets e. of the Cascades. Rare in winter on the coast, but small groups from unknown populations winter in many yrs in Coos Bay, and occasionally in Yaquina Bay and at Bandon. Willets are very rare spring and fall migrants in the Willamette V. and other inland areas w. of the Cascades. In coastal areas, birds are rare during spring and fall.

Lesser Yellowlegs *Tringa flavipes*

COOS	CLAT	LANE	BENT	PORT	CENT	MALH
					21 Apr	13 Apr

Uncommon to common migrant, most birds in fall. In the eastern one-third of Ore., it usually outnumbers Greater Yellowlegs in fall. Numbers drop significantly farther w., where Greater is usually far more common w. of the Cascades. However, some yrs bring remarkably large flights to w. Ore. On the outer coast this is one of the less common regular migrant shorebirds, with numbers usually much lower than those of

Greater Yellowlegs. Southbound movements of adults begin fairly early, with outriders appearing the last few days of June in some yrs. The bulk of movement begins in early Jul and continues through Sep, with a peak in Aug at Malheur NWR involving chiefly juvs. Unlike those of the Greater Yellowlegs, fall movements have a narrow peak in late Aug-early Sep and then drop off sharply. Very rare in winter, mostly on the s. coast and interior sw. Ore. Spring movements involve far fewer birds than are seen in fall. Migration begins with small numbers in late Mar, including birds in e. Ore.

Wood Sandpiper *Tringa glareola*
Vagrant. Breeds across n. Eurasia; rare but regular migrant to w. Aleutians.

One accepted Ore. record: a bird was photographed and seen by many observers at Fern Ridge Res., Lane Co., 30 Sep – 8 Oct 2008, although the bird may have been present for a wk or more before the first report.

Upland Sandpiper *Bartramia longicauda*
A rare breeder in large montane meadows within forests of e. Ore., mostly in Bear V. and Logan V., Grant Co. It also bred at Sycan Marsh, Lake Co., in 1981. Also reported irregularly from Big Summit Prairie, Crook Co., Bridge Cr. W.A., and Campbell Flats on Starkey Forest (both Union Co). In Umatilla Co., reported at Pine Cr., Albee, and at French Ranch in the n. Ukiah Basin. In 1991, a pair was reported from Cable Cr., e. Ukiah Basin, and in 1992 and 1993 pairs were reported from several sites in the Marley Cr. area on Starkey Forest. At Bear and Logan valleys, birds return in the first wk of May. Fledging was observed 15 Jul-12 Aug. No departure information is available.

Upland Sandpipers are almost never observed away from the breeding grounds in Ore. Transient records from and adjacent to Malheur NWR are on 31 May 1964, 2 May 1987, and 12 Aug 1987. There are 2 records from the Boardman Bombing Range, Morrow Co., in 1995 and 1996. One was at Papersack Canyon, Gilliam Co., on 30 May 1994. There are 5 records from w. Ore.: 23-28 Jul 1987 at Hatfield Marine Science Center, Lincoln Co.; 22 May 1999 at Cape Blanco, Curry Co.; 16 Sep 2000 at McKenzie Ranch near New L., Coos Co.; 20 Jun 2001 at Coos Spit and 28-30 Jun 2008 at Wahl Ranch, Curry Co.

Whimbrel *Numenius phaeopus*
Common spring and fall migrant in coastal areas although found rarely in small numbers inland as well. All reports in Ore. have been of the N. American subspecies *N. p. hudsonicus*, with the exception of 2 sight

records showing enough white that they could have been the e. Eurasian subspecies *N. p. variegatus*.

Whimbrel is a rare spring migrant in the Willamette V. with about 1 record annually, typically in late Apr or early May. It is a rare spring migrant in e. Ore. with most records occurring in May at favored migratory shorebird stopovers. It is a casual fall migrant inland. The earliest coastal spring record is 14 Mar in Newport but northward migrants generally first appear in early Apr. Peak numbers occur in late Apr and early May. Few are seen after mid-May. A few non-breeding birds usually summer at favored estuaries such as Yaquina Bay and Necanicum Estuary as well as on open beaches in Clatsop Co. Adult fall migrants generally begin arriving in early Jul with the peak of fall migration occurring in Aug. Juvs. do not arrive before late Aug and reach peak numbers in Sep. Southbound migrants may be seen as late as Nov. Winters in small numbers on the s. Ore. coast, primarily at Bandon (less regular since the 1990s) and Coos Bay and also sometimes at Yaquina Bay.

Bristle-thighed Curlew Numenius tahitiensis

vagrant occurrence

Vagrant. Very restricted breeding range in w. Alaska, winters on Hawaii and other islands in the tropical Pacific. Rare in spring to coastal s. Alaska, vagrant along the W. Coast.

Eight accepted Ore. records, 6 of which occurred during the unprecedented weather-related landfall made by this species from n. Cal. to Wash. in 1998:

1. Two were observed at Bandon, Coos Co., on 16 Sep 1981.
2. One was observed at Yaquina Bay, Lincoln Co., on 14 May 1998.

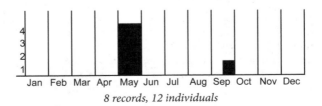

8 records, 12 individuals

3. Three birds were photographed at the s. jetty of the Columbia R., 9-21 May 1998.
4. One bird was at New River, Curry Co., on 6 May 1998.
5. One bird was at New River, Coos Co., on 19 May 1998.
6. One was photographed at Bandon Marsh NWR, Coos Co., on 22 May 1998.
7. One was observed at Pony Slough, Coos Bay, Coos Co., on 13 May 1998.
8. One was photographed at Clatsop Beach, Clatsop Co., on 22 May 2006.

In addition, a bird was reported flying past the Boiler Bay Viewpoint, Lincoln Co., on 29 Sep 2000. This record is still under review by the OBRC.

Long-billed Curlew *Numenius americanus*

COOS	CLAT	LANE	BENT	PORT	CENT	MALH
					2 Apr	26 Mar

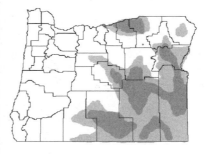

The Long-billed Curlew is a locally common breeder in open grassland areas e. of the Cascades in Klamath, Lake, Harney, Crook, Umatilla, Morrow, Union, Malheur, and Baker cos. It is not known to nest in Wallowa Co. in recent yrs. It is most abundant in the Columbia R. basin followed by the Harney/Malheur L. area; small numbers of breeders likely occur in most short-grass habitats at L. Abert and other alkaline lakes in sc. and se. Ore.

During migration, this species occurs in the same habitats as during the breeding season; rare in the Willamette V., more commonly observed in spring than fall; also found in small numbers in estuaries along the coast. Have been observed during all months on the coast. It is not present in winter along the coast in all yrs; most regular at Coos Bay. Long-billed Curlews arrive on breeding areas beginning mid-Mar. Some females depart breeding grounds by mid-Jun; a few birds arrive on the coast beginning in late Jun. Most adults remain on breeding areas till late Jul; juvs. are noted into mid-Aug. Near Malheur NWR, fall migration peaks 5-25 Aug, most are gone by mid-Sep, and the latest record is 5 Oct; elsewhere e. of the Cascades birds have been reported as late as Nov.

*Hudsonian Godwit *Limosa haemastica**

vagrant occurrence

Vagrant. Breeds locally across w. and s. Alaska, n. Canada and the s. shore of Hudson Bay. Winters mainly in s. S. America.

A casual vagrant to Ore., with 16 accepted records to date. Thirteen of those are fall records from early Aug through Oct, mostly on the coast. Spring records include 1 at the s. jetty of the Columbia R., Clatsop Co., on 31 May 1983; 1 at Ankeny NWR, Marion Co., 10-11 May 1994; and 1 at Miller I. W.A., Klamath Co., on 30 May 2000. All records but 1 are of single birds; a flock of 16 was at Bayocean Spit, Tillamook Co., on 17 Aug 1980.

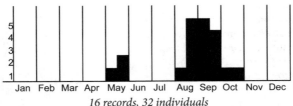

16 records, 32 individuals

*Bar-tailed Godwit *Limosa lapponica**

vagrant occurrence

Vagrant. Breeds across n. Eurasia and in n. and w. Alaska. Alaskan breeders fly across the Pacific Ocean to winter in New Zealand and e. Australia.

Casual vagrant to Ore., with 21 accepted records to date, all along the coast. Rare but regular in fall, not annual. Ore. spring records range from late Apr to early Jun. A group of 4 at Bandon Marsh NWR, Coos Co., on 14 May 1988 is the largest reported Ore. flock. Ore. fall records range from late Jun to mid-Oct. One was at Coos Bay 3 Nov –7 Dec 2001 for an unusual winter record.

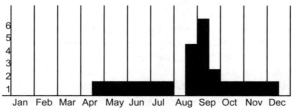

Bar-tailed Godwit: 21 records, 25 individuals

Marbled Godwit *Limosa fedoa*
Regular spring and fall migrant on the Ore. coast; irregular in winter, mainly from Coos Bay southward. Rare and irregular spring and fall migrant (single birds) in the Willamette V. Occasional spring migrant in the Rogue V., but absent in fall. Irregular spring and fall migrant in e. Ore. Absent in summer and winter in inland valleys; casual in e. Ore. in winter. Spring migration commences in early Apr and extends through early Jun on the coast. In e. Ore., average arrival at Malheur NWR is 27 Apr; latest record is 7 Jun. Flocks generally consist of fewer than 50 birds on the coast. Most spring records in e. Ore. consist of 1-10 birds at any one locality. The first southbound migrants appear in mid-Jun. Two peaks occur on the coast, the first from late Aug to early Sep, and the second in late Sep. Juvs. migrate south several wks later than most adults. After mid-Nov, a few stragglers are seen until late Dec and thereafter become scarce until spring migration resumes. The latest record in e. Ore. is 13 Oct 1990.

Ruddy Turnstone *Arenaria interpres*
The species is an uncommon to common spring and fall transient along the coast; a few birds remain to winter there each yr, mainly on the s. coast. Largest migrant flocks seen at Bandon. Irregular spring and occasional fall transient inland, including e. Ore. This species is usually found singly or in small flocks. Larger flocks are occasional in fall and spring. Earliest fall arrivals are generally the second wk of Jul, rare to 30 Jun. Juvs.' arrival dates are scattered throughout the fall migratory period, beginning in late Aug. In some yrs there are fewer juv. than adult migrants. Numbers decrease during Sep and birds are scarce by Oct, rare through winter. Fall records inland w. of the Cascades include 11 Aug -15 Sep. E. of the Cascades, there are numerous fall records from 3 Aug to 30 Sep. Spring migrants usually arrive late Apr; absent by end of May. Inland w. of the Cascades, seen 24 Apr to 4 Jun.

Black Turnstone *Arenaria melanocephala*
A common transient and winter visitant on the coast; rare in early summer. The only e. Ore. record is of 2 individuals at Ochoco Res., Crook Co., 8 Sep 1985. There are fewer than a dozen inland records of single individuals w. of the Cascades at all seasons. First migrants arrive in early Jul; migration continues through mid-Dec. Adults arrive first; juvs. begin to arrive 6-17 Aug. Wintering birds scatter along the coast in small flocks. Generally gone by mid-May, rare late May to early Jul.

Surfbird *Aphriza virgata*
Strictly coastal with no inland records. Fairly common migrant along the coast during fall and spring with large numbers resident during the winter months. Fall movement begins in early Jul (earliest arrival date reported is 23 Jun) with peak number noted during the latter two wks in Jul; adults arrive first followed by juvs. Spring migration appears as a gradual reduction in numbers (from early Mar through Apr) with no noticeable peak departure period. Latest departure date recorded is 28 May.

***Great Knot** *Calidris tenuirostris*
Vagrant. Breeds in the mtns. of ne. Siberia and winters from the Persian Gulf e. to the Philippines and Australia. Casual spring migrant in sw. and w. Alaska.
     One accepted Ore. record of a juv. seen by many and photographed at Bandon Marsh and the lower Coquille R., Coos Co., 1-17 Sep 1990, for the first N. American record of this species s. of Alaska.

Red Knot *Calidris canutus*
See *BOGR* for complex taxonomy. In contrast to Cal. and Wash., most Red Knots bypass Ore. Primarily found on the coast, where they are regular transients in spring and fall. Casual in summer and occasional in winter along the Ore. coast. Casual in spring and fall in the Willamette V. Occasional in the Rogue V. in spring, but casual in fall. It is a rare transient in spring and fall in e. Ore. Red Knots are rapid transients through Ore. in spring. They arrive in mid-Apr and depart by the end of May. In e. Ore., they have been seen as late as 6 Jun. Reported more frequently from the Rogue V. and e. of Cascades than the Willamette V. Numbers are usually low, singles and small flocks.
     Fall migration is underway by the third wk of Jul, peaks the last wk of Aug and first wk of Sep when juvs. arrive, and thereafter dwindles into mid-Nov. There are only 3 fall records from the Willamette V.: St. Paul sewage pond, Marion Co., 13 Sep 1991; Fern Ridge Res. on 14 Oct 2003 (Geier 2004) and 10-20 Sep 2006 (Irons 2007a), all single birds.

There are 8 records in e. Ore. (all single birds); dates recorded for 5 range from 24 Aug to 26 Sep. A few scattered individuals winter on the Ore. coast in some yrs. There are no records from inland valleys or e. Ore. in winter.

Sanderling *Calidris alba*
Common to locally abundant on open sand beaches from fall through spring. Rare to locally uncommon migrant inland statewide; most often reported along the Columbia R. and at e. Ore. lakes. Present in Ore. except in late Jun. First southbound migrants appear in early Jul; birds are common to abundant on coast from Jul onward. Fall migrants tend to be in small flocks but build through the season until flocks of 1,000 or more are found on beaches by Nov. Can be somewhat local in winter, with large clusters separated by mi. of empty beach.

Away from the outer coast this species moves in very small numbers from Jul through Oct, rarely Nov. It is regular in small numbers at Malheur NWR, with records from 11 Jul to 2 Oct and peak of passage in Aug. Winter populations move somewhat along the outer beaches, with a noticeable tendency to concentrate by late Feb as birds begin staging to move n. Beaches from Coos Bay to Florence and in Clatsop Co. are principal spring staging areas. Peak of passage on the coast is late Apr through mid-May, with extended buildups in some areas (especially near the Columbia R.) and fewer birds in other locations by mid-May. The earliest spring date at Malheur NWR is 24 Apr, with a late date of 8 Jun.

> I.D. Note: Juvs. are occasionally mistaken for Semipalmated Sandpipers. Adults in alternate plumage (or in molt) are occasionally mistaken for Red-necked or Little Stints, especially when seen alone. Note particularly the unique lack of a hallux (rear toe) in Sanderlings, as well as the rather heavy bill and tendency to show a dark "shoulder" mark near the bend of the wing when on the ground.

Semipalmated Sandpiper *Calidris pusilla*
Rare irregular spring transient throughout Ore., very uncommon coastal and rare but regular inland fall transient. Least common in sw. part of state. Most spring sightings in Ore. are late Apr through late May; the earliest spring record w. of the Cascades is 14 Apr 1964; early spring record e. of the Cascades is 3 May 1987. There are no records between 21 May and 29 Jun. Adults return in early Jul (earliest coastal fall date 29 Jun 1986; earliest interior fall date 7 Jul 1984). The peak of adult movement (which involves very few birds) is in mid-Jul, with some

reported through early Aug. Juvs. arrive in late Jul and peak mid-Aug to mid-Sep (again, very few birds are involved); the latest coastal fall date is 25 Sep 1987; the latest interior fall date is 25 Sep 1983. There are no verified Ore. records from 25 Sep to 2 Apr.

Western Sandpiper *Calidris mauri*

COOS	CLAT	LANE	BENT	PORT	CENT	MALH
					21 Apr	21 Apr

winter distribution

The most abundant shorebird in estuaries and along beaches during migration from Jul through Sep and, briefly, in spring. Small numbers can appear statewide. Generally, larger flocks are seen in fall than in spring. The largest concentrations of migrant birds are usually found at Tillamook Bay, Bandon Marsh, and the Columbia R. estuary. During winter along the coast, Westerns are occasional to uncommon at larger estuaries. Rare at w. interior sites during the winter, although a few birds are found most winters at Fern Ridge Res. near Eugene. Generally absent e. of the Cascades in winter.

Spring migration of Western Sandpipers is more compressed than fall migration, and individuals pass through the region quickly. Main spring migration w. of the Cascades is from mid-Apr to early May, with a peak generally in last few days of Apr and first few of May. E. of the Cascades, the first arrival and peaks of Westerns are approximately a wk later. The first southbound adults appear in the last wk of Jun. Along the coast, peak of adult movement is late Jul and early Aug, followed by a higher peak of juvs. in late Aug; e. of the Cascades, the pattern is similar but high counts have been recorded late into Sep.

*Red-necked Stint *Calidris ruficollis*
Vagrant. Breeds in Siberia and rarely in n. and w. Alaska. Rare but regular migrant in the Bering Sea.

Nine accepted Ore. records, including 4 different adults that were photographed in the shorebird congregation on Bayocean Spit at Tillamook Bay, Tillamook Co., during the fall of 1982:

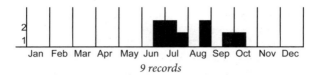

9 records

1. A bird in breeding plumage was photographed at Bayocean Spit, Tillamook Co., on 20 Jun 1982.
2. A bird in breeding plumage was photographed at Bayocean Spit, Tillamook Co., on 3 Jul 1982.

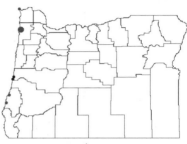

vagrant occurrence

3. One was at Bayocean Spit, Tillamook Co., 19-22 Aug 1982.
4. One bird in mostly breeding plumage was photographed at Bayocean Spit, Tillamook Co., on 21, 22, and 26 Aug 1982.
5. A bird in breeding plumage was at Bandon, Coos Co., on 25 Jun 1984.
6. A bird in breeding plumage was at the s. jetty of the Columbia R., Clatsop Co., on 19 Jul 1997.
7. An adult in breeding plumage was at the N. Spit Coos Bay, Coos Co., on 15 Jul 1999.
8. A juv. was on Siltcoos Beach, Lane Co., on 19 Sep 2004.
9. A juv. was photographed at the s. jetty of the Siuslaw R., Lane Co., 4-6 Oct 2006.

*Little Stint *Calidris minuta*
Vagrant. Breeds across n. Eurasia to nc. Siberia. Casual migrant in w. and n. Alaska.
   Four accepted Ore. records:
1. A juv. was photographed at Bayocean Spit, Tillamook Co., on 7 Sep 1985.
2. A juv. was photographed at Bandon, Coos Co., on 12 Sep 1986.
3. A juv. was photographed at the s. jetty of the Columbia R., Clatsop Co., 10-11 Aug 1995.
4. An adult in mostly alternate plumage was photographed at the N. Spit Coos Bay, Coos Co. on 13 Jul 2002.

This species can be very difficult to separate from the similar Red-necked Stint, especially in juv. plumage, and all future records should be carefully documented.

*Long-toed Stint *Calidris subminuta*
Vagrant. Breeds locally from sw. Siberia to Kamchatka. Very rare spring migrant and fall vagrant on the w. Aleutian Is.
   Two accepted Ore. records:
1. A juv. was photographed and its voice recorded at the s. jetty of the Columbia R., Clatsop Co., 2-6 Sep 1981.
2. An adult was observed at the s. jetty of the Columbia R., Clatsop Co., on 17 Jul 1983.
Often very similar to Least Sandpiper, and all records should be carefully documented.

Least Sandpiper *Calidris minutilla*

COOS	CLAT	LANE	BENT	PORT	CENT	MALH
					20 Apr	25 Apr

winter distribution

An uncommon to locally abundant peep statewide in migration, with most birds along the coast and at larger lakes and marshes inland. Found in appropriate habitat statewide. Locally common on the coast in winter; smaller numbers winter in the w. interior valleys, where small flocks can be found at larger lakes, locally in flooded fields and sometimes even at marginal sites such as sewage ponds. A few birds sometimes winter e. of the Cascades where appropriate habitat remains open. A few southbound adults appear in the last wk of Jun, with most adult movement in Jul. However, single adult Least can be found well into Sep mixed into flocks of other peeps, where their plumage seems anomalous and therefore attracts the attention of observers looking for stints. Juv. movement is extended and peak numbers can be found from mid-Aug through Nov, though late Aug and early Sep are typical peak times. Peak of southbound passage at Malheur NWR is 25 Jul to 25 Aug.

Spring movement is more compressed, with most birds moving from early Apr through early May. Peak of passage at Malheur NWR is 20

Apr to 5 May. Spring peaks at some inland locations are very high, e.g., 23,150 at Summer L., 1 May 1987 and 6,000 at L. Abert, 1 May 1971. Numbers at coastal sites are lower but still substantial, e.g., 3,500 at Tillamook Bay, 30 Apr 1991.

I.D. Note: Plumage variation in Least Sandpiper is an underappreciated I.D. problem that is poorly handled in most field guides. This is one of the most variable peeps in all but its dullest basic plumage. Observers afield in September can see a bewildering array of Least, with oddly splotched adult stragglers mixed with duller juvs., brilliant juvs. that recall illustrations of Long-toed Stint or Sharp-tailed Sandpiper, a few birds already in dull winter garb and every gradation in between. Recognition of this problem is an important aspect of learning the "basic" shorebirds.

*White-rumped Sandpiper *Calidris fuscicollis*
Vagrant. Breeds from ne. Alaska across arctic Canada to Baffin I. Fall migration mostly along the Atlantic coast, spring migration across the Great Plains.

One accepted Ore. record of an adult photographed at New River, Coos Co., on 28 Jun 2003.

Baird's Sandpiper *Calidris bairdii*
Uncommon migrant statewide, with most birds southbound juvs. Can occur in suitable habitat anywhere in Ore., but numbers are usually very low and sizable flocks almost nonexistent. Most often reported from the high Cascades eastward and on the coast; less common in the w. interior valleys, perhaps owing to paucity of habitat. Sometimes occurs at alpine lakes. Annual numbers are quite variable. Southbound movements of adults begin by early Jul, although most yrs bring few birds. Peak of passage of juvs. is from mid-Aug to early Sep. Most birds have gone by late Sep, but stragglers have been reported at Malheur NWR as late as 14 Oct, at Fern Ridge Res. 20 Nov, and on the coast as late as 20 Nov at Coos Bay and 28 Nov at Yaquina Bay. Any birds found after Oct should be photographed for confirmation.

Peak fall numbers are unimpressive compared to other shorebirds, typically under 10 birds in a flock and rarely more than 30. In recent yrs, sizable flocks have been seen in ne. Ore. in fall. There are no valid winter records from Ore. Spring numbers are even lower, sometimes absent, and those few that are seen are often e. of the Cascades. The peak of this very limited passage at Malheur NWR is 20-30 Apr, with the earliest report 8 Apr and the latest 8 May. The latest record for w. Ore. is 6 Jun at Yaquina Bay.

Pectoral Sandpiper *Calidris melanotos*
Found statewide in migration; largest numbers in fall, sometimes all but absent in spring. Common on the outer coast but also in wet coastal pastures. More local inland but large flocks can be found in preferred habitat. Fall numbers vary considerably from yr to yr. Very few adult birds move through Ore.; the few that occur pass through from early Jul through Aug. Peak of juv. passage is later than for many other shorebirds, with numbers not building until Sep and sometimes remaining quite high through Oct. A few birds linger into early Nov. Most winter reports are probably referable to Least Sandpipers. Any records after Nov should be documented. Spring movement is much smaller; in some yrs essentially invisible. Movement can begin early, e.g., 9 Apr and is usually over by mid-May, though there are records to early Jun on the outer coast.

Sharp-tailed Sandpiper *Calidris acuminata*
Irregular transient in fall on the Ore. coast; only one spring record. Occasional in the Willamette V. and in e. Ore. In coastal Ore., 1-12 birds (but usually <6) have been reported each yr since 1980. One to 4 birds occasionally seen in the Willamette V.; most reported from Sauvie I. and Fern Ridge. Five records in e. Ore.

The earliest fall records are Aug 22, 1973 (*NAB* 28:95) and Aug 28, 1987 (Contreras 2006); these are the only known multiple-observer records before Sep. The latest is 12 Nov 1991 on the coast. Most migrate though Ore. in the last few days of Sep, tapering off through mid-Oct. The single spring record was 24 May 2000 at New R., Coos Co.

> I.D. Note: Some juv. Pectoral and Least Sandpipers are remarkably bright, and when feeding alone or near duller Pectorals can be reminiscent of Sharp-tails. Fall juv. Sharp-tails usually have a very bright whitish supercilium that is more obvious behind the eye; this whitish spot can be remarkably visible at a distance. Also, the more "capped" look and the peachy breast without heavy streaking are diagnostic.

Rock Sandpiper *Calidris ptilocnemis*
Of 4 subspecies described, only *C. p. tschuktschorum* occurs in Ore. However, an individual of the distinctive large, pale Pribilof subspecies *C. p. ptilocnemis* was found in December 2000 at Ocean Shores jetty, Grays Harbor Co., Wash. This large subspecies in basic plumage resembles a pale Surfbird in coloration. Rare to locally uncommon; flocks larger than 10 are rare and singles are common. Strictly coastal with no inland records. Uncommon to rare migrant and winter visitor along the entire rocky coastline although greater numbers recorded for the n. counties.

Since the 1990s, has become much less frequent on the s. half of the Ore. coast. A late fall migrant with the major influx into Ore. occurring during the last wk in Oct and into early Nov. The earliest arrival date reported is 21 Aug, which is anomalous. Spring migration involves few birds and is rather protracted with no discernable peak; most birds depart by the third wk of Apr. Latest departure date recorded is 14 May.

Dunlin *Calidris alpina*

COOS	CLAT	LANE	BENT	PORT	CENT	MALH
					9 Apr	27 Apr

Abundant transient and winter visitant in estuaries and occasionally on beaches along the coast of Ore. Thousands winter in the Willamette V., especially the s. part. Small numbers appear during migration and winter in the Rogue and Umpqua valleys. In e. Ore., smaller numbers (up to a few thousand) are seen

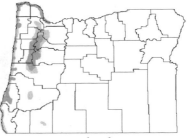

winter distribution

at a variety of wetlands during migration, mainly in spring, especially around Klamath Basin and se. alkaline lakes such as Summer L. and L. Abert. Dunlin are rare spring and fall migrants at lower elevations in ne. Ore. Records for Dunlin on the coast mainly occur from mid-Sep to early May. Birds are largely absent in Jun, Jul, and most of Aug, although there are occasional records in these months. In the Willamette V., high concentrations (10,000 +) of Dunlin are reported Jan-Mar, with major movements in Mar. Mid-Apr to mid-May appears to be the main spring migration period for Dunlin in this region. Timing of fall passage of Dunlin e. of the Cascades is not well understood, although it is rare to see birds Jul to mid-Sep, and uncommon to see them late Sep into Nov, with a few records in Dec. Dunlin generally do not winter e. of the Cascades.

Curlew Sandpiper Calidris ferruginea

Vagrant. Breeds in arctic w. and c. Siberia. Casual visitor to the e. U.S and in w. Alaska and the Aleutians.

Casual fall visitor to Ore., with 14 accepted records to date. All but 1 were seen on the coast, the majority between late Jul and early Oct. A late juv. was at the n. jetty of the Siuslaw R., Lane Co., on 24 Nov 2005, and

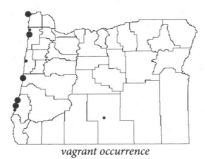

1 was photographed in the company of Sanderlings and Dunlin at Bastendorff Beach, Coos Co., on 18 Dec 2005 for an unusual winter record. The sole inland record was of an adult male at Summer L. W.A., Lake Co., 17-21 Jul 2004.

vagrant occurrence

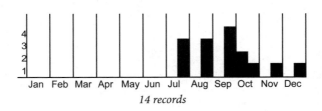

14 records

Stilt Sandpiper *Calidris himantopus*

Rare fall and occasional spring transient, most frequently found in estuarine habitat along the coast. Also found along shorelines of the Great Basin region of sc. and se. Ore. However, it has occurred in appropriate habitat throughout the state. Spring sightings are truly exceptional, with only 4 records, each e. of the Cascades: "early May" 1962 at Klamath Marsh; 8 May 1991 at Malheur NWR; 3 on 12-15 May 1995 at Summer L. W.A.; and 1 on 22 Apr 1998 at Malheur.

First migrants heading s. from their breeding grounds are adults, which pass through Ore. from early Jul through mid-Aug. Adult records are quite unusual, averaging only about 1 sighting every 3 yrs. The earliest southbound record was 2 Jul 1993 at the s. jetty of the Columbia R. Latest record of an adult was 8 Sep 1993 at L. Abert. Juv. birds migrating southward to wintering grounds make up the bulk of occurrences in Ore. Found primarily 19 Aug-24 Sep, peaking the last wk of Aug. There are only 7 records after 1 Oct. Latest fall records were both in 1989, 1 on the very late date of 25 Nov at Ochoco Res. in c. Ore., the next-latest record a month earlier, 1 on 22 Oct at Bandon, Coos Co. Tends to be found singly or in pairs, but occasionally in small flocks.

Buff-breasted Sandpiper *Tryngites subruficollis*
This is a rare but regular fall migrant on the Ore. coast. Sporadic fall migrant on Sauvie I. Casual in the Rogue V. and at Fern Ridge. Two fall records e. of the Cascades, 1 near Prineville, 24 Sep – 5 Oct 1990, and 1 at the Redmond sewage ponds 24-25 Aug 2001. There is only a single spring record, 1 seen 12 Apr 1981 in alternate plumage at Wilson R. Meadows, Tillamook Co. There are no winter records. Generally 1-6 birds can be found at favored sites along the Ore. coast. Counts at Sauvie I. range 1-3 birds. Peak number at a single site was 14 near the s. jetty of the Siuslaw R., Lane Co., 11 Sep 1985, one of the largest flocks ever found on the W. Coast. Fall migration through Ore. extends from mid-Aug to mid-Oct. Early dates are 13 Aug 2001 and 15 Aug 1985; migration peaks from the last wk of Aug to mid-Sep; latest record 17 Oct 1988.

Ruff *Philomachus pugnax*
Rare fall transient and very rare spring transient, usually on the coast. Casual in winter. Some records are from inland in w. Ore., particularly from Sauvie I. near Portland and from the wetlands near Fern Ridge Res. There are 4 records from e. Ore. Peak period of occurrence is late Aug–early Sep. Earliest fall record for a juv. is 11 Aug and latest are 23 Nov 1980 at Coos Bay (Contreras 1998) and at Bandon 14-15 Nov 2008 (K. Andersson, L. Miller et al.); possibly the same bird was nearby at Coos Bay on 30 Nov (R. Hoyer, ALC). Adults reported between 25 Jul and 11 Oct. Five spring records, all of single birds, include 3 from e. Ore. and 2 from the coast as follows: near Klamath Falls, 3-9 Apr 2001; White L., Klamath Co., 30 Apr 2000; Summer L., 12-14 Apr 1991; Coos Bay, 18 Apr 1997; and Tillamook Co., 2 Jun 1984. Two winter records for Ore.; 1 in the Coquille V., 18 Jan 1980, and 2 that remained w. of Eugene in the winter of 2002-03 (Contreras 2006).

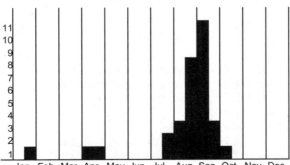

27 records, 38 individuals (through 1991)

Short-billed Dowitcher *Limnodromus griseus*
Three subspecies that differ somewhat in the field; see references and field guides for details. Common to locally abundant coastal migrant, less common and more local in w. interior valleys, rare but regular e. of the Cascades. Records e. of the Cascades are widespread but numbers reported are very low, often consisting of 1 or 2 birds in large flocks of Long-billed Dowitchers. Has been recorded as far e. as Malheur Co. and ne. Ore. Except in winter, when usually absent, this is the commonest dowitcher on the outer coast. Spring movements begin in late Mar and the peak of passage is in late Apr. Stragglers appear through May. E. of the Cascades single birds or very small numbers are the norm.

Southbound movements begin with the arrival of the first adults in the last days of Jun. Peak of passage for adults is mid-Jul, with numbers similar to those found in spring migration. Imms. begin arriving in early Aug and peak in late Aug and early Sep, with stragglers through early Oct. Numbers are somewhat higher, with flocks of several hundred not uncommon, and a record high of 2,000 on 18 Aug 1990 at Bandon, Coos Co. There are reliable reports of calling birds found as late as Dec and a few CBC reports of calling birds, but there are no winter records confirmed by specimen or voice recording.

Long-billed Dowitcher *Limnodromus scolopaceus*

winter distribution

Common to locally abundant migrant statewide. This is by far the most common dowitcher (sometimes the most common shorebird at a given site) found in migration e. of the Cascades. It is also the dowitcher most likely to be found at most inland locations in the state and the only dowitcher that regularly winters. In migration can be found at almost any shallow-water site in the state, from Malheur L. to small potholes in the w. interior valleys and the mudflats of the outer coast. Winter distribution is more limited, with most birds on the coast but small numbers in the w. interior valleys. Rare in winter e. of the Cascades.

Adults appear in early Jul (mostly e. of the Cascades until mid-Jul), with a peak of passage in late Jul and very early Aug. Juvs. begin arriving in numbers in Aug, with a buildup in late Aug and a lower extended peak throughout Sep, with some movement still underway in early Oct.

Numbers (sometimes in the thousands) peak at Malheur NWR in late Aug. Peak counts w. of the Cascades are much lower, with 2,000 at Sauvie I., 13 Oct 1988, the highest reported at one site and normal numbers in the dozens to hundreds at a given site. Most are gone from Ore. e. of the Cascades by Dec, with only rare stragglers reported during winter. Latest record at Malheur is 26 Nov 1971. A few birds can be found most winters in the w. interior valleys. Small flocks remain along the coast all winter, but total numbers and locations of large flocks vary from yr to yr. Northbound movements are smaller and blend somewhat with wintering flocks on the coast, but significant movements are underway by Mar and a noticeable peak occurs in late Apr.

*Jack Snipe *Lymnocryptes minimus*
Vagrant. Breeds across n. Eurasia and winters s. to tropical Africa, se. China and Taiwan.

Two accepted Ore. records, both of birds taken during snipe hunting season in the marshes along the Lane Co. coast:
1. One bird was shot and the specimen photographed on 20 Oct 2004.
2. One bird was shot and the specimen photographed on 16 Nov 2007.

Recently, small snipe matching the description of this species were observed at Stewart Pond, Eugene, Lane Co., on 19 Feb 2008; near Astoria on 18 Oct 2008; and near Fern Ridge Res., Lane Co. on 6 Jan 2009. None of these records have been reviewed by the OBRC, but they hint at the possibility that this secretive species has been overlooked in the past. It should be watched for wherever migrating Wilson's Snipe occur.

Wilson's Snipe *Gallinago delicata*

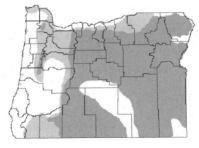

Breeds in the Blue and Wallowa mtns. region, and also breeds throughout freshwater wetland complexes of sc. and se. Ore. Uncommon and local w. of the Cascades in summer. Uncommon local breeder in the Willamette V.; also n. Clatsop Co. and n. Jackson Co. Uncommon and local in the Cascades in the breeding season, and at isolated sites in the c. Coast Range. Uncommon to common in winter at lower elevations along the coast and in inland valleys, and can be locally abundant where birds gather to feed in coastal pastures and other wetlands. Uncommon to fairly common winter resident throughout interior w. Ore. valleys. Uncommon e. of the Cascades in winter, and in especially severe cold may not be present at all. Can be found almost anywhere statewide during spring and fall. Birds breeding in wetland complexes of sc. and se. Ore. typically begin arriving in Mar. Spring influx at Malheur NWR occurs 20-30 Mar, with pairs on territory by Apr. By mid-Jul presumed fall migrants sometimes observed away from breeding areas. Numbers at Malheur NWR begin declining in Sep, with migrants still seen through Oct. In w. Ore., fall arrivals appear in Aug-Sep and depart Mar-Apr.

Subfamily Phalaropodinae

Wilson's Phalarope *Phalaropus tricolor*

COOS	CLAT	LANE	BENT	PORT	CENT	MALH
					30 Apr	25 Apr

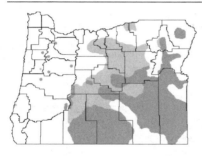

Common transient and breeder e. of the Cascades. Largest numbers breed on the great marshes of se. Ore. In the Cascades, breeds to at least 5,100 ft, mainly in Deschutes, Douglas (rare), and Klamath cos. Local breeder in wet valleys e. of the Cascades. Rare breeder w. of the Cascades, but increasing, with several recent records in Lane, Linn, Benton, Polk, and Jackson cos. Occasionally seen during migration on coastal estuaries and salt marshes. Spring movements in recent yrs in w. Ore. have shown an average arrival in Benton Co. of 10 May (earliest 20 Apr) and most arrival records in the mid-valley and Wash. Co. from the middle third of May. The earliest Willamette V. report is 9 Apr. Arrival patterns in the Rogue V. (where few birds occur) are similar. They depart nesting grounds as soon as breeding is completed. Abundant in se Ore. during the fall. Present in Ore. until Sep (latest 22 Sep). There are no documented winter records from the state.

Red-necked Phalarope *Phalaropus lobatus*

COOS	CLAT	LANE	BENT	PORT	CENT	MALH
					3 May	12 May

Common to abundant migrant along the coast and over the ocean within 31 mi of shore. Coastal and w. Ore. sightings fluctuate markedly from yr to yr. There is a secondary flyway through c. Ore. that brings large numbers to L. Abert and to other alkaline lakes. Over most of the state small groups of up to 10-12 birds are regularly seen. Small numbers occasionally remain to summer e. of the Cascades. Early fall migrants begin arriving in late Jun at interior alkaline lakes staging areas. They increase through Jul to a peak in Aug and early Sep; most are gone by late Sep with stragglers into Oct. A late bird was at Hatfield L., Deschutes Co., 17 Nov 1984. Fall movements w. of the Cascades are inconspicuous and involve mostly small flocks. Early birds begin passing offshore in early Jul, with the main movement occurring from late Jul through Sep, with stragglers to early Nov. Spring movements are often highly conspicuous along the coast and much less so inland. Main movements e. of the Cascades occur during May. Early birds arrive during Apr, and the last leave by mid-Jun. Main coastal movements occur from late Apr to early Jun, with peak numbers during the first wk of May. Early birds arrive during Mar.

Red Phalarope *Phalaropus fulicarius*
Uncommon to common spring and fall transient, primarily offshore; small numbers regular onshore; irregularly rare to common in winter. Blown inshore, and occasionally inland, nearly annually w. of the Cascades, especially during Nov storms. Recorded e. of the Cascades about 20 times; half the records are from May-Jun and are not storm-related, indicating a small number of birds migrate overland in spring. Migrate offshore from late Apr to early Jun (earliest 14 Apr) and mid-Jul to Dec. Migration peaks for the Pacific Northwest in mid-May, Aug-Sep (adults), and late Oct to early Nov (juvs.). Odd records exist for every wk of Jun and Jul. Fall adult migration begins in late Jul; juvs. arrive in late Aug with peak numbers from late Sep to mid-Dec. In general, prefer deeper waters and migrate 1 mo later during spring and fall than Red-necked Phalaropes. High count 15,000 at Cape Arago 25 Nov 1990. May occasionally winter offshore Jan-Mar; thousands were blown to shore in Ore. and Wash. after a storm 18 Jan 1986.

Family Laridae
Subfamily Larinae

*Laughing Gull *Larus atricilla*
Vagrant. Breeds on the Gulf of Cal., the Gulf of Mexico and along the e. coast of the U.S.
  Three accepted Ore. records:

1. One bird in alternate plumage was photographed at the Lower Klamath NWR, Klamath Co., on 24 Apr 1983.
2. One adult in basic plumage was photographed at Bay City, Tillamook Co.; it was present through most of Oct 1998.
3. One adult in alternate plumage at the s. jetty of the Columbia R. on 31 Jul 1999.

In addition, 1 was reported at Crane Prairie Res., Deschutes Co., on 24 Sep 2008. This record has not yet been reviewed by the OBRC.

Care should be taken to separate this species from similar black-hooded gulls, especially Franklin's Gull.

Franklin's Gull *Larus pipixcan*

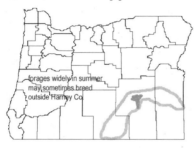

forages widely in summer
may sometimes breed
outside Harney Co.

Breeds in the se. portion of the state, especially the Harney Basin, rare w. of the Cascades. Nests locally in most yrs only at Malheur NWR and Hart Mtn. Nat. Ant. Ref., abundantly at the former and in small numbers at the latter. Rare in Klamath Basin May-Aug. In fall, may be found throughout e. Ore.; rare but regular on coast and in interior valleys where very rare in winter and spring. Average arrival date at Malheur NWR is 13 Apr, with earliest record nearly a month earlier. Young fledge in Jul and early Aug at Malheur NWR, with most departed by Sep.

*Little Gull *Larus minutus*

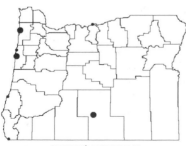

vagrant occurrence

Vagrant. Breeds across c. Eurasia. It is a sporadic breeder and regular winter visitor around the Great Lakes.

There are 11 accepted Ore. records, 8 from the coast (Curry, Coos, Lincoln and Tillamook cos.), 2 from Summer L., Lake Co., and 1 from John Day Dam, Sherman Co. The majority of records are from the fall and winter, with only 3 spring records.

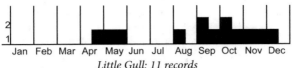

Little Gull: 11 records

*Black-headed Gull *Larus ridibundus*

Vagrant. Breeds widely across Eurasia and in w. Greenland and Newfoundland, winters regularly along the Atlantic coast and at the Great Lakes.

Three accepted Ore. records:
1. An adult was near Warrenton, Clatsop Co., on 20 Dec 1981.
2. One imm. was photographed at the Bay City sewage ponds, Tillamook Co., 3-19 Dec 1992 .
3. One adult was near Grass V., Sherman Co., on 19 Oct 1996.

Bonaparte's Gull *Larus philadelphia*

Abundant spring and fall transient along the coast, primarily over the ocean just offshore. Fairly common and widespread transient elsewhere in Ore., usually in flocks of less than 100. Larger flocks have occurred at Fern Ridge Res., Lane Co.; in the Klamath Basin; and occasionally about coastal estuaries. The number of individuals occurring away from the coast varies considerably each yr, probably owing in significant part to weather patterns, and movements are often unpredictable. Rare but regular in summer. Irregular in winter along the coast (small numbers present in most yrs), and rare in the Willamette V.

Spring migration is rapid and often spectacular. Early birds arrive during the later half of Mar with the main movement occurring during Apr and continuing to mid-May; numbers drop rapidly to straggling flocks which continue to mid-Jun. Inland records during the spring are plentiful but seldom involve large numbers. A few non-breeding individuals and small groups, almost all subadults, remain to summer and might be found anywhere in the state. Up to 100 are often found at coastal spots. Early birds from the n. begin to arrive in Jul with a general movement by early Aug, which includes brown juvs. Peak numbers occur from late Oct through Nov with most gone by mid-Dec.

Heermann's Gull *Larus heermanni*

Locally common on outer seacoasts, beaches, bays, and estuaries. A few wander inland during the fall southward retreat. Fewer than 20 inland records from w. of the Cascades. Three of the 5 records e. of the Cascades have been along the Columbia R.; the other 2 were 18 Oct 1998 at Klamath Falls and 16 Oct 1990 at Thompson Res., Lake Co. They move n. to the Ore. coast in late spring, becoming locally common by mid-summer. Flocks of hundreds are sometimes observed, but a few score is the usual limit of local concentrations. Earliest observations vary from 18 Apr to 11 Jul but are normally in the last half of Jun, usually coincident with influxes of Brown Pelicans. Northward movement usually peaks in the second half of Jul. In recent yrs, Heermann's Gulls have been observed earlier with increasing frequency. Southward movement begins in Sep, peaks in Sep and Oct, and has been observed over coastal waters in Nov. Most leave by mid-Nov. Latest observations vary from 30 Nov through late Dec, merging with the few noted mostly along the s. coast during CBCs and later in winter.

> I.D. Note: In flight, all ages of this dark gull may suggest a jaeger at first glance because of their size, strong wing-beats, dark color, and occasional pale or even white patch in the primaries. Also, their habit of coursing low and fast through the wave-troughs and occasionally pursuing other gulls tends to deceive observers.

Mew Gull *Larus canus*

winter distribution

See *BOGR* for taxonomy. This is an abundant migrant and winter visitor along the coast, the lower Columbia R. and in the Willamette V.; rare along the Columbia R. e. of the Cascades and in the Klamath Basin; very rare elsewhere. Occasional in summer. The first southbound migrants arrive in late Jul (rare), usually adults in heavy molt; occasionally juvs. Their numbers build slowly through Aug (very few) and Sep to a conspicuous movement along the coast starting in mid-Oct. A very heavy movement the last wk of Nov brings wintering numbers to the Willamette V. Flocks of 10,000 or more along the n. coast are not uncommon into early winter, after which they scatter into smaller groups. Large flocks are sometimes seen in the Willamette V., especially in late winter. Gradually leave wintering areas from late Mar (bulk of movement) through Apr, with lingering birds noted to mid-May.

I.D. Note: In flight the black wingtips of Mew show a larger white spot (from two adjacent primaries) than do those of other small gulls. More likely than other gulls to stand or land in the wettest part of beaches or the edge of surf wash. Has a more obvious white trailing edge to wings than does Ring-billed Gull.

Ring-billed Gull *Larus delawarensis*

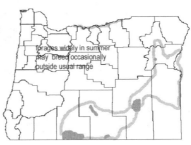

The Ring-billed Gull is a local breeder e. of the Cascades and a fairly common wintering gull throughout Ore. Breeding is fairly widespread, with small colonies occurring at major lakes and marshes, sometimes along larger rivers. Non-breeding birds are uncommon in summer in w. Ore., the Cascade lakes, and occasionally along the coast, but are fairly common in e. Ore. at lakes and large rivers. Widespread and common during spring and fall. During the winter, common in the Willamette V., locally along the coast (mainly in pastures and towns, avoids outer beaches), in the Klamath Basin and along the Columbia R.

Casual from early Jul through late Apr in the Umpqua V.; during Aug it is rare to very uncommon. Local and uncommon in winter near open water in e. Ore. First appear at nesting sites in Ore. during the last wk of Feb, with an average arrival date of 22 Feb. By mid-Jul or Aug, populations in non-breeding areas begin increasing. Large flocks numbering in the thousands are frequently reported from e. Ore. lakes in fall. Thereafter numbers decline although there is another peak during Mar. Most have left the coast by May, although a few remain through the summer.

California Gull *Larus californicus*

Local breeder in e. Ore. and widespread migrant and winter resident. The most regular colony sites are in the major lake basins of se Ore. and along the Columbia R. Very small colonies may appear elsewhere as habitat is available. They first appear back on their colonies during the second wk of Mar. Non-breeding birds are widely scattered throughout e. Ore. and are uncommon at montane lakes and along the coast. Birds begin arriving in mid-Jul on the coast. These birds are typically subadult birds that presumably did not breed, but these flocks also include post-breeders and many hatch-yr birds. They are casual from late Jun through early May in the Umpqua V., except during Aug when rare to very uncommon.

Very large numbers gather on coastal beaches during Sep-Nov. Most southbound movement is very close to shore, typically over the beaches or surf line, while other gulls tend to move beyond the surf line. Two subspecies are recognized; *albertaensis* is thought to arrive later than *californicus* on the coast in fall: ALC found small numbers of large, pale California gulls probably referable to *albertaensis* at all Lane Co. coastal gull roosts during Oct 2007; none had been at these sites from summer through early Sep. During winter, locally common in the Willamette V., along the coast, in the Klamath Basin and along the Columbia R. to Hood R. Rare elsewhere in e. Ore. during the winter with the exception of a small population near Baker City. Both *californicus* and *albertaensis* winter, but *californicus* is by far the more common.

Herring Gull *Larus argentatus*

status along Snake R poorly known

winter distribution

The taxonomic relationship of many of the large gull species is complex; see *BOGR* for a full discussion of Herring Gull. *L. a. smithsonianus* is the only subspecies that regularly occurs in Ore. The darker-backed Asian race, *L. a. vegae*, occurs regularly to w. Alaska and 1 specimen is known from Ore. There have been several reports of possible *vegae* in winter in Ore.

Common migrant and winter visitor. Hundreds sometimes appear onshore after storms; small numbers are more regular. Moderate numbers winter in the Willamette V. Flocks of 500 or more have been noted (rarely) in the Portland metropolitan area, but numbers seldom exceed 100 elsewhere in the Willamette V. and in most yrs only a few are present in flocks of other gulls. Most common near Portland and Eugene, least regular in the c. valley. Fairly common in winter e. of the Cascades near Klamath Falls, and along the Columbia R. Scattered individuals occur elsewhere. The majority of Herring Gulls wintering in Ore. are adults. Summering individuals are occasionally reported. Begins arriving in early Aug and becomes common by Oct. The coastal movement is mostly offshore and is usually inconspicuous. Herring Gulls are common between the coast and 600 mi offshore in winter. The main northward movement in spring occurs in Apr and May. Wintering numbers in the Willamette V. decline during Mar and Apr. Spring movements along the coast are often very conspicuous with large numbers flying low over the beaches and offshore. Large numbers of subadult birds regularly trail the movement of adult birds.

Thayer's Gull *Larus thayeri*
Common migrant and fairly common winter visitor along the coast; uncommon on the s. coast. The largest wintering numbers are found in the Portland metropolitan area, where flocks of several hundred are not uncommon. Lesser numbers winter elsewhere in the Willamette V. Rare along the Columbia R. e.

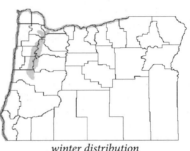

winter distribution

of the Cascades; and in the Klamath Basin. Very rare elsewhere. The majority of Thayer's Gulls wintering in Ore. are adults.

Early fall migrants arrive along the coast during late Aug. Numbers remain very low until the main movement arrives in mid-Oct, and it is mid-Nov before wintering numbers arrive in the Willamette V. No obvious migratory movement usually noted. The coastal population becomes less conspicuous by Dec with most coastal CBCs recording fewer than 10 individuals. However, severe winter storms can bring large flocks to protected roosts on the outer coast, suggesting that many winter offshore. Wintering numbers in the Willamette V. begin to decline by late Feb and most are gone by mid-Mar; small groups, mostly subadults, remain to mid-Apr. There is an increase in numbers along the coast during Mar each yr, but there is no noticeable migration. Most are gone by late Mar, but small numbers remain into May.

*Iceland Gull *Larus glaucoides*
Vagrant. This arctic gull breeds along the coast of Greenland (pale-winged subspecies *glaucoides*) and in arctic Canada (subspecies *kumlieni* with darker wing tips). The nominate subspecies winters along the coasts from Greenland and Iceland to Scandinavia and Great Britain, while

kumlieni winters along the Atlantic coast from Labrador to N. Carolina and in the Great L. region.

Three accepted Ore. records:
1. One adult was at Moolack Beach, Lincoln Co., on 24 Feb 1991.
2. A bird in second winter plumage was photographed at Salem, Marion Co., 15 Feb – 8 Mar 1996.
3. One was photographed at Florence, Lane Co., on 10 Feb 2002.

In addition, there are a number of unconfirmed reports of this sometimes difficult to identify species. The darker-winged subspecies *kumlieni* in particular can show a great resemblance to pale or bleached individuals of the closely related Thayer's Gull (with which it is sometimes considered conspecific), which renders identification difficult. Small individuals of the similarly colored Glaucous Gull as well as various hybrids pose additional identification pitfalls; future records should therefore be carefully documented.

**Lesser Black-backed Gull *Larus fuscus*

Vagrant. Breeds mainly across Europe and in Iceland and has recently expanded its range to Greenland. Since the 1970s, the species occurs with increasing frequency as a winter visitor to e. N. America, especially in the Great L. region, the mid-Atlantic states, and the se. U.S.

One accepted sight record for Ore. of an adult observed at Fern Ridge Res, Lane Co., 17-20 Mar 2001.

In addition, an adult was photographed at Newport, Lincoln Co., on 29 Aug 2008. This record is currently under review by the OBRC.

*Slaty-backed Gull *Larus schistisagus*

Vagrant. Breeds from e. Siberia to Kamchatka and n. Japan. Casual visitor yr-round in w. Alaska (where it has bred occasionally).

Five accepted Ore. records:

vagrant occurrence

1. Up to 6 adult and subadult Slaty-backed Gulls were photographed among a large gull concentration at a food-processing plant on Sauvie I., Multnomah Co., 29 Dec 1992 – 20 Mar 1993.
2. One adult in winter plumage was photographed at Sauvie I., Multnomah Co., 7-23 Jan 1995.

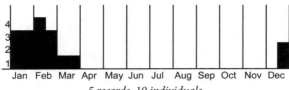

5 records, 10 individuals

3. One subadult bird was photographed at Westmoreland Park in Portland, Multnomah Co., 1-18 Feb 1998.
4. An adult was photographed at Sauvie I., Multnomah Co., 27 Dec 1997 – 22 Feb 1998.
5. An adult was photographed at Astoria, Clatsop Co., on 8 Feb 2004.

In addition, 1 was photographed in Portland, Multnomah Co., from 29 Jan to early Feb 2009. This record has not yet been reviewed by the OBRC. There are also a number of unsubmitted and unconfirmed sightings. The species can be difficult to separate from dark-backed forms of the Western Gull or potential hybrids, and future records ought to be carefully documented.

Western Gull *Larus occidentalis*

There are 2 subspecies. The n. subspecies *L. o. occidentalis* breeds from Wash. to c. Cal. and is larger with slightly paler upperparts (especially n. birds) and usually darker eyes than the s. subspecies *L. o. wymani*. During the non-breeding season birds that may be *wymani* by appearance are very rare in Ore. Present all yr and breeds along the entire coast. At all times of the yr abundance at sea highest from Reedsport s.; numbers at sea n. of Reedsport are highest in summer. Seldom more than 35 mi seaward off the shelf break; most birds occur on the inner and mid-shelf regions. Non-breeders occur yr-round n. of the breeding range, although their distribution shifts towards the s. during winter. Small numbers of imms. and adults are found in fall and winter along the Columbia R. and as far inland as the John Day Dam and the Portland and Eugene areas. Rare inland records include sightings in Umatilla and Klamath cos. and Summer L., Lake Co. Returns to colonies mid-Feb.

Glaucous-winged Gull *Larus glaucescens*

Breeds in small numbers in nw. Ore., rarely as far s. as Parrot Rock, Lane Co. The largest breeding colony in Ore. is at East Sand I. in the Columbia R. Small numbers breed inland in Ring-billed and California Gull colonies at Memaloose I. in the Columbia R. near The Dalles, and Miller Rock, upstream from the mouth of the Deschutes R. They breed occasionally farther e. along the Columbia R. as habitat permits. These gulls are abundant fall through spring at the coast, up coastal rivers, and

very infrequent breeder south of Yaquina Head

in flooded areas. CBCs show numbers of Glaucous-winged Gull and Western/Glaucous-winged Gull hybrids in the hundreds in the Portland and Sauvie I. counts, with smaller numbers upriver as far as Salem and Hood R. They are present in winter in the Willamette V., rare but regular in e. Ore. along the Columbia R. and occasional in interior sw. Ore. Never as abundant offshore as Western Gulls, they occur over the continental shelf fall through spring. They have been recorded over 600 mi offshore. The first birds arrive at colonies in early Feb; most have arrived by late Apr. Fall dispersal brings increasing numbers to the c. and s. Ore. coast during October; significant movements into the Willamette V. occur in early Nov.

Glaucous Gull *Larus hyperboreus*

Two N. American subspecies, *L. h. leuceretes* of e. Canada and nw. Europe and the smaller, slightly darker *L. h. barrovianus*, the Alaska breeding subspecies. Specimens of *barrovianus* have been collected in Ore. and no specimens of any other subspecies have been reported from the W. Coast of N. America. However, there is exceptional variation in bill size and in body size of Glaucous Gulls wintering in Ore., which suggests that different populations may be involved.

Rare but regular along the coast and the Columbia R.; local and rare in the Willamette V. It can be uncommon midwinter at Sauvie I. Very rare elsewhere; unrecorded in the Umpqua and Rogue valleys. Present every winter in coastal Ore. and up the Columbia R. to Portland, but numbers vary. Most coastal CBCs record the species with some regularity, usually only 1 or 2 birds, but less frequent farther s. Rare e. of the Cascades, with fewer than 10 records along the Columbia R. and 2 from Klamath Falls. Arrives rather late in autumn and leaves fairly early in spring, with most birds first reported in late Oct or Nov and few reliable reports after Apr., however, a few confirmed as late as June.

I.D. Note: From spring to mid-summer beware of pale, worn first-yr Glaucous-winged Gulls, which are often whiter than real Glaucous Gulls, most of which when viewed at close range show very fine light brown scalloping or barring on much of their plumage through their second winter.

Sabine's Gull *Xema sabini*
Common to abundant spring and fall transient over continental shelf well offshore. Irregular but fairly common in fall and uncommon in spring along the coast; casual inland. Casual in summer and winter. Pelagic migrations are taken individually or in medium-sized flocks of up to 60 birds. Fall movement occurs from mid-Jul to late Nov with the peak from late Aug to mid-Sep. Rare but regular fall migrant inland. Rare e. of the Cascades between early Sep and mid-Nov with up to 5 reports annually, some involving 2-3 individuals. Two spring and 2 fall records in the Rogue V.

Little is known of the pelagic status of the species during the winter and early spring because offshore sea conditions preclude regular boat trips. However, a few are clearly present in early winter, contrary to some sources. An imm. was off Cape Arago, Coos Co., 17 Dec 1978; an adult was off the s. jetty of the Columbia R. 15 Dec 1979; 1 was off Cape Arago 20 Dec 1981, and 5 were there 5 Dec 1987; 1 was off Curry Co. 7 Jan 2001. A bird in breeding plumage at Yaquina Bay 22 Feb 1992 may have been an early spring migrant. Early spring migrants arrive by mid-Mar increasing to the main movement during May. Rare in early June. There are few spring inland records.

Black-legged Kittiwake *Rissa tridactyla*
Uncommon to common migrant and winter resident along the outer coast and offshore. Rare in interior nw. Ore. s. to Fern Ridge Res, mainly at large bodies of water after storms. Very rare e. of the w. interior valleys. One was at John Day Dam 24 Nov to 5 Dec 1995. One was in Heppner, Morrow Co., on 12 Nov 1967. One was near Frenchglen in late May 2001. First reports in fall are usually in early Sep near shore. Kittiwakes are often present in the mouth of the Columbia R. well before they are seen along the remainder of the Ore. coast or offshore. Early fall movement may be largely coastal. Regular offshore in winter, uncommon but regular onshore. In some yrs large numbers are present. Early spring numbers can be quite high. Movements in Apr and early May are often composed mainly of first-winter birds. Generally absent in summer, but a few summer stragglers are sometimes found, with some yrs having extraordinary concentrations of birds.

*Red-legged Kittiwake *Rissa brevirostris*

vagrant occurrence

Vagrant. Endemic to the Bering Sea, where it breeds on the Pribilofs, the Aleutians, and the Russian Commander Is. After breeding, it disperses at sea in the n. Pacific and s. Bering Sea.

Eight accepted Ore. records, all but 1 involving birds found dead or moribund:

1. A decomposed bird was found at Sunset Beach, Clatsop Co., on 24 Jan 1982. The wing and foot were collected.
2. An adult was photographed on a ship railing 15 nautical mi. w. of Tillamook Head, Clatsop Co., on 7 Aug 1983.
3. One was found dead on the beach at Waldport, Lincoln Co., on 25 Mar 1951. The wings and one foot are in the Royal Ontario Museum, Toronto, Canada.
4. One was found dead on the beach at DeLake [D L.], Lincoln Co., on 28 Jan 1933. The specimen is at the U.S. National Museum.
5. An adult female was found dead on the beach at Nehalem, Tillamook Co., on 12 Mar 1955. The specimen is at the Royal Ontario Museum, Toronto, Canada.
6. One was found dead on the beach at Cannon Beach, Clatsop Co., on 30 Dec 1981. The specimen is at the Burke Museum, U. of Wash., Seattle.
7. A winter-plumaged adult was found moribund at Rockaway Beach, Tillamook Co., on 16 Jan 1989. It later died at a rehab center.
8. A moribund bird was found on a highway near Jewell, Clatsop Co., on 28 Dec 2003 and brought to Astoria Rehab Center, where it died.

An additional record of a bird found at the N. Spit of Coos Bay, Coos Co., on 5 Mar 1999 has not been reviewed by the OBRC.

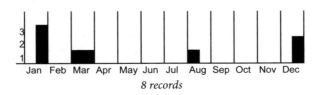

8 records

*Ross's Gull *Rhodostethia rosea*
Vagrant. Breeds in arctic ne. Siberia, with isolated populations in Greenland and Canada. It is presumed to winter in the Bering, Beaufort, and Okhotsk seas.

Two accepted Ore. records:
1. A basic-plumaged adult was photographed at Yaquina Bay, Lincoln Co., where it remained from 18 Feb to 2 Mar 1987.
2. A bright adult was photographed at McNary Dam on the Columbia R., Umatilla Co., 27 Nov – 1 Dec 1994.

Subfamily Sterninae

*Least Tern *Sternula antillarum*
Vagrant. Breeds along the Pacific coast from c. Cal. s., on the Atlantic and Gulf coasts, and locally along rivers in the interior U.S.

Seven accepted Ore. records, mostly from the coast:
1. Four adults were at the s. jetty of the Siuslaw R., Lane Co on 19 Aug 1973.

vagrant occurrence

2. One was photographed at the s. jetty of the Columbia R., Clatsop Co., on 31 May 1976.
3. Two males were collected at the mouth of the Columbia R., Clatsop Co., on 21 May 1964. The specimens are in the Tillamook Co. Pioneer Museum.
4. An adult was photographed at the s. jetty of the Siuslaw R., Lane Co., on 8 Jun 1997.
5. An adult was photographed at Yaquina Bay, Lincoln Co., 26 Jul – 1 Aug 1998.
6. An adult was at Harris Beach SP, Curry Co., on 9 Jul 1998.
7. A subadult was photographed at Fernhill Wetlands, Wash. Co., 6-10 Mar 1999.

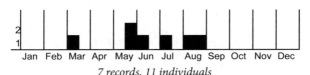

7 records, 11 individuals

In addition, 1 was observed at Malheur NWR, Harney Co., in Jun 2005, and another was photographed at Tualatin NWR, Wash. Co., on 24 Jun 2008. These records have not yet been reviewed by the OBRC.

Caspian Tern *Hydroprogne caspia*

COOS	CLAT	LANE	BENT	PORT	CENT	MALH
1 Apr	1 Apr			9 Apr	19 Apr	27 Apr

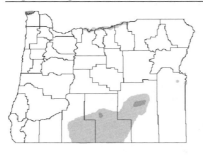

The largest Caspian Tern nesting colony in the world is on E. Sand I. in the Columbia R. estuary, but the future of this colony is uncertain. Other recent breeding colonies have been on the mid-Columbia R. e. of the Cascades in nc. Ore.; Malheur and Harney lakes in se. Ore.; Summer L. and lakes in the Warner V. in sc. Ore. Most colony sites have a history of intermittent use. Reaches Ore. in early Mar; 3 Mar 2002 at Brookings the earliest recent arrival. Arrival of breeding adults at colonies begins in late Mar/early Apr; continues to mid-May. Most young fledge and leave natal colony by late Jul. Breeding adults may depart colonies in Jun if nesting attempt fails, or from mid-Jul through Aug if accompanied by fledglings. Adults feeding young can be seen (and heard) hundreds of mi. from the nearest active colony. Most birds drift s. along the coast from late Jul to mid-Sep; sightings trail off in late Sep and Oct; few records of stragglers in early Nov. Two at Coos Bay 18 Dec 2007 (J. Heaney *fide* T. Rodenkirk) are the only records later than Nov. A few migrate inland and appear at lakes and reservoirs.

Black Tern *Chlidonias niger*

COOS	CLAT	LANE	BENT	PORT	CENT	MALH
		4 May			16 May	3 May

Breeds in marsh wetland complexes of se., sc., and c. Ore. Three records from Malheur Co. at Batch Is. and Bully Cr. Res., but not known to breed there. Infrequent spring and summer sightings from Union and Wallowa cos., but not suspected to breed there. Has bred regularly at Fern Ridge Res. since 1992. Black Terns were also reported in May and Jun from small marshes in Linn Co. s. and se. of Corvallis since at least 1995, and there have been regular summer sightings of a few from Baskett Slough NWR, Polk Co. This is a widespread transient e. of the Cascades during

Apr and May; very rare w. of the Cascades except at Fern Ridge Res., where fairly common. It typically arrives on breeding grounds in e. Ore. in the first wk of May. Most adults and fledged young leave breeding areas by 1 Aug. In w. Ore., breeding season may be extended as evidenced by record of black 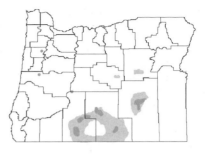 downy chick on a nest at Fern Ridge Res., Lane Co. on 27 Jul 1992. Peak autumn migration at Malheur NWR is 10-20 Aug. Occasional in w. Ore. and along the coast through Dec.

Common Tern *Sterna hirundo*
Common to abundant spring and fall transient over the ocean, usually within 15 mi, irregularly along the coast and in the estuaries. Casual in w. Ore. away from the coast. Rare spring and uncommon fall transient e. of the Cascades, casual in summer. The spring offshore movement is primarily from mid-Apr to mid-May with smaller numbers to mid-Jun. Spring records e. of the Cascades (very few birds) are during the same time period as the coastal movement. Two in Jackson Co. 11 May 1994 is the only w. Ore. spring record away from the coast. Very rare in summer, with both coastal and interior records. The fall movement occurs from mid-Aug to late Oct with a peak period in late Aug and early Sep.

Arctic Tern *Sterna paradisaea*
An uncommon offshore transient in Ore. waters and an occasional migrant along the coast. The bulk of the population is thought to migrate 10-40 mi from land. Rarely reported inland but may turn up nearly anywhere. During spring, Arctic Terns may appear as early as mid-Apr, but are most regular during May, with some birds passing through until mid-Jun. Accidental in Ore. during summer. Fall migration is more extended, and occurs from mid-Aug through mid-Oct with the bulk of reports in mid-Sep. It has been recorded as early as mid-Jul and as late as 25 Nov. Most inland records refer to only 1 or 2 birds.

Forster's Tern *Sterna forsteri*

COOS	CLAT	LANE	BENT	PORT	CENT	MALH
					3 May	23 Apr

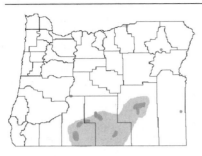

This is an uncommon but highly visible colonial breeder e. of the Cascades. It is fairly common at Malheur NWR and in sc. Ore. at Sycan Marsh. Known to have bred some yrs at Upper Klamath L., Klamath Marsh NWR, Summer L., Silver L., and Warner V. lakes. Sometimes breeds at Rufus Bar below John Day Dam. Transients are common and widespread e. of the Cascades during spring as far e. as the Malheur R. and Owyhee R. watersheds. Arrives mid- to late Apr; migration peaks early May. Nesting at Malheur NWR begins early Jun. Small groups and non-breeding individuals are occasionally seen during summer away from breeding colonies. Small numbers are reported in w. Ore. interior valleys, along the Columbia R., and along the coast during fall. Migration begins in Jul, and peaks late Aug to early Sep. Rare transient through mid-October. A single bird seen after storms at Bandon 13 Dec 1995 is the only winter record for Ore.

Elegant Tern *Sterna elegans*

Recorded in about 2/3 of yrs since the mid 1980s. Numbers vary widely from yr to yr. Virtually all records are coastal. Peak counts include 319 at the Necanicum R. mouth in Aug 1984, 200 at the Rogue R. mouth in Sep 1984, 200 in lower Coos Bay in Jul 1992, and 215 at the Rogue

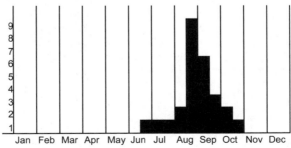

20 records, several hundred birds (through 1992)

R. mouth in Sep 1992. Post-breeding birds disperse n. and enter Ore. beginning in late Jun; the earliest record is 10 Jun 1997. Most records have been of adults. Numbers usually diminish rapidly along the Ore. coast after late Aug; the latest record is 13 Nov 1983.

Subfamily Rynchopinae

[**Black Skimmer *Rynchops niger*]
Vagrant. This unmistakable black-and-white bird is reminiscent of a large tern with an oversized red beak. It breeds along the coasts of Baja Cal. and in s. Cal., where the population is expanding, as well as on the Gulf of Mexico and along the E. Coast of N. America up to New England. Casual visitor to n. Cal., with a small wintering population in San Francisco Bay.

There is 1 sight record from Ore. currently under review by the OBRC. A well-described adult in non-breeding plumage was reported from the mouth of the Pistol R., Curry Co., on 26 Jan 2008. In addition, a well-described Black Skimmer was reported at Coos Bay on 24 Apr 2002. This record has not been submitted to the OBRC.

Family Stercorariidae

South Polar Skua *Stercorarius maccormicki*
Rare to uncommon fall transient offshore, primarily over the continental slope. Six sightings from shore, mostly in Sep. Skuas arrive in late Jun (earliest 1 Jun), present in low numbers from late Jul-Aug, peak from 8 Sep-9 Oct (latest 18 Oct), 3 records from Dec (1 beached alive), 1 from Apr. Record numbers in any one day: 8 on 5 Oct 1996, 7 on 30 Sep 1978, 4 on 29 Sep 1979, and 4 on 12 Sep 1998, all off the c. coast.

The majority of birds seen off the W. Coast are dark. These may be imms. as some have assumed, but more observations are needed to clarify this. Skua taxonomy is in flux, and identification and migration routes are still being determined. The possibility certainly exists that some of these dark birds might be something other than South Polar Skuas. Interestingly, a wash-up on a Coos Co. beach on 9 Jul 1980 had been banded 22 Feb 1980 in Antarctica on the Indian Ocean, rather than on the Pacific.

I.D. Note: Sometimes dark-phase Pomarine Jaegers are misidentified as skuas. Also, imm. dark-morph Parasitic Jaegers can show large white wing patches and may cause confusion. Onshore reports of skuas should be well documented to eliminate the possibility of misidentified jaegers.

Pomarine Jaeger *Stercorarius pomarinus*
Uncommon spring and fairly common fall transient offshore 2-50 mi,
following shearwaters. Sightings centered near the continental shelf edge.
More than 90% are seen >5.6 mi from shore. Occasionally observed from
shore in fall. Seven inland records: 2 storm-driven on 10 Nov 1975 at
Fern Ridge Res.; 1 adult dark-morph photographed at Summer L., Lake
Co., during a fall in the 1980s; 1 each on 2 Sep 1985 and 28 Sep 1997 at
McNary Dam; 1 n. of Corvallis, Benton Co., on 23Sep 1992; 1 at Fern
Ridge 9 Sep 1998 (D. Farrar p.c.) and 1 found alive that later died 28-30
Jun 1999 at Halfway, Baker Co. Rare winter visitor. Spring migration
begins in Mar, uncommon to May; rare Jun; return migration begins in
Jul, peak Aug-Sep, common through Oct; rare Nov-Feb. An astounding
750 were observed on a full-day cruise 50 mi. off the Ore. coast 17 Sep
2000. Other high numbers include 50-200 daily 25-27 Jul 1989, 80-100
on 29 Jul 1975, and 31 on 30 Sep 1978. An amazingly high number so
late in the season was 15 seen from Cape Arago after a storm on 25 Nov
1990. This is the most frequently encountered jaeger at sea beyond 10
mi from shore.

Parasitic Jaeger *Stercorarius parasiticus*
Uncommon fall and rare spring transient offshore. Most within 14 mi
of coast. Rare fall migrant inland—at least 25 records (some of multiple
birds), 10 at lakes of Harney Co. and 7 at Fern Ridge Res., Lane Co (D.
Farrar p.c.; dates range 2 Sep–14 Nov). Rare spring migrant Mar-Jun.
Fall migration begins in Jul, peaks in Sep when common, corresponding
to migration of Arctic Terns. Rare Nov-Dec, absent Jan-Feb. High
number on Ore. pelagic trip was 40 on 20 Sep 1980. Regularly viewed
from shore in fall; however largest number, 10 from Bandon on 1 Jun
1980, were apparently very late spring migrants. Inland fall migrants
range from 5 Jul-18 Oct. This is the most frequently seen jaeger from
shore and sometimes enters estuaries. Best chance for detection is in Sep,
within 3 mi of shore. Also, some pass over beaches where shorebirds
have gathered.

Long-tailed Jaeger *Stercorarius longicaudus*
Rare to fairly common fall transient and rare spring (7 records) transient
far offshore—the most pelagic of jaegers. Fall migration peak comes
earlier than for other species; rarely straggles to late fall. In 68 at-sea
observations where distance was recorded, sightings ranged from 12 to
140 mi offshore; median 36.5 mi (G. Gillson p.c.). Sixteen sightings from
shore. Ten records of inland fall migrants, with 4 at Fern Ridge Res. (D.
Farrar p.c.) and several e. of the Cascades. One specimen from 25 mi sse.
of Burns, 14 Aug 1976. Spring migration dates range 19 Apr-27 May with

main movement in mid-May. Fall migration dates extend 7 Jul-6 Nov with peak numbers occurring during a 4-wk period centered in late Aug. Absent Dec-Mar. Astonishing were 925 observed on a full-day cruise 50 mi. off the Ore. coast 17 Sep 2000. Other high numbers include 62 on 20 Aug 1987 about 37 mi off Lincoln Co.; 62 on 12 May 1997 about 140 mi off s. Ore. coast;, and 125 on 25 Aug 2001 about 32 mi off Newport. Inland fall records range 21 Jul-25 Sep but most records occur 14 Aug-6 Sep, corresponding to peak abundance offshore. Best chance of detection mid-late Aug or early Sep at least 25 mi from shore.

Family Alcidae

Common Murre *Uria aalge*
Major nesting concentrations in Ore. are on the s. and n. coasts reflecting the availability of suitable nesting habitat. The largest colony complex in Ore. is Three Arch Rocks NWR. Murres are the most abundant bird over the continental shelf during all months although winter densities are lower than in summer. They are commonly present in large estuaries in late summer and fall. Some begin moving onto nesting rocks as early as late Dec, more often in Jan and Feb. Chick/adult pairs are first seen at sea on the central coast during late Jun or early Jul. The colony at Yaquina Head is abandoned by early Aug. Colonies may be adversely affected by active Bald Eagle nests nearby. There is some evidence of a general movement of adults n. after the breeding season.

> I.D. Note: Murre chicks leave the nest site at 20-25% of their adult weight and are frequently mistaken for murrelets in late summer.

*Thick-billed Murre *Uria lomvia*
Vagrant. Breeds circumpolar from Greenland across n. Eurasia and from n. and w. Alaska to ne. Canada. There is a small, isolated population off n. Vancouver I.

Six accepted Ore. records, most pertaining to dead or moribund birds:

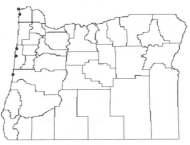

vagrant occurrence

1. One was found dead on the beach near Mercer, Lane Co., on 30 Jan 1933. The specimen is now in the Ore. State U. collection.

6 records

2. A female was collected at Depoe Bay, Lincoln Co., on 14 Jan 1933. The specimen is at the Yale Peabody Museum, New Haven, Connecticut.
3. One was found dead on the beach at the s. jetty of the Columbia R., Clatsop Co., on 15 Sep 1972. The specimen is now in the Ore. State U. Collection.
4. An oiled bird was found at Nye Beach near Newport, Lincoln Co., on 25 Aug 2001. It was rehabilitated at the Ore. Coast Aquarium and released on 6 Oct 2001.
5. A moribund bird was found and photographed on the beach at Sunset (Clatsop) Beach, Clatsop Co., on 27 Feb 2007.
6. One was photographed at Whiskey Run Beach, Coos Co., on 10 Mar 2007.

Due to its great similarity to the Common Murre, this species is not always safely identified at sea, and all records should be carefully documented.

Pigeon Guillemot *Cepphus columba*

COOS	CLAT	LANE	BENT	PORT	CENT	MALH
15 Mar	27 Mar					

Occurs during the breeding season all along the coast wherever offshore islands or rocky cliffs are present. Most breed in small colonies of <40 birds, sometimes on human structures such as old piers or wrecked ships. Occasionally seen in winter as solitary individuals close to shore or in estuaries; they prefer sheltered inshore waters rather than exposed coastlines. Adults return to Ore. breeding sites in early to late Mar. Guillemots have been observed lingering in the vicinity of breeding areas into Nov and Dec although most often have moved away by early Sep.

*Long-billed Murrelet *Brachyramphus perdix*
Vagrant. The Asiatic counterpart of the Marbled Murrelet, with which it was considered conspecific until 1997. It breeds along the coast of e. Asia from Kamchatka to n. Japan, and winters from the sea of Okhotsk to s. Japan and Korea. Vagrants have occurred widely across the U.S., many at inland locations.

There is a single accepted Ore. record of a bird photographed at Arago Reef, Coos Co., on 13 Aug 1994.

In addition, there are a number of convincing reports that have not yet been reviewed by the OBRC, most from Jul and Aug. It may also be vagrant on inland lakes; a probable sighting of this species occurred in early Aug 1997 on Leaburg Res., Lane Co.

Marbled Murrelet *Brachyramphus marmoratus*

Breeds on forested slopes of the Coast Range. Distribution at inland nesting sites is fragmented, as birds occur only in areas where suitable habitat remains. Visits inland breeding sites at all times of yr, except during the prebasic molt in early fall. Present yr-round on nearshore waters. Uncommon to rare along entire coast, but densities greatest off the c. coast between Cascade Head and Cape Arago. Generally found within a few mi. of shore during the breeding season and up to 6 mi in winter. Egg laying begins in Apr and extends until Jul. Young fledge between mid-Jun and late Sep and fly directly to sea. Marbled Murrelets are considered non-migratory, although they are found farther offshore in winter compared with breeding season.

*Xantus's Murrelet *Synthliboramphus hypoleucus*

Vagrant. Breeds off s. Cal. and along the w. coast of Baja Cal. There are two subspecies (*S. h. hypoleucus* and *S. h. scrippsi*), which may represent separate species. Both have been recorded in Ore. waters.

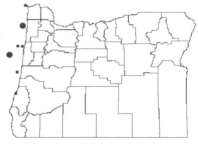

vagrant occurrence

Ten accepted Ore. records, most of the expected subspecies *scrippsi* (unless noted otherwise):

1. Two were captured and photographed 65 mi. off Newport, Lincoln Co., on 19 Nov 1969.
2. One was captured and photographed 65-165 mi. off Newport, Lincoln Co., in Jun 1973 (subspecies *hypoleucus*).
3. Two in basic plumage were photographed 12 mi. offshore in Lane Co. on 31 Aug 1985.
4. One was photographed 12 to 18 mi. offshore in Tillamook Co. on 14 Sep 1985.
5. One was seen close to shore at Boiler Bay State Wayside, Lincoln Co., 7-8 Nov 1987.
6. One was found dead on the beach at the N. Spit Coos Bay, Coos Co., on 26 Jun 1998. The specimen is now at Ore. State U.

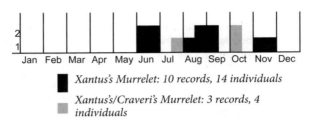

■ *Xantus's Murrelet: 10 records, 14 individuals*

▨ *Xantus's/Craveri's Murrelet: 3 records, 4 individuals*

7. One adult was observed in flight at the s. jetty of the Columbia River, Clatsop Co., on 14 Jun 2001.
8. One was seen 25 mi. w. of Boiler Bay, Lincoln Co,. on 10 Aug 2001.
9. Two were observed 18 mi. w. of Tillamook, Tillamook Co., on 15 Sep 2001.
10. One was photographed 25-30 mi. w. of Newport, Lincoln Co., on 25 Aug 2007.

In addition, there are several records that have not been reviewed by the OBRC. One was collected 115 mi. w. of Cape Falcon 28 Jul 1970, and an astonishing 42, including both *scrippsi* and *hypoleucus*, were observed offshore between 10 Aug and 20 Oct 2001 by multiple observers.

Furthermore, the OBRC has accepted the following 3 records of small murrelets that could not safely be identified to species as either Xantus's or Craveri's Murrelet (*Synthliboramphus craveri*): 1 was close to shore at Brays Point, Lane Co., on 23 Jul 1991; 2 birds were 45 mi. w. of Newport, Lincoln Co., on 7 Oct 1995; and 1 was 35 mi. off Yachats, Lincoln Co., on 5 Oct 2002.

Ancient Murrelet *Synthliboramphus antiquus*

Uncommon to common fall migrant and winter visitant in shelf waters near shore; rare to uncommon in spring; absent to rare in summer. Possible rare irregular local breeder, not proven. Vagrant inland, particularly in fall. After breeding there is a general dispersal southward, and birds typically arrive in Ore. in Sep. Most sightings are in the late fall and winter with flocks of 10-20 normal. Larger concentrations of hundreds are less frequent. Inland reports are irregular and very rare, mostly Sep-Nov, but 1 was in Medford in Mar. Summer sightings are occasional from land; in Jun and Jul 1997 they were seen at numerous locations along the Ore. coast. Most leave by Mar or early Apr.

Cassin's Auklet *Ptychoramphus aleuticus*
Although fewer than 1,000 Cassin's Auklets nest in Ore., nesting sites are found along the entire coast where offshore rocks provide appropriate habitat. During the non-breeding season this is the most abundant alcid seen at sea in Ore. They are present offshore all yr. During summer and fall large numbers have been seen moving s. offshore and from land. They are widespread at sea, occurring within a few mi. of the coast out to at least the continental slope. There are 3 inland records, all from the Columbia R., which suggests the possibility that they were brought in by ships.

*Parakeet Auklet *Aethia psittacula*
Vagrant. Breeds from w. and c. Alaska across the Bering Sea and the Aleutians to e. Siberia.

   There are 13 accepted Ore. records, including 6 specimen records between 1913 and 1933. Recent accepted records include dead birds found at Bayocean Beach, Tillamook Co, on 3 Dec 1977; at Wandamere

vagrant occurrence

Beach, Lincoln Co., on 18 Apr 1982; at Clatsop Beach, Clatsop Co., on 12 Dec 1994; and on Beverly Beach, Lincoln Co., on 24 Feb 1996. Live sightings include 4 birds that were observed 20 mi. w. of Garibaldi, Tillamook Co., on 7 Sep 1986; a flying bird 45 mi. off Seaside, Clatsop Co., on 17 Sep 2000; and a bird w. of Yachats, Lane Co., on 3 Jan 2008.

   In addition, 2 live birds were observed off Cape Lookout, Tillamook Co., on 13 Aug 1977, and 1 live individual was reported 50 mi. w. of Curry Co., on 17 Sep 2000. Seven dead birds were found on the beaches in Coos Co. following the Feb 1999 *New Carissa* oil spill, suggesting a more significant near-shore presence than previously known. These records have not yet been reviewed by the OBRC.

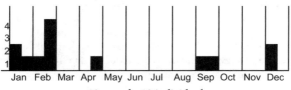

13 records, 18 individuals

Rhinoceros Auklet *Cerorhinca monocerata*

Nest in small numbers (<1,000) in Ore. with Goat I. and Hunter I. having the largest concentrations of breeding birds. Offshore in winter months, detected as far out as the seaward side of the continental slope. Occasionally found in lower estuaries, primarily during late summer and fall. Burrows on Goat I. are occupied by the end of Mar. In the non-breeding season they move offshore, but for a brief period in late summer and early fall they are often found close to shore and in the mouths of estuaries. There are occasional records of small flocks of birds close to shore after the breeding season. Birds from British Columbia probably winter off the Ore. and Cal. coasts. This may account for the extraordinary migratory movement seen 12 and 13 Mar 2002 off Boiler Bay, when 2,500 and 6,500, respectively, were seen.

Horned Puffin *Fratercula corniculata*

Rare to sometimes abundant visitor to the offshore waters of the ne. Pacific. Occasionally found dead on beaches, most commonly in winter, and occasionally in large numbers. Live birds occasionally seen onshore in winter and spring. Occasional off the Ore. coast in small numbers during the summer months. Individual birds, or possibly pairs, occasionally stay in Ore. for the breeding season and are seen attending colonies with Tufted Puffins, but there are no records of breeding in Ore. Individuals were seen in seabird colonies during the breeding season at Yaquina Head in 1973 and 1974; Island Rock, south of Port Orford, in 1979; Hunter I., Curry Co., in 1984 and 1987; at Cape Lookout, Tillamook Co., in 1968, 1976, 1977, and 1981; and at Goat I., Curry Co., in 1998.

Tufted Puffin *Fratercula cirrhata*

COOS	CLAT	LANE	BENT	PORT	CENT	MALH
15 Apr	8 Apr					

It nests along the entire Ore. coast where soil-covered islands are present. It also nests on headlands such as Cape Meares, Cape Lookout, Cape Foulweather, and Yaquina Head. Major nesting concentration is in the n. of the state, with two-thirds of nesting birds at Three Arch Rocks. During the non-breeding season, puffins disperse offshore, where they forage as individuals often far past the continental slope. There are records of their presence offshore in all months of the non-breeding season although numbers appear low in Nov and Dec. Rarely seen from land in winter. They have been recorded as early as 7 Mar at Bandon. The only study of Tufted Puffins nesting in Ore. was conducted on Goat I., Curry Co., where 40 artificial nest boxes were monitored for two breeding seasons. At this site puffins returned to their nesting sites in early Apr. Adults leave the colonies in late Aug to early Sep.

Order COLUMBIFORMES
Family Columbidae

Rock Pigeon *Columba livia*
Introduced. Common to abundant statewide in cities, towns, and agricultural areas. Distribution is more scattered in steppe habitats east of the Cascades according to available habitat. Pigeons are not found in forested areas, but occur in some small towns and villages in otherwise forested landscapes on w. slopes of the Cascades. Nest in colonies and singly. They can breed during any month of the yr over most of their range. The only Ore. study was at Succor Cr. Canyon, Malheur Co., where mating activity commenced in Feb and Mar.

Band-tailed Pigeon *Columba fasciata*

COOS	CLAT	LANE	BENT	PORT	CENT	MALH
1 Mar		13 Mar	12 Mar		9 May	

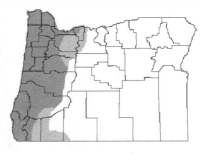

This is a common summer resident in forested areas w of the Cascade crest. Most abundant in the Coast Range with abundance increasing from e. to w., most likely in response to the distribution of food. Rare e. of the Cascade crest, occurring as a vagrant in riparian habitat and at desert oases from late Mar to Oct. Occur more often e. of the Cascades in Wasco Co. In winter, uncommon and highly local resident, mainly in Portland and in sw. Ore. Usually begin arriving in Mar, in some yrs earlier, e.g., multiple arrivals were reported throughout w. Ore., 17-18 Feb 2002. Use of mineral sites occurs Jun-Sep with a peak in Aug. Most birds leave in Oct. Those that remain form nomadic aggregations throughout winter.

Eurasian Collared-Dove *Streptopelia decaocto*
A new arrival in Ore., quickly spreading throughout the state. The OBRC accepted 17 records before dropping the species off its review list in 2007. Occurs statewide in small numbers, with a significant population in Burns and Hines and small clusters forming elsewhere. Population is increasing rapidly throughout the state.

White-winged Dove Zenaida asiatica

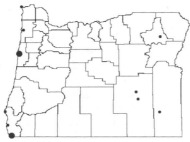

vagrant occurrence

Vagrant. Breeds across the s. U.S. from s. Cal. to Florida; disperses widely after breeding.

Casual vagrant in Ore., with 17 accepted records to date. The first records for the state were of 1 observed at the s. jetty of the Columbia R., Clatsop Co., on 28 Aug 1976 and 1 photographed at the Hatfield Marine Science Center on Yaquina Bay, Lincoln Co., 28-30 Oct 1979. Since then, there have been at least 14 additional records, the majority from the coast, with additional sightings at Malheur NWR, near Burns Junction, Malheur Co.; Harney Co., at Cove, Union Co.; and at Pendleton, Umatilla Co.

Most records have occurred in the fall and early winter (Sep to Jan), several involving birds that remained for multiple days. A smaller peak occurs from May to early June, and 1 was photographed at Cape Blanco, Curry Co., on 18 July 2006.

In addition, 1 was photographed s. of Yachats, Lane Co., on 29 Sep 2008. This record has not yet been reviewed by the OBRC.

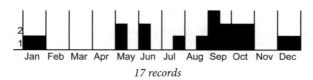

17 records

Mourning Dove *Zenaida macroura*

Abundant in spring, summer, and early fall statewide in open landscapes, except along the coast and in the higher elevations of the w. Cascades, where it is uncommon to rare. It is absent from alpine areas and densely forested sites, especially at the highest elevations. Fairly common to uncommon in valleys in winter. Migrants return late Mar-early Apr in e. Ore., but it is difficult to discern migration in many areas because of presence of birds yr-round. Aside from wintering birds, the typical pattern is for imms. that are independent of their parents to gather in wandering flocks of up to about 50 beginning in Jul. They are subsequently joined by adults. Southward migration begins as early as late Jul at Malheur NWR with a peak 25 Aug to 10 Sep.

*Common Ground-Dove *Columbina passerina*
Vagrant. Breeds across the s. U.S. from s. Cal. to S. Carolina. Post-breeding wanderers have reached many n. states, incl. c. Cal. and Nevada.

There is 1 accepted Ore. record of a bird photographed at Cape Blanco, Curry Co., on 3 August 2006.

Order CUCULIFORMES
Family Cuculidae
Subfamily Coccyzinae

*Yellow-billed Cuckoo *Coccyzus americanus*

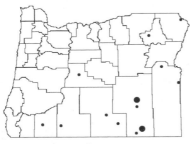

vagrant occurrence

Currently a rare, irregular visitor e. of the Cascades; very rare and sporadic w. of the Cascades. There is no known breeding population in the state, but there is some evidence that cuckoos bred in Ore. within the last 30 yrs. Reports of a nesting in La Grande in 1980 remain unconfirmed. One found dead and photographed after hitting a window in Bend had a brood patch.

Single individuals have been reported almost every yr from riparian areas e. of the Cascades. The OBRC has accepted 18 eastside records to date, some involving photographs and birds found dead, but there have been about 40 reports (many not submitted to the OBRC) from e. Ore. in the 1970s-90s. Eleven of these were from Malheur NWR and 10 from Fields. Other locales included Pueblo Mtns. (also Harney Co.), Cow Cr. and Owyhee R. near Adrian (both Malheur Co.), Logan V. (Grant Co.), Haystack Res. (Jefferson Co.), Imnaha (Wallowa Co.), Umatilla, Bend, Hart Mtn., Upper Klamath L., and L. Abert.

During the same period, only 4 w. Ore. reports were published; 2 were from Sauvie I. and 1 each from Sams V. (Jackson Co.) and West Linn (Clackamas Co.). Of these, only the Jackson Co. record has been accepted by the OBRC.

Over half of all reports were for Jun; but the months of Jul and Aug were also represented. Extreme dates for observations are 19 May-5 Sep. This is a late arrival to Ore. in spring, with most reports in Jun.

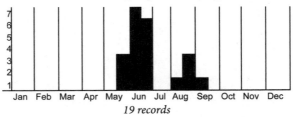

19 records

Order STRIGIFORMES
Family Tytonidae

Barn Owl *Tyto alba*

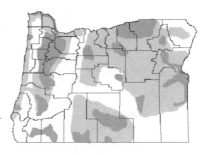

A fairly common permanent resident in open country w. of the Cascades. E. of the Cascades it is more local in its distribution, being most common in agricultural areas. It is absent from much open country, most notably in the se. corner of the state. It is an occasional resident of Malheur NWR, but experiences high winter mortality in some yrs. Less common over much of its range in winter. While Barn Owls breed most frequently in the spring, they are known to breed at any time of the yr when voles are abundant. Most Ore. breeding is in late spring. Most Barn Owls are resident, and evidence for migration in any population is weak. However, juvs. often disperse great distances.

Family Strigidae

Flammulated Owl *Otus flammeolus*

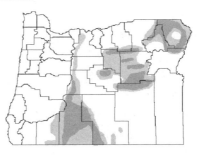

See *BOGR* for taxonomy. Breeds on the e. slope of the Cascades, in the Blue and Wallowa mtns., and in small numbers in the mtns. of sw. Ore. W. of the Cascade crest, it has been reported in extreme se. and s. Douglas Co., throughout Jackson Co., and w. to nc. Josephine Co. No systematic study has been made of sw. Ore. populations; their status is poorly known. It likely migrates throughout its range; also known from Great Basin sites including Hart Mtn. and Malheur NWR. Thought to arrive in Ore. primarily during May, but the capture of 16 between 29 May and 25 Jun 1977 at Hart Mtn. indicates the species may be a regular and uncommon late-spring migrant in the Great Basin. Records from Malheur NWR span 30 Apr-7 Jun; 26 of 36 (72%) spring records at Hart Mtn. were from the period 21 May to 10 Jun. Autumn migration probably begins in Aug, and appears to peak in Sep or Oct. Small numbers may linger through mid-Nov, but records beyond late Oct are rare. The late record from Ore. is 13 Nov 1991 in Harney Co.

Western Screech-Owl *Megascops kennicottii*

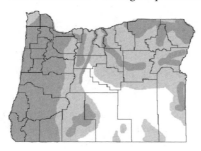

See *BOGR* for taxonomy. Fairly common yr-round resident in lower-elevation woodlands throughout the state. Usually found below 3,000 ft in w. Ore., but has occurred at least to 4,100 ft in the w. Cascades. In w. Ore., common in lowlands; fairly common in Siskiyou Mtns., along the coast, in the Coast Range, and in low to mid-elevations of w. Cascades. E. of the Cascades, it is uncommon at low to moderate elevations. Breeding phenology is poorly understood. There are few nesting data for Ore. Throughout range, courtship commences in Jan and Feb. OBBA data indicate majority of fledglings seen Jun-Jul, but observations ranged from 27 Apr to 31 Aug. There is no evidence of migration in this species, though there may be some movement downslope into lowlands or residential areas in winter.

Great Horned Owl *Bubo virginianus*
A fairly common permanent resident throughout the state, but generally absent in areas above timberline. Although Great Horned Owls occasionally disperse long distances, the majority of banded juvs. are recovered within 15 mi of their natal sites. Can be found on nests as early as Jan.

Snowy Owl *Bubo scandiacus*
Irregular in small numbers to Ore.; generally associated with large-scale irruptive events. They occur occasionally in non-irruption yrs, most often on coastal dunes of the n. coast or in high deserts and agricultural areas of c. and ne. Ore. Snowy Owls begin to appear from late Nov to Dec during irruption yrs, and peak in mid-Jan. Snowy Owls seen in Ore. during the irruption of 1996-97 remained into mid-Mar. In peak yrs, typically found s. to Eugene, the c. coast, and the n. part of e. Ore.; less often farther s.

*Northern Hawk-Owl *Surnia ulula*

Vagrant. Breeds in the taiga belt across n. Eurasia and from w. and c. Alaska across n Canada to the n. Great Lakes. Significant southward movements occur in some winters.

Three accepted Ore. records:

1. One was observed on Sauvie I., Multnomah Co., 4 Nov – 22 Dec 1973.
2. One was photographed near Palmer Junction, Union Co., 15-20 Jan 1983.
3. One was photographed and seen by many in Bend, Deschutes Co., 3-23 Feb 2005.

Northern Pygmy-Owl *Glaucidium gnoma*

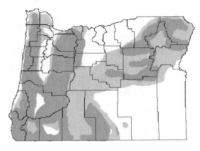

Taxonomy of the Northern Pygmy-Owl is controversial; see *BOGR*. Fairly common throughout forested areas of Ore., including the Coast Range, Klamath Mtns., Cascade Mtns., and Blue Mtns. It is rare or absent in the isolated mtns. of se. Ore. (Steens Mtn., Pueblo Mtns.) and in deciduous woodlands of the Willamette, Umpqua and Rogue valleys. Considered a resident, but little is known about seasonal movements. During winter, sometimes observed in areas not used for breeding, including suburban backyards, deciduous riparian areas, and w. juniper shrubland, but rarely far from forests. Apparent movements to lower altitudes during winter have been reported, especially in e. Ore., but source of lowland birds not proven. Ore. populations may exhibit both altitudinal migration and yr-round residency depending on latitude, elevation, and regional climate.

Burrowing Owl *Athene cunicularia*

COOS	CLAT	LANE	BENT	PORT	CENT	MALH
					8 May	27 Mar

A spring and summer visitant in open grassland and shrub-steppe habitats in all ecoregions of e. Ore. (except higher mtns.). Probably most common in the Columbia Basin and in se. Ore. Formerly bred in the Rogue and Umpqua valleys. Rare annual visitor to the Willamette V. and s. coast, especially during winter. In the Columbia Basin, adults

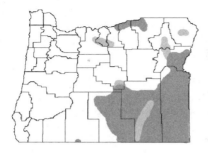

and juvs. begin leaving the nesting territory between Jul and Sep, and are generally gone from the region before Oct. Burrowing Owls are observed as early as late Oct in w. Ore., but more typically appear in Nov or Dec, and are often seen into late Feb or Mar. Return as early as Mar to breeding areas.

Spotted Owl *Strix occidentalis*

Permanent resident in forested regions of w. Ore., from the coastal mtns. to the e. foothills of the Cascade Range. A few pairs also occur in the Saddle Mtn. area immediately e. of Klamath L. Absent from lowland interior valleys of w. Ore. and from high-elevation subalpine forests, except for occasional stragglers. Normally resident on the same territory throughout the yr, but home range areas are largest during winter when some individuals wander extensively. Juvs. leave the nest in late May or Jun and disperse Sep-Oct.

Barred Owl *Strix varia*

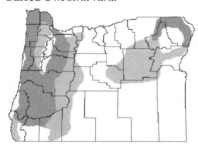

Rapidly expanding, now found essentially statewide. A permanent resident in forests of the Cascades, Coast Range, Blue, Wallowa, Strawberry and Klamath mtns., recently reached w. Curry Co. Rare or absent in non-forested regions of the Willamette, Umpqua, and Rogue valleys, and high desert region of se. Ore., but have been found in the cities of Portland and Eugene along forested ridgelines.

Great Gray Owl *Strix nebulosa*

Uncommon to rare inhabitant of forests adjacent to openings above 3,000 ft in the Cascade, Blue, and Wallowa mtns. Somewhat local. Most observations in the Cascades are from e. of the crest, though they have been discovered breeding w. of the crest in the Willamette NF. Recently, a population has been discovered in the Siskiyou Mtns. Unlike birds

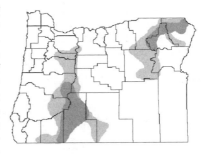

elsewhere in Ore., most of the Siskiyou Mtn. birds occur at lower elevations (1,400-3,000 ft). Although some disperse during winters of prey scarcity, they are largely resident. Calling occurs most frequently from late Feb through Apr. Young leave the nest between mid-May and mid-Jun. Juvs. move to thicker cover and climb to an elevated perch.

Long-eared Owl *Asio otus*

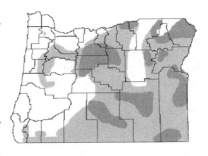

A fairly common breeder in open country e. of the Cascades in wooded riparian areas and junipers. Uncommon in conifer forests in ne. Ore. below about 5,500 ft., and in pine forests at low to moderate elevations on the e. slope of the Cascades. A rare breeder in foothills of the Willamette V., where fewer than 5 nesting records have been reported. Its status is particularly unclear in the w. Cascades and Coast Range, where there are no confirmed nesting records except at Hagg L., Wash. Co. Rare and probably breeds in e. Lane Co. (Contreras 2006); also reports from Linn, Douglas, Tillamook, Coos, and Curry Cos.

May winter throughout the breeding range, but sites at higher elevations are probably vacated in winter. Birds breeding in more northerly locations may winter in the state. Movements are largely speculative and lack sufficient research. In e. Ore., groups of 10 or more birds may roost together in thickets during winter, but there are no winter records for ne. Ore. Uncommon in winter in the Willamette and Rogue valleys, where regular wintering groups have been found at Finley NWR and E. E. Wilson W.A. Two winter (Dec) and 1 possible migration (Mar) record, for the Umpqua V. Very little is known about migration routes, or which populations might be more migratory vs. sedentary. Spring migration thought to be primarily in Mar, but little is known about the timing or migratory habits of these birds. Winter roosts in the Columbia Basin begin breaking up during the last wk in Feb. In ne.

Ore., males actively singing in the vicinity of a nest in Mar and Apr. Fall migration is thought to primarily occur in Oct, but virtually nothing is known about the distances that Ore. birds move, the routes they use, or which populations are relatively migratory vs. sedentary.

Short-eared Owl *Asio flammeus*

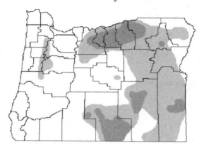

Locally common to rare in open country throughout the state. Considerable variation in its distribution from yr to yr is likely due to fluctuations in prey base. E. of the Cascades it is locally common in the breeding season, particularly in the large wetland complexes. It may have largely disappeared as a breeder from Klamath, Deschutes, and Crook cos., where it was historically considered common. It is very uncommon locally w. of the Cascades. It is uncommon yr-round in the Willamette V., becoming more rare in the n. portion, but breeding status is currently unknown and it may possibly be extirpated as a nesting species there.

Uncommon in winter. In ne. Ore. it is most common in the Grande Ronde V. and s. Union Co. Some remain in winter along the Columbia R. lowlands. Numbers increase in w. interior valleys and along the coast in winter. An uncommon to rare visitor to the Rogue V. and occasional to rare along the coast with usually at least 1 found in most yrs on coastal CBCs. Widespread in migration. Periodically irruptive during breeding and non-breeding seasons. Spring migration occurs in Mar and Apr. Dispersing juvs. can be found in Aug as fall migration begins. At Malheur NWR autumn migration peaks in late Oct and into Nov. Location of winter populations is quite variable and apparently related to prey abundance. Short-ears tend to concentrate at favored locations, particularly in winter.

Boreal Owl *Aegolius funereus*
Presumed to be a permanent resident but breeding unconfirmed. Regularly observed about the Wenaha-Tucannon Wilderness in ne. Umatilla and nw. Wallowa cos.; near Todd L. and the s. slopes of South Sister Mtn., Deschutes Co.; above Waldo L., Lane Co.; and on Mt. Pisgah, Wheeler Co. USFS surveys found birds in the Willamette, Deschutes, and Umatilla NFs in 1993. Most detections were of birds attracted to

recorded songs and calls played during Sep and Oct. Little Ore. information is available. In Idaho, males give the primary song on territory as early as 20 Jan, reaching greatest intensity by late Mar. Males resume territorial defense Aug-Nov. No information is available on Ore. birds during the winter months.

local in Cascades; range somewhat speculative and poorly documented

Note: Similarity of size and some calls to Saw-whet Owl can cause confusion and some misidentification. Boreal Owls are usually found in remote high-elevation forests where travel is difficult and conditions uncomfortable, especially at night. Responds well to recorded calls played in spring and fall but mostly silent and unresponsive during the nesting season.

Northern Saw-whet Owl *Aegolius acadicus*

Widespread breeder in low- to mid-elevation coniferous and mixed deciduous/coniferous forests statewide. Found at higher elevations to tree line in lower numbers. Relatively uncommon in dry oak forests, juniper woodlands, and chaparral. In the Coast Range, this is the most common forest owl detected during Apr-May. Occasionally found during the non-breeding season in isolated woodlots and riparian thickets within the Willamette V., coastal pastures and high desert regions of e. Ore. Nesting begins in Apr and May when males begin calling. Flight-capable juvs. are observed in late Jun in the Coast Range. A significant fall movement takes place in the w. Rocky Mtns. and other, poorly understood movements are reported. Banders trapped 96 Saw-whets in mist nets at a single location near Florence, Lane Co., in Oct-Nov of 1996-98. We do not know if this represents directional migration or random dispersal of young owls.

Order CAPRIMULGIFORMES
Family Caprimulgidae
Subfamily Chordeilinae

Common Nighthawk *Chordeiles minor*

COOS	CLAT	LANE	BENT	PORT	CENT	MALH
31 May		31 May	4 Jun	8 Jun	27 May	24 May

Breeds and migrates at all elevations throughout the state. Fairly common to locally common within and e. of the Cascades; rare to locally uncommon w. of the Cascades. One of the latest migrants to arrive in Ore. Reported early arrival dates include 4 May in Oakridge, 9 May in the s. Willamette V., 10 May in Philomath, and 12 May at Eugene. Migration flights occur both during day and night, but most often in early evening, and often in large flocks. Peak fall migration is 15-31 Aug at Malheur NWR, and early Sep in the s. Willamette V. Occasional birds are reported annually throughout the state in the last 10 days of Sep. Late autumn records include 3 Oct at Malheur NWR, 5 Oct in Portland, 9 Oct in the s. Willamette V., and 17 Oct s. of Salem. There are no winter records.

I.D. NOTE: Extremely early arrival dates of 17 Apr and 28 Apr at Malheur NWR may be vagrant occurrences of Lesser Nighthawk, a species which arrives much earlier than Common Nighthawk in n. Cal. There are a few Apr reports of nighthawks in western Ore., and a Lesser was photographed off the coast of British Columbia on 5 Jun 2006. Lesser Nighthawk is more likely than Common before early May. Any nighthawk seen in Ore. before mid-May should be identified with care.

Subfamily Caprimulginae

Common Poorwill *Phalaenoptilus nuttallii*

COOS	CLAT	LANE	BENT	PORT	CENT	MALH
					10 May	14 May

Uncommon to locally common e. of the Cascades; locally uncommon in Jackson Co., uncommon to rare farther w. in Josephine Co. Uncommon summer resident in chaparral-oak in Rogue Butte V., particularly Roxy Ann Peak, where it has bred successfully, and on open, lower-elevation serpentine sites in Josephine Co. Numerous records from spring through fall in the w. Cascades from Douglas Co. n. to Linn Co., on isolated buttes of the s. Willamette V., and south of Hood R., but breeding status unknown. Spring migrants have reached Portland as well as other n. Willamette V. sites. Several records from spring and fall for Coos and Curry cos.

The migratory period is not well known. Some spring migrants arrive in late Apr. Records on 14 Mar 1964 at Malheur NWR and 30 Mar 1992 at the Hermiston airport, Umatilla Co., are the earliest known. The breeding period extends from early Jun through early Jul. At Malheur NWR numbers 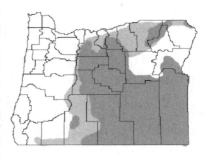 decline in early Sep with the latest noted on 3 Oct 1977. Elsewhere, small concentrations have been noted in mid-Sep. There are many records from late Oct through late Nov from throughout the state. Late records have included active birds, birds in torpid condition, and dead birds, all indicating possible attempts at local overwintering.

Whip-poor-will *Caprimulgus vociferus*

Vagrant. Breeds widely across the e. U.S. (subspecies *vociferus*), with a disjunct population (*arizonae*) in s. Cal., Arizona, and New Mexico.

One accepted Ore. record of a calling bird that was heard and recorded near Frenchglen, Harney Co., on 14 May 2005.

Order APODIFORMES
Family Apodidae
Subfamily Cypseloidinae

Black Swift *Cypseloides niger*
Rare to uncommon spring and fall transient and summer visitant (presumed breeder) throughout state. Nests at Salt Cr. Falls, e. Lane Co., and at a waterfall in e. Lane Co., about 3 mi wnw. of Diamond Peak and 7 mi sw. of the Salt Cr. Falls site, ironically in the Swift Cr. basin. The species is strongly suspected to breed in other locations along the coast, in the Cascades, the Columbia R. gorge, and other canyons and mountain ranges in e. Ore. Breeding season (Jun to mid-Aug) records away from e. Lane Co. include Lincoln, Coos, Curry, Linn, Multnomah, Jefferson, Deschutes, Crook, Wallowa and Harney cos. First arrivals are usually about 10-16 May. They are most often seen as singles or in flocks of fewer than 15 birds, at times in association with a larger number of Vaux's Swifts. Usually gone from the Salt Cr. Falls site by early August. Fewer birds are detected in fall migration, which occurs from late Aug through Sep. Usually absent after about 20 Sep; latest sighting is 11 Oct in Eugene.

Subfamily Chaeturinae

Vaux's Swift *Chaetura vauxi*

COOS	CLAT	LANE	BENT	PORT	CENT	MALH
10 Apr	4 May	9 Apr	19 Apr	12 Apr	18 Apr	7 May

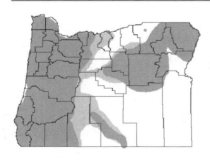

A transient and summer resident nesting in older forests and brick chimneys statewide except in se. Ore., where it occurs only during migration. Fairly common throughout forested regions of the state and in urban areas having brick chimneys. Rare in extensive, treeless areas such as the desert regions of e. Ore. Concentrations of more than 10,000 swifts may be seen at roosts during migration. Early migrants reach sw. Ore. during the second wk of April. Most arrive in Ore. in late Apr and early May and depart from mid-Aug to mid Oct. They congregate at communal roost sites, especially in Sep, and migrate in large flocks.

Subfamily Apodinae

White-throated Swift *Aeronautes saxatalis*

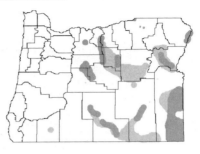

A locally common to
abundant breeder, primarily
on c. and e. Ore. cliffs.
Occasional spring and
sporadic fall migrant in w.
Ore. along the coast, in the
Willamette V., and on the
w. slope of the Cascades. A
small colony may still exist
at Lower Table Rock, Jackson
Co. Breeding may also occur
near Davis L., Deschutes/Klamath Co.; at Crater L., Klamath Co.; and
in the Kalmiopsis Wilderness, Curry Co. Earliest arrival date is 17
Mar. Regular at nesting cliffs by Apr. Sometimes seen in migration and
at breeding colonies with Violet-green Swallows and Cliff Swallows.
Moves away from breeding areas in late summer. May form flocks to
migrate. Gone from the state by mid- to late Sep. Of fall reports from e.
of the Cascades, 2 Oct 1989 (at Summer L., Lake Co.) is the latest. An
11 Oct 1997 report at Toketee, Douglas Co., is the latest for the state.
No winter records.

Family Trochilidae
Subfamily Trochilinae

*Broad-billed Hummingbird *Cynanthus latirostris*

Vagrant. Breeds from se. Arizona s. through w. and c. Mexico.
  Two accepted Ore. records:
1. A subadult male was photographed at John Day, Grant Co., 12-14
   Sep 1998.
2. A male was photographed at Gearhart, Clatsop Co., 6-14 Oct 2001.

*Ruby-throated Hummingbird *Archilochus colubris*

Vagrant. Common breeder across much of s. Canada and the e. U.S.
  One accepted Ore. record of an adult male photographed at a feeder
in Pendleton, Umatilla Co., where it remained from 14 to 17 Sep 2006.
  In addition, a male was photographed at a feeder in Keno, Klamath
Co., in early Sep 2008. This record is still under review by the OBRC.

Black-chinned Hummingbird *Archilochus alexandri*

COOS	CLAT	LANE	BENT	PORT	CENT	MALH
	26 Apr				10 May	26 Apr

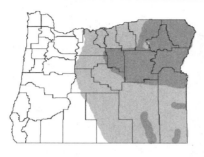

A rare to locally common summer resident e. of the Cascades. Least common in Klamath and Lake cos. Fairly common in foothills near the Blue, Wallowa, and Steens mtns. in summer, also in areas of Wasco Co., and in the Snake and Owyhee valleys. Migrates through se. and sc. Ore. They begin arriving in mid- to late Apr with peak migration mid- to late May. Males wander and migrate early, arriving on breeding grounds before females. W. of the Cascades there is little documented evidence of nesting. There are a few records from the Willamette V. and more in the Cascade foothills, especially in spring. Rare spring migrants have been recorded along the coast in Coos, Lincoln, Tillamook, and Clatsop cos., usually at feeders. It is also occasionally reported from the Rogue V. in spring and summer. There are at least 4 late Mar reports, all from w. of the Cascades: 2 at Coos Bay, 1 at Shady Cove, Jackson Co., and 1 at Eugene. There are no reliable winter records. Most males leave by early Aug, and females and imms. leave by late Aug, although females or imms. are seen regularly at Malheur HQ in early Sep. Latest detection was a male 30 Sep 1998 at a feeder in Reedsport, Douglas Co.

Anna's Hummingbird *Calypte anna*

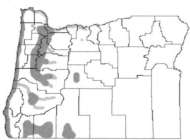

A rare to locally common summer resident w. of the Cascades in interior valleys and along the coast; also along the Columbia R. e. to The Dalles. Occurs and probably breeds into the w. Cascades at some urban developments such as Oakridge. In winter, uncommon to fairly common in w. Ore. at lower elevations, especially where feeders are present. Casual winter visitor in s. Cascades. In e. Ore., locally uncommon in spring and summer in several locations along the e. flank of the Cascades, with most reports from the Klamath Basin and c. Ore. (Deschutes, Crook, and Jefferson cos.). Breeds in and around Bend, where it is the most common hummingbird species in summer. Has been found as far e. as Ukiah, Umatilla Co.

Though generally absent e. of the Cascades in winter, birds have overwintered in Bend. Arrives in c. Ore. in late Apr or early May, but breeding activities begin earlier in w. Ore. Displaying males are sometimes seen as early as Jan in sw. Ore. Nesting occurs as early as late Jan in mild areas of w. Ore. Post-breeding movements are difficult to assess. They usually depart c. Ore. by mid-Oct, and numbers in w. Ore. begin increasing during Sep and Oct. Wintering populations appear to be greater than breeding populations, suggesting some northward migration from Cal. or possibly concentration of family groups.

Costa's Hummingbird *Calypte costae*

Very rare spring and summer visitor to c. and sw. Ore. and coastal locations. Records exist during spring and breeding months in Clatsop, Clackamas, Lane, Jackson, Josephine and Deschutes cos., and during post-breeding in Lincoln, coastal Lane, Clackamas, Multnomah, Douglas, and Jackson cos. A breeding attempt occurred near Harbor, Curry Co. Males are sometimes present for the entire yr in the Rogue V. Costa's is a very rare fall and winter visitor to coastal and Portland area locations. Arrival dates in the Bend area are 30 Mar to 20 May; in the Roseburg-Sutherlin area 4 Apr 1990, 27 Apr 1989. A displaying male was seen late Apr 1989 in the n. Umpqua V. Departure dates not well documented; 1 individual was seen 11 Nov 1977 in the Roseburg area. Ore. sight reports include all months of yr.

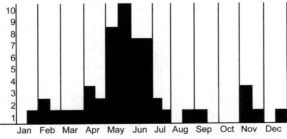

28 records (through 2000)

Calliope Hummingbird *Stellula calliope*

COOS	CLAT	LANE	BENT	PORT	CENT	MALH
28 Apr				29 Apr	22 Apr	2 May

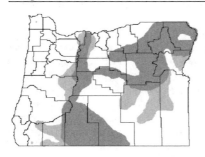

A common summer resident of the Blue and Wallowa mtns. and other high ranges e. of the Cascade summit, including Steens and Hart mtns. Spring and fall migrants are rare to locally uncommon at lower elevations elsewhere e. of the Cascades. The Alvord Basin might be an important migration corridor to and from mtns. in e. Ore. In the w. Cascades, scattered records exist from Mt. Hood to Crater L. NP, but repeat observations are rare and nesting has not been documented. At Thorn Prairie, Douglas Co., this species is a regular summer resident. Generally very uncommon to rare n. of there, at moderate to high elevations.

W. of the Cascades, it is locally uncommon in the Siskiyou Mtns. and the Rogue V. Spring migrants are rare in the Willamette V. and along the coast, though reports appear to be increasing. It has been a rare but regular spring migrant in the foothills of central Lane Co. since at least the mid-1970s. Multiple females and/or juvs. have been seen almost annually in Jun-Jul on Saddle Mtn., Clatsop Co., since 1995; its status there is unknown. Most arrive mid-Apr to early May. The earliest detection is 22 Mar 1998 at Lebanon, Linn Co. Based on rangewide migratory patterns, males are assumed to arrive first. By the end of May, birds have traveled to montane breeding territories. Most adult males have left Ore. by early Jul, and most females and imms. leave late Aug-early Sep. A few records exist for late Sep.

Broad-tailed Hummingbird *Selasphorus platycercus*

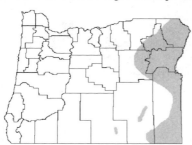

A very irregular, uncommon and somewhat local summer resident and migrant in e. Ore. The Blue and Wallowa mtns. of ne. Ore. harbor small local populations, at least in some yrs. A few records hint at birds on breeding territories: an adult male at Spring Cr. near La Grande on 3 Jul 1981 appeared to have been displaying, and similar sightings have been reported from the Eagle Cap Wilderness Area, Wallowa Co. In se. Ore. they are reported fairly often from Steens Mtn. and Mahogany Mtn. and encountered on Hart Mtn. during breeding season. The OBBA found summering birds of both sexes in mtns. of s. Malheur Co. Probably breeds locally in many of these areas, but nesting remains unconfirmed. Some of the records from se. Ore. such as those from Fields, Andrews, and Adel, probably involve migrants, as these places are below the usual breeding elevations. Generally absent w. of the Cascades, with a few notable exceptions. Probably arrive in mid-Apr; arrival data are scarce. The earliest reliable observation is 12 Apr 1997 at Mosier, Wasco Co. The latest detection is 4 Sep 1994 on Steens Mtn. No winter records.

Rufous Hummingbird *Selasphorus rufus*

COOS	CLAT	LANE	BENT	PORT	CENT	MALH
15 Feb	2 Mar	21 Feb	2 Mar	25 Feb	18 Apr	

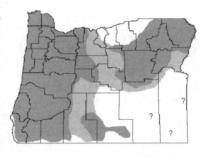

Common transient and breeder throughout most of w. Ore., especially in forested regions. It is uncommon on the e. slope of the Cascades, uncommon at higher elevations of the Blue Mtns., and uncommon to fairly common in the Wallowa Mtns. Summering birds are rare in se. Ore.; breeding has not been confirmed in Harney and Malheur cos., the Columbia Plateau, or c. Ore. In most yrs, they begin to arrive in w. Ore. in mid-Feb. First detections are invariably along the s. Ore. coast; the earliest arrival date is 19 Jan at Coos Bay, Coos Co. W. interior valley arrival dates fall behind coastal dates by about 1 wk. Peak migratory movements occur from late Mar through the first wk of Apr. There are very few first detection reports e. of the Cascades, but arrival is probably discretionary and weather dependent, ranging from late Mar through Apr. Arrival in the Blue Mtns. is typically during the first wk of Apr.

Males arrive about 2 wks before females, presumably to set up territories. Males move away from breeding territories as early as Jun. Some females and imm. birds begin dispersal in Jul but a female has been found feeding young in the nest as late as 28 Jul 2001 near Zigzag, Multnomah Co. Post-breeding dispersal has confused the issue of breeding ranges somewhat and many high Cascades, Wallowa, and se. Ore. montane records may be of dispersed birds rather than breeders. Males will use displays generally associated with breeding purely in defense of feeding territories. Most leave the state by late Aug, though a few are encountered into Sep. There are scattered winter records of *Selasphorus* hummingbirds from CBCs, most in the Willamette V. All recent winter records are associated with hummingbird feeders. Most winter records of *Selasphorus* hummingbirds in w. Ore. have been assumed to be this species, but no thorough documentation of these individuals has been obtained.

Allen's Hummingbird *Selasphorus sasin*

This is a fairly common spring and summer resident along the s. Ore. coast as far n. as Bandon and is uncommon up the Coquille V. to Powers; breeding has been verified only in Curry Co. It is very uncommon at Coos Bay and rare n. to Reedsport. In s. Curry Co., Rufous Hummingbird is thought to be limited to higher-elevation inland areas while Allen's breeds on the outer coast. There are no confirmed winter records, but see the Rufous Hummingbird account for identification issues. Spring migrants arrive early, beginning in late Feb. Males arrive first, followed by females, and by late Mar most have returned. Males mist-netted in mid-Jun at higher elevations in e. Curry Co. and Josephine Co. suggest a post-breeding dispersal upslope into the Siskiyous. This is a very rare summer visitant in the Rogue V., probably transients rather than breeders. Fall migration begins early, peaking in Jul, and few are recorded after early Aug, though this may be a result of identification uncertainties with females and imms.

It occurs as a very rare vagrant in other parts of w. Ore., but physical similarities to Rufous Hummingbird make reports difficult to evaluate. A specimen obtained in 1983 from Philomath, Benton Co., was confirmed as an Allen's. A pair of *Selasphorus* hummingbirds that was netted, measured, and photographed 10 Mar 1988 at Astoria, Clatsop Co., was identified with near certainty as this species—but that far n. of their expected range they were most likely accidentals.

Order CORACIIFORMES
Family Alcedinidae
Subfamily Cerylinae

Belted Kingfisher *Megaceryle alcyon*
Common permanent resident throughout most of the state, except in n. Lake and e. Deschutes cos., where open water is generally absent. It is local in s. Harney and Malheur cos., in agricultural areas along the Columbia R., and at high elevations where habitat is limited. During winter, kingfishers withdraw from areas where ice is present on feeding sites. It remains throughout e. Ore. where open water permits; in Klamath Co. it uses open water found along geothermal water routes in towns. Somewhat difficult to determine onset of breeding. Adults entering probable nest sites were reported 30 Apr to 15 Jul and fledged young observed 24 May to 3 Aug. Fall movements are poorly known. Over 200 were along the Deschutes R. between Warm Springs and Sherar's Bridge, 22-25 Sep 1987. A Lincoln Co. survey Nov 1993 to Jan 1994 found 13 males and 7 females, which could indicate an unequal sex ratio in winter. Can be very common in good habitat: 38 pairs were found during a survey of the lower Luckiamute R., Polk Co., on 27 Jul 1974.

Order PICIFORMES
Family Picidae
Subfamily Picinae

Lewis's Woodpecker *Melanerpes lewis*

COOS	CLAT	LANE	BENT	PORT	CENT	MALH
					3 May	26 Apr

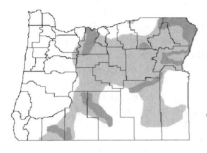 

winter distribution

Common yr-round only in the white oak-ponderosa pine belt e. of Mt. Hood. Also, breeds in low numbers in open habitat along e. Ore. river and stream valleys; most common in Baker Co. Winters in oak savannah e. of Mt. Hood, in the upper Rogue R. V. and along Bear Cr. in the Medford area; uncommon and very local in the Willamette V., occasional in Josephine Co.; casual in Umpqua V. A regular movement of these woodpeckers occurs along Cascade ridges in fall, beginning in mid-August. A regular transient in small numbers w. of the Cascades, uncommon e. of the Cascades, and most common in open habitats (e.g., burns) in and near Cascade forests. Very rare on the coast. In a detailed study e. of Mt. Hood, courtship began in Apr and continued through May; birds fledged in Jul and left the nest area seeking additional forage in early Aug. Winter residents returned to oak habitat and began storing acorns in late Sep. At Malheur NWR, where transient, average spring arrival is 26 Apr, peak of passage is 1-12 May; fall peak is 10-25 Sep.

**Red-headed Woodpecker *Melanerpes erythrocephalus*
Vagrant. Breeds from se. Canada across most of the e. U.S.

One accepted sight record for Ore. of an adult observed at P-Ranch, Harney Co., on 21 June 1987.

In addition, 1 was observed at Malheur NWR on 6 Jul 2008. This record has not yet been reviewed by the OBRC.

Acorn Woodpecker *Melanerpes formicivorus*

Fairly common in the Rogue V. and adjacent hills. Locally common in the Klamath R. Canyon in sw. Klamath Co. Uncommon to fairly common in the Klamath Mtns. n. to n. Curry Co. and the Umpqua R. V. Likely extirpated in Coos Co., where it existed until the 1990s. Locally common in the s. Willamette V., becoming uncommon and local just s. and w. of Portland. Probably extirpated at The Dalles, where it was found intermittently from 1960 through 1991. Colony sites change intermittently and individuals may be noted away from colonies at any time of yr. There are only about a dozen extralimital records; near Upper Klamath L. is the only repeat location with at least 3 sightings. One near Frenchglen in Sep 2008 (G. Grier p.c.) is the easternmost record. One extralimital specimen from Crater L. NP, 14 Aug 1961.

Williamson's Sapsucker *Sphyrapicus thyroideus*

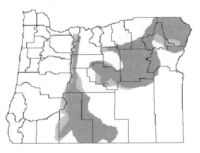

A common to uncommon summer resident of forests in the Blue Mtns., and on the e. slope of the Cascades, se. to Warner Mtns. in the s. A few breed w. of the Cascade summit, where they are locally common in the high Cascades of e. Jackson Co., and may breed in the Siskiyou Mtns., s. Jackson Co. Post-breeding dispersants and transients are found to the high Cascades and lower elevations of e. Ore.; casual in winter. A casual vagrant to w. Ore. below the high Cascades. Spring migration occurs Mar to early May. Early birds arrive in Ore. during Mar, but most arrive during Apr. Males arrive up to 2 wks earlier than females. Fledging dates for 19 nests in ne. Ore. were 19 Jun–20 Jul. Families usually disperse immediately after young fledge. Southward movements are not conspicuous with birds remaining scattered. Most leave late Aug to mid-Oct, with lingerers noted through Nov.

Yellow-bellied Sapsucker Sphyrapicus varius

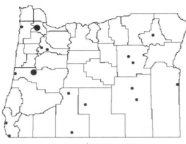

vagrant occurrence

Vagrant. Breeds e. of the Rocky Mts. across Canada and the ne. U.S. Winters across the se. U.S. to C. America.

There are 18 accepted Ore. records from all parts of the state, 15 between early Oct and late Feb. In addition to birds in the typical fall-winter occurrence pattern, an adult male and an imm. female were at Scoggins V. Park, Wash. Co., on 9 Jul 1976; an adult female was photographed near Gilchrist, Klamath Co., on 5 Jul 1983; and an adult male was observed at La Grande, Union Co., on 11 Jul 1980.

In addition, there are several unreviewed sightings. This species can be very difficult to separate from the similar Red-naped Sapsucker, with which it is known to hybridize occasionally, and future records should be carefully documented.

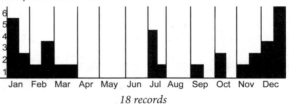

18 records

Red-naped Sapsucker *Sphyrapicus nuchalis*

COOS	CLAT	LANE	BENT	PORT	CENT	MALH
					10 Apr	6 Apr

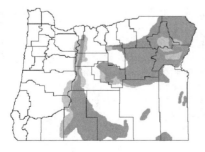

winter distribution

A common summer resident throughout forested mtns. e. of the crest of the Cascades. A spring and fall migrant through the same mtns. and lower elevations. Rare in winter along the e. slope of the Cascades and very rare elsewhere e. of the Cascades. Casual in all seasons w. of the Cascade summit; most often during spring migration. Hybridizes with Red-breasted Sapsucker, mostly along the e. slope of the Cascades and in sc. Ore. In the Fremont NF in sc. Ore., about 1/3 of sapsuckers are hybrids. In spring, arrives at Malheur NWR as soon as early Feb and peaks late Apr to early May. On the c. e. slope of the Cascades, some arrive as early as late Feb, with an average first arrival of mid-Apr. May be dependent on conifer sap for food until deciduous trees bud and insects are available. Young are still in the nest cavity from mid-May to late Jul. Fledglings are typically observed early to late Jul. Fall migration at Malheur NWR occurs mid-Aug to mid-Oct, with most sightings from mid- to late Sep. A few individuals winter at lower elevations in sc. Ore.

> I.D. Note: Winter and w. Ore. observations of Red-naped should be made with care since the very similar Yellow-bellied Sapsucker is casual in Ore. and is probably just as likely in winter w. of the Cascades.

Red-breasted Sapsucker *Sphyrapicus ruber*

Two well-marked subspecies; both occur in Ore. *S. r. ruber* is a fairly common breeder in the n. part of the state from the coast to the Cascades and s. to the s. Cascades. Breeds locally on the e. slope, particularly in c. Ore. In sw. Ore., *S. r. ruber* intergrades with *S. r. daggetti*, which gradually replaces it to the s.,

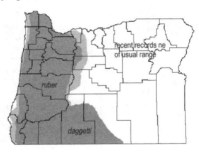

probably near s. Douglas Co. *S. r. daggetti* is found from s. Douglas and Josephine cos. e. to the Warner Mtns. S. coastal birds may be intergrades but more specimens are required to verify ranges in sw. Ore. Recently a vagrant visitant to the Ochoco, Wallowa, and Blue mtns. and an irregular transient in the Harney Basin. Winters in the Coast Range and lowlands of w. Ore., with small numbers found in river valleys of the w. Cascades, the Klamath Basin, and sc. Ore.

Both subspecies are known to hybridize with Red-naped Sapsuckers in localized zones of overlap e. of the Cascades summit: near Sisters, Ft. Klamath, and Warner V., and especially in the Warner Mtns. Possibly arrives on territory earlier than Red-naped Sapsucker, which may limit hybridization. In the Klamath Basin, the bulk of migrants arrive in mid-Mar. Departure and/or downslope movement of birds in fall from the Cascades may depend on weather conditions. Dates of movement are unclear, as the species winters throughout much of its Ore. breeding range. It is also unknown whether birds that leave higher elevations in Ore. move to local valleys or migrate southward. It is not clear whether winter influxes into w. Ore. are from the Cascades or from more northerly populations. Specimens of *S. r. ruber* have been collected in s. Cal. and Arizona in winter, suggesting that at least some migration occurs out of the Northwest, but it is not clear whether these are Ore. birds or "leapfrogging" birds from Alaska or British Columbia.

Nuttall's Woodpecker Picoides nuttallii
Vagrant. Resident of oak and riparian woodlands from n. Cal. w. of the Sierras to nw. Baja Cal.
Two accepted Ore. records:
1. A male and a female were collected near Ashland, Jackson Co., on 3 and 4 Feb 1881. The specimens are in the British Museum.
2. One was found dead near Trail, Jackson Co., in the fall of 1991.
In addition, 1 was reportedly collected in the Umpqua V., Douglas Co., during Aug 1855. This record has not been reviewed by the OBRC.

Downy Woodpecker *Picoides pubescens*

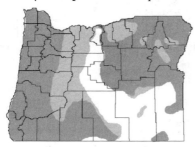

See *BOGR* for complex taxonomy. Breeders in w. Ore. are distinctly duller, especially underneath, than birds from e. Ore., which are bright white underneath. Found mostly at low to moderate elevations in deciduous and mixed deciduous-coniferous forests, and less often in coniferous forests. Most abundant in riparian areas and red alder. In the w. Cascades, it occurs in deciduous river corridors and in some large patches of deciduous habitat. Fairly common in towns. In fall/winter some local movements occur as a few individuals move to lower elevations and/or populated areas, such as Malheur NWR or Bend.

Hairy Woodpecker *Picoides villosus*

See *BOGR* for complex taxonomy. Resident in forests throughout Ore. with the exception of juniper. Common throughout most of range, but uncommon to fairly common along the coast and in w. interior valleys. Most common in burns or in areas with trees that are dead from or 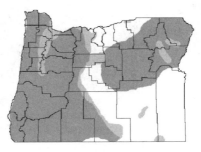 infested with mountain pine beetles. Few consistent seasonal movements are known. Some wandering occurs outside the breeding season. At Malheur NWR spring migration begins in Mar or Apr and ends by late May. Fledglings are typically observed mid-Jun to late Jul. Fall migration at Malheur NWR begins in early Oct, peaks in late Oct, and ends by mid-Nov; small numbers winter. Regular movement into residential areas (more commonly e. of the Cascades) has been noted in winter, especially when montane conditions are severe.

White-headed Woodpecker *Picoides albolarvatus*

An uncommon permanent resident in open ponderosa pine or mixed-conifer forests dominated by ponderosa pine of the Ochoco, Blue, and Wallowa mtns., and the e. side of the Cascades, but suitable habitat is restricted. Local w. of the Cascade crest, mainly in the upper reaches of the Umpqua R. basin and 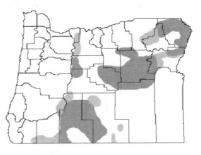 in the Siskiyou Mtns. Fewer than 10 records exist outside this range, including coastal sites and Malheur NWR. There is a small population in true firs in the Siskiyou Mtns. sw. of Ashland. This population has not been studied and could show variations from results of studies conducted in ponderosa pine habitat. No consistent seasonal movements are known, but limited movements or wandering outside breeding areas and seasons occur as noted in the distribution sections above.

American Three-toed Woodpecker *Picoides dorsalis*

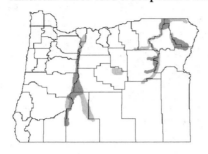

Rare and local, particularly near and w. of the Cascade summit, often near high-elevation lakes or beetle outbreaks; sometimes in or near burns but not as attracted to them as is the Black-backed Woodpecker. Found mainly in lodgepole pine and spruce. Reports come sparingly from both slopes of the Cascades and the Blue Mtns. including the Wallowas. Southernmost records are from Mt. McLoughlin. There is 1 record from Hart Mt. and 2 from w. of the Cascades (Roxy Anne Butte and Mt. Ashland, Jackson Co.). Begins breeding in late May to late Jun. This species may breed relatively late in the season owing to its tendency to occupy high-elevation forests. Status in Ore. is not well known.

Black-backed Woodpecker *Picoides arcticus*

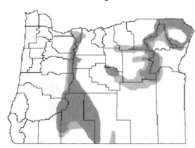

A rare to locally common resident near the summit and on nearby plateaus and ridges on the w. side of the Cascades; more widespread on the e. slope. Uncommon in the Blue Mtns., where it is less common than the Am. Three-toed Woodpecker (the reverse of the rest of Ore.). In nw. Ore., there have been several sightings from the Clackamas R. drainage. The westernmost extent of its range is in the Siskiyou Mtns, with 3 records to Curry Co. (Munson et al. 2004) and 1 to Cape Arago, Coos Co. (Contreras 1998). The reported center of abundance is the lodgepole pine forest e. of the Cascade crest between Bend and Klamath Falls. Inhabits the Warner Mtns. They begin nesting in mid-May. The breeding schedule can vary among yrs by at least 3 wks due to weather conditions, and may begin later at higher elevations.

Northern Flicker *Colaptes auratus*
A common resident throughout Ore. (red-shafted *cafer* group). One subspecies of the *auratus* (yellow-shafted) group, either *C. a. borealis* or *C. a. auratus*, is a rare winter visitor or transient throughout Ore. Hybrids showing characteristics of red- and yellow-shafted birds are often seen in Ore., especially in fall and winter. In spring some individuals appear at higher elevations and winter visitors leave, though it is not clear whether this represents a simple upslope movement or multiple northerly movements of different populations. A conspicuous influx occurs at Malheur NWR from early Mar to early Apr. Fall movements into lower elevations and migration into Ore. make for decreased numbers in winter at higher elevations and increased fall and winter numbers in farmland, towns, and other areas, such as lowland parts of n. and c. Malheur Co. from Sep to Jan, on the w. slope of the s. Cascades during late Sep and Oct, and at Malheur NWR from mid-Oct to mid-Nov. Yellow-shafted birds often appear during late Sep and early Oct.

Pileated Woodpecker *Dryocopus pileatus*

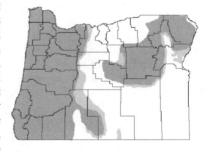

An uncommon permanent resident in older forests in the Blue, Cascade, and Klamath mtns.; Coast Range; and Willamette, Umpqua, and Rogue valleys. Limited altitudinally by habitat availability; higher and lower elevations may lack large enough trees for nesting, roosting, and foraging. No significant seasonal movements. Individuals are regularly seen in deciduous and coniferous stands that seemingly lack large trees in the major w. Ore. valleys and foothills, and in the Coquille V., particularly in winter.

Order PASSERIFORMES
Family Tyrannidae
Subfamily Fluvicolinae

Olive-sided Flycatcher *Contopus cooperi*

COOS	CLAT	LANE	BENT	PORT	CENT	MALH
30 Apr	11 May	27 Apr	7 May	2 May	16 May	17 May

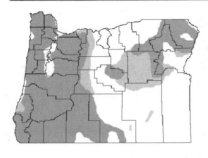

Breeds in low densities throughout conifer forests in Ore. from near sea level along the coast to timberline in the Cascades and Blue Mtns. Most abundant throughout the Cascades. In migration, may occur in any forested habitat including forest patches in desert oases of se. Ore., urban forest, and deciduous or mixed deciduous/coniferous riparian forest. Breeding habitat is conifer forest, particularly in semi-open habitats with tall live trees and snags. Spring migration and arrival of residents well documented because of loud, distinctive song. Spring migration peaks in late May, earlier in sw. and coastal Ore., and later in montane areas and e. Ore. Rare migrant as early as mid-April. Late migrants occasionally occur at desert oases in early Jun. Timing of fall migration is less known, but peaks late Aug and into first wk of Sep. A few late Sep records; latest 28 Sep 1986 at Emigrant L., Jackson Co.

Western Wood-Pewee *Contopus sordidulus*

COOS	CLAT	LANE	BENT	PORT	CENT	MALH
1 May	14 May	3 May	3 May	2 May	13 May	10 May

Common migrant and fairly common to common breeder statewide in open groves of trees or along forest edges at all elevations. Rare in landscapes dominated by dense conifer forests in the w. Cascades and Coast Range, even in open habitats, but occasionally present along riverine woodlands adjacent to open areas or at lower elevations. Uncommon summer resident along the n. coast. In vast expanses of agriculture or sagebrush steppe, found only in patches of trees at homesteads and near water. Spring arrival in Ore. is comparatively late. There are a few records in sw. Ore. for the last wk of April. Peak of passage is typically the latter half of May, and migrants are noted in se. Ore. into early Jun. According to most observers reporting on fall

Common plumages of some Northwest Sandpipers

*Adult Least Sandpiper,
midsummer.
Photo: Don Munson*

*Least Sandpiper, mostly molted from
juvenile to winter plumage.
Photo: Russ Namitz*

*Adult Least Sandpiper.
Photo: Lois Miller*

*Least Sandpiper, juvenile.
Photo: Don Munson*

*Breeding Western Sandpiper.
Photo: Don Munson*

*Juvenile Western Sandpiper, fall.
Photo: Russ Namitz*

*Adult Western (above)
and Semipalmated (below)
Sandpipers, early summer.
Photo: Wink Gross*

*Juvenile Semipalmated
Sandpiper, fall.
Photo: Russ Namitz*

*Western Sandpiper, winter.
Photo: Owen Schmidt*

Juvenile Swallows

Birds in flight: *top row: Vaux's Swift, Violet-green Swallow,*
Tree Swallow, Bank Swallow
second row: Northern Rough-winged Swallow, Cliff Swallow
Perched birds *(from top to bottom): Cliff Swallow, Tree Swallow,*
N. Rough-winged Swallow, Violet-green Swallow (left),
Bank Swallow (right)

Juvenile Sparrows

top row: Chipping Sparrow, Sage Sparrow, Brewer's Sparrow
bottom row: Vesper Sparrow, Lark Sparrow, Black-throated Sparrow

Female and young Carpodacus Finches

Pair of Cassin's Finches.
Photo: Steve Berliner

Cassin's Finches. Note modest eye-ring, whitish ground color underneath, crisp streaks and heavy bill that is slightly longer than it is deep.
Photos: Alan Reid (above), Steve Dowlan (left)

Purple Finches. Note dark around eye, slightly dull ground color underneath, fuzzy streaks and fairly short, triangular bill.
Photos: Don Munson

Hutton's Vireo and Ruby-crowned Kinglet

*Hutton's Vireos, showing equal-weight wingbars,
thicker gray legs and feet, and heavy bill.
Photos: Lois Miller (left, right) and Ed McVicker (center)*

*Ruby-crowned Kinglets,
showing tiny bill, thin
obscure upper wingbar, thin
dark legs and yellowish feet
(brightness varies).
Photos: Lisa Ladd-Wilson
(right), Don Munson
(above right) and Lois
Miller (above left)*

Flying Seabirds

top row: Brandt's Cormorant, Pelagic Cormorant
second row: Red-throated Loon, Pacific Loon
third row: Common Loon (above), Red-necked Grebe (below)
fourth row: Horned Grebe, Red Phalarope

Flying Alcids

All birds depicted in breeding plumage.
top row: Common Murre (2 birds on left), Pigeon Guillemot (right)
second row: Rhinoceros Auklet (2 birds)
third row: Cassin's Auklet (2 birds on left),
Marbled Murrelet (2 birds on right)
fourth row: Ancient Murrelet (2 birds)

migration, many wood-pewees have left the state by Sep and there are very few Oct reports; among the latest are 1 at Baskett Slough NWR 2 Oct 1989, 1 in the Rogue V. 3 Oct 1984, and 1 at Malheur NWR, P Ranch, 8 Oct 1978.

*Eastern Wood-Pewee *Contopus virens*
Vagrant. Breeds from se. Canada s. across most of the e. U.S.

One accepted Ore. record of a singing bird recorded and photographed at Malheur NWR, Harney Co., 28-30 May 1994.

In addition, another singing bird was mist-netted and banded there 28-31 May 1998. This record has not been reviewed by the OBRC. This species is very similar to the Western Wood-Pewee, from which it cannot always be reliably separated in the field except by voice.

*Alder Flycatcher *Empidonax alnorum*
Vagrant. Breeds from c. Alaska across Canada to the ne. U.S.

There is only 1 accepted Ore. record to date: a bird was photographed and its voice recorded at E. Ingram I. Road, Benton Co., 29 May – 2 June 2007. The identity of this bird was confirmed through spectrograms of its recorded song and call notes.

In addition, there are about 10 older records (from 1980 to 1992), mostly of singing birds from Malheur NWR, Harney Co., and locations in ne. Ore., which had originally been accepted as Alder Flycatchers by the OBRC. The identification was based mainly on vocalization. However, recent research has revealed that some call and song notes of Willow Flycatcher bear a strong resemblance to those of the Alder Flycatcher, which led the OBRC to question and reconsider these earlier records. Whenever possible, any future sightings in Ore. should be documented by voice recordings that allow spectrographic analysis.

Willow Flycatcher *Empidonax traillii*

COOS	CLAT	LANE	BENT	PORT	CENT	MALH
15 May	2 Jun	12 May	16 May	14 May	19 May	14 May

Habitat of breeding Willow Flycatchers is characterized by dense shrubs and/or tall herbaceous plants with scattered openings of shorter herbaceous vegetation. Nesting and migratory habitat in e. and sw. Ore. is almost exclusively riparian zones, typically willows. In nw. Ore., both riparian and upland habitat (including shrub growth in clear-cuts or burns) is used for nesting, from low-elevation valleys to high mountain areas. Most birds arrive in s. Ore. in mid-May, with the peak of migration occurring throughout the state in the last few days of May through the first wk of Jun. Late migrants extend to mid-Jun. Rare migrant

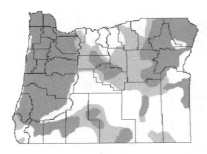

as early as mid-April. Fall migration occurs mostly during mid-Aug to mid-Sep with the peak of migration e. of the Cascades in late Aug and w. of the Cascades in early Sep. There is limited fall migratory movement through the Willamette V. Riparian habitat used during fall migration in nw. Ore. is primarily moderate- to high-elevation wet meadows with a shrub component. A few stragglers to late Sep, rarely early Oct.

Least Flycatcher *Empidonax minimus*
A rare but regular migrant and local summer resident in the state. The spring migration ranges from mid-May to mid-Jun with the majority of sightings from e. of the Cascades, especially Harney Co. In Ore. the Least Flycatcher is found in deciduous groves along streams and in wet lowlands. It desires a deciduous overstory with at least some low brushy undergrowth. Territorial birds have been regularly observed during the summer at Clyde Holliday SP, along the John Day R. near Mt. Vernon, Grant Co. Up to 5 singing males have been reported from there during some summers. Nesting was confirmed in 1985, 1995 and 1997, and probably occurred there on other occasions. Occasionally found singing at other e. Ore. sites but breeding not confirmed elsewhere. A territorial pair was on Sauvie I. from 2 Jun to 4 Jul 1991 and was suspected of successfully fledging young. The fall movement ranges from early Aug to late Sep with sightings reported from both e. and w. Ore. Extremely rare in early winter. One bird at Tillamook, 20-28 Dec 1992 was mist-netted, measured, and photographed before being released.

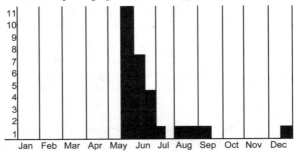

26 records, 29 individuals (through 1999)

Hammond's Flycatcher *Empidonax hammondii*

COOS	CLAT	LANE	BENT	PORT	CENT	MALH
30 Apr		17 Apr	21 Apr	19 Apr	21 Apr	

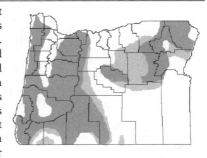

Common summer resident of older montane coniferous forests throughout state. Breeds in true fir- and Douglas-fir-dominated forest types. Present in conifer and riparian forests of isolated mountain ranges of se. Ore., including Hart and Steens mtns. Uncommon spring migrant in conifer and deciduous woods in the Willamette V. Arrive mid-Apr to early May w. of the Cascade crest. Arrive early to mid-May in e. Ore.; early date 22 Apr at Malheur NWR. Late dates for 13 yrs of fall observations in Lincoln Co. were from 19 Aug to 21 Sep. Recorded in Malheur NWR into late Sep. Other late records for e. of the Cascades are mid-Oct. One winter sight record from Roseburg.

Gray Flycatcher *Empidonax wrightii*

COOS	CLAT	LANE	BENT	PORT	CENT	MALH
					27 Apr	20 May

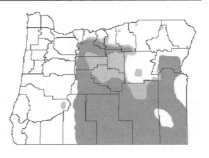

An uncommon to locally fairly common breeder e. of the Cascade summit, including the Columbia Plateau southward throughout the Great Basin. Breeds in isolated locations in the ne. portion of the state. The accuracy of records outside normal range must be viewed skeptically because identification is challenging. Rare but annual along the w. slope of the Cascades during spring migration, including 1-5 individuals detected per yr at Detroit Flats (at upper end of Detroit Res.), Marion Co., since 1995. Rare in the Rogue V. and very rare in the Willamette and Umpqua valleys during spring migration.

There have been no breeding records w. of the Cascade summit, although they have been reported occasionally during breeding season along the w. slope of the Cascades. Only 3 s. coastal records. Breeds in arid woodlands and shrublands to elevations as high as 6,000 ft. During migration less selective of habitat; often found in riparian areas frequented by other migrating *Empidonax* species. Spring migration begins mid- to late Apr and is complete by the end of May. Most records w. of the Cascades are in the last wk of Apr and the first wk of May. There appears to be no pronounced peak e. of the Cascades, but the largest influx occurs in the first and second wks of May. Southward migration extends from mid-Aug to late Sep. The latest fall record is 2 Oct 1991 at Malheur NWR. The only fall record w. of the Cascades was a vagrant reported at Gold Beach on the out-of-season date of 4 Nov 1998. There are no documented winter records.

Dusky Flycatcher *Empidonax oberholseri*

COOS	CLAT	LANE	BENT	PORT	CENT	MALH
30 Apr				1 May	3 May	2 May

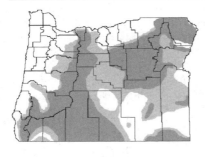

The Dusky Flycatcher is an uncommon to common summer resident in most of its breeding range in Ore. It is found the entire length of the Cascades, but habitat is limited w. of the summit in the n. Generally found at 3,000-6,000 ft elevation on the w. slope of the s. Cascades; in the Klamath Mtns. generally above 2,900 ft. Also breeds in higher mtns. e. of the Cascades, including ne. Ore. (except lowlands of Columbia Basin) above about 4,500 ft. Locally uncommon summer resident in the w. Cascades and Rogue-Umpqua Divide in the c. Umpqua Basin, w. to near Mt. Bolivar (se. Coos Co.) and Iron Mtn. (n. Curry Co.), as low as 2,000 ft. Breeding habitat e. of the Cascade summit includes mountain aspen stands, juniper woodlands, open ponderosa and lodgepole pine forests, or other open mountain areas with scattered trees; openings in grand fir forests. Spring migration habitat less restrictive, includes lowland valleys.

Fairly common spring migrant and rare to uncommon fall migrant in most lowland valleys in the vicinity of breeding territories. Also a rare migrant in the Willamette V., Columbia R. estuary, n. coast, and c. coast. Rare to occasional migrant along s. coast. Arrival of spring migrants and establishment of breeding territories appear to overlap statewide; mid-

Apr to mid-May. Departure from breeding territories and fall migration occurs early Aug to early Sep. Late dates include 4 Sep 1998 in the n. Cascades; 9 Sep 1990 near Ashland; 9 Sep 1992 at Summer L.; 27 Sep 1986 at Malheur NWR; and 22 Oct 1963 at Malheur NWR. There is 1 unverified mid-Dec sighting near Coos Bay thought to be this species by an experienced observer.

The "Western" Flycatcher complex

Formerly classified as a single species (Western Flycatcher, *E. difficilis*), Pacific-slope Flycatcher and Cordilleran Flycatcher differ genetically, vocally, and morphologically in color, shape, and size, but are nearly identical in the field. The two species are sympatric in n. Cal. and s. Ore. The term "Western" Flycatcher may be useful for reporting sightings of some birds just as the term "empidonax" is sometimes used for unidentified individuals in the genus. Song types in the two species may be more complex and overlapping than previously understood. Further study of these species is needed.

COOS	CLAT	LANE	BENT	PORT	CENT	MALH
20 Apr	3 May	20 Apr	27 Apr	24 Apr	3 May	14 -May

Pacific-slope Flycatcher *Empidonax difficilis*

Common to abundant breeder in forests of Coast Range and w. Cascades below about 4,000 ft elevation; common transient in w. Ore. "Western" Flycatchers of uncertain taxonomy are locally common to uncommon breeders in moister forested habitats e. of the Cascade crest (e. Cascades and Blue Mtns.). They are uncommon transients in e. Ore. Common in a variety of

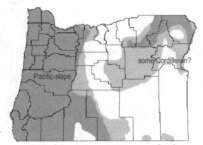

breeding range map covers both Pacific-slope Flycatcher and Cordilleran Flycatcher

low- to mid-elevation forest types in w. Ore., including Sitka spruce, red alder, western hemlock, Douglas-fir, and western red cedar. At higher elevations, uncommon in Pacific silver fir forests. In e. Ore. "Western" Flycatcher occurs locally in black cottonwood, quaking aspen, ponderosa pine, lodgepole pine, and high-elevation spruce/fir forests, particularly in moist riparian corridors; during migration "Western" Flycatcher occurs in a variety of wooded or brushy habitats throughout the state, and at oases in arid country e. of the Cascades.

Spring migrants usually begin to arrive in w. Ore. in mid- to late Apr, breeders common by mid-May. In e. Ore. first "Western" Flycatcher arrivals are in late Apr and early May, peaking in late May and early Jun. At Malheur NWR, spring migrants observed from 23 Apr to 17 Jun, average 14 May. Fall migration peaks in late Aug and early Sep, mostly complete by mid-Sep. Late dates: 20 Sep on upper Calapooia R.; 4 Oct along Beaver Cr. at Lebanon; 8 Nov. At Malheur NWR, fall migrant "Western" Flycatchers observed from 12 Aug to 3 Oct, with peak passage 25 Aug to 15 Sep. A few winter reports have accrued, but no winter records have yet been verified.

Cordilleran Flycatcher *Empidonax occidentalis*

The Cordilleran Flycatcher was recently designated a species distinct from the Pacific-slope Flycatcher, with which it was formerly lumped under the name Western Flycatcher. The two species are almost identical in appearance, and the population in e. Ore. is in some respects vocally intermediate between the Cordilleran and Pacific-slope types, so the distribution and status of the Cordilleran Flycatcher in Ore. is unclear. "Western" Flycatchers in e. Ore. are relatively uncommon by comparison to Pacific-slope Flycatchers w. of the Cascade crest. For further information see discussion under Pacific-slope Flycatcher.

The identity of populations in e. Ore. is unclear and birds are most safely identified as "Western" Flycatchers. "Western" Flycatchers are locally common to uncommon breeders in the e. Cascades, and in the Ochoco and Blue mtns. They breed in low numbers at elevations >4,500 ft in the drier s. Blue Mtns. of Grant, Harney, and n. Malheur cos., locally in w. Baker Co. and locally in the Pueblo and Ore. Canyon mtns. The status of Cordilleran Flycatcher in w. Ore. is uncertain; it is likely very rare if it occurs at all. See discussion under Pacific-slope Flycatcher.

Black Phoebe *Sayornis nigricans*

Expanding. Uncommon to common local resident in lowlands of Rogue, Applegate, and Illinois R. valleys and tributaries, generally below 2,500 ft; s. coast lowlands north to Coos Bay. In the 2000s, has expanded n. to breed locally in Douglas Co., in coastal Lane Co,. and around Fern Ridge Res. The Black Phoebe's display commences in Feb; they occasionally sing in winter. Irregular breeder but expanding n. of Lane Co. Has bred or attempted breeding n to Yamhill Co. Casual visitor in the Klamath Basin. Sometimes wanders to unlikely locations. An individual was observed at Gold L. bog (e. Lane Co.) on 8 Jul 1988 at 4,800 ft. Great Basin reports include individuals at Fields 20 May 1990 and Malheur NWR 5 Apr 1991 (without details). Black Phoebes are strongly associated with water. Slow-flowing, idle, or slack water of large rivers, streams, and creeks, ephemeral and permanent ponds, lake shorelines, irrigation ditches, and even water tanks are used. Not strongly associated with any particular vegetative species; generally at riparian edge, or habitats adjacent to water; less restricted during winter.

Eastern Phoebe Sayornis phoebe

Vagrant. Breeds from nw. Canada s. across much of the e. U.S.

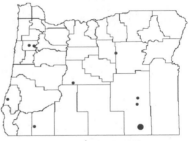

vagrant occurrence

Ten accepted Ore. records:

1. A territorial bird was photographed and its voice recorded at Falls City, Polk Co., 6-23 Jun 1992.
2. One was photographed at Fields, Harney Co. 1-7 Nov 1994.
3. One was at Independence, Polk Co., 19-20 Feb 1996.
4. One was at Buena Vista Station, Malheur NWR, Harney Co., 31 May – 7 Jun 1998.
5. One was photographed near Bandon, Coos Co., and remained 28 Dec 1998 – 20 Mar 1999.
6. One was at the Valley of the Rogue SP, Jackson Co., 10-12 Jun 1999.
7. One was along Hwy 26 at John Day R., Wheeler Co., on 14 May 2000.

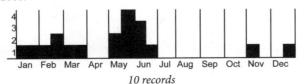

10 records

8. One was photographed near LaPine, Deschutes Co., 8-19 May 2004.

9. One was photographed at Fields, Harney Co., on 19 May 2004.

10. One was photographed at Fields, Harney Co., on 28 May 2006.

In addition, there are several records that have not yet been reviewed by the OBRC, including a bird photographed at Corvallis, Benton Co., on 24 Apr 2004.

Say's Phoebe *Sayornis saya*

COOS	CLAT	LANE	BENT	PORT	CENT	MALH
				4 Mar	25 Feb	22 Feb

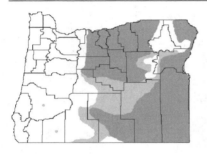

Breeds in arid, sparsely treed, open country such as sagebrush plains, dry foothills, canyons, rimrock country, and dry farms from the e. base of the Cascades eastward. Common breeder from se. to nc. Ore. and Snake R. in extreme ne. Ore. Uncommon breeder in sc., c., and ne. Ore. Common migrant e. of the Cascades. Uncommon to very uncommon spring and fall migrant w. of the Cascade summit to the coast. In most springs 3-4 individuals are reported w. of the Cascades, but some yrs are exceptional, such as 1999, when 31 were reported. At the other extreme, no spring migrants were reported 1991-94. Fall migrants w. of the Cascades average 2-3/yr; however, as many as 12 were reported in 1998.

Very uncommon but regular winter resident in the w. interior valleys. Occasional in winter along the s. coast. Occasional winter resident in lowlands e. of the Cascades. Earliest of our insectivorous migrants, first arriving in mid- to late Feb. Spring migration peaks in mid-Mar and continues through mid-Apr, although a few stragglers may continue to arrive into early May. Although not always possible to distinguish from winter residents, most of the early Feb records likely represent spring migrants. Late records of individuals in w. Ore. include 17 Jun 1978 at Eugene, and 2 Jun 1998 at the n. spit of Coos Bay. Southward migration occurs from late Aug to the end of Sep without a discernable peak. Most records later than Sep (through winter) are w. of the Cascades, although single individuals have been reported e. of the Cascades most yrs since 1990.

*Vermilion Flycatcher *Pyrocephalus rubinus*
Vagrant. Breeds in the s. U.S. from s. Cal. to w. and c. Texas, also in C. and S. America.

Four accepted Ore. records:
1. An imm. male was photographed at Bend, Deschutes Co., and remained 10 - 25 Oct 1992 .
2. An adult male was observed at Myrtle Point, Coos Co., 6-7 Dec 1992.
3. An adult male was photographed at Irrigon, Morrow Co., on 7 Nov 2000.
4. An adult male was photographed at Woodburn, Marion Co., and remained from 8 Jan into Mar 2003.

Subfamily Tyranninae

*Dusky-capped Flycatcher *Myiarchus tuberculifer*
Vagrant. Breeds from se. Arizona and sw. New Mexico s. through Middle America to n. S. America.

There is 1 accepted Ore. record: 1 was photographed and its voice recorded at Newport, Lincoln Co., 2-11 Jan 1996.

Ash-throated Flycatcher *Myiarchus cinerascens*

COOS	CLAT	LANE	BENT	PORT	CENT	MALH
					12 May	18 May

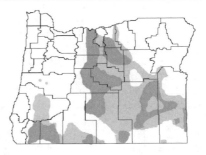

Uncommon to locally common summer resident in the Rogue and Applegate valleys; locally uncommon summer resident in the Illinois and Umpqua valleys. Rare wanderer to the Willamette V.; most regularly sighted at Mt. Pisgah, Lane Co. Fairly common to locally common from Bend-Sisters area n. to The Dalles, including Crooked R., Bear Cr., and mid- to upper John Day V. Accidental in the n. Blue Mtns. Uncommon summer resident in the s. Blue Mtns. and areas of se. Ore. with semi-arid slopes and canyons containing large western juniper, sometimes with an understory of sagebrush, bitterbrush, and/or rabbitbrush. Uses oak-pine habitat in the e. Columbia Gorge, dry, mixed woodlands of western juniper, mountain-mahogany, and ponderosa pine in the Klamath Basin, or oak woodlands in Klamath R. canyon.

Ash-throateds arrive w. of the Cascades from late Apr to early May, and e. of the Cascades primarily early to mid-May. After fledging, adults and juvs. leave breeding territories from mid-Jul to mid-Aug. During this time, in the Rogue V. they may be found in open willow riparian habitat, where they do not breed. Late departures from breeding areas include 18 Aug 1991 and 11 Sep 1997 from the Rogue V. Reverse fall migration, or dispersing juvs., may account for fall coastal and Willamette V. sightings. There are few winter reports, and none confirmed after Nov. Rare to occasional migrant in coastal Ore., mainly s. A possible nesting pair was recorded at Brookings into late May 1993.

> Note: any small *Myiarchus* observed in late fall or winter should be observed carefully in case it is a Dusky-capped Flycatcher.

Tropical Kingbird *Tyrannus melancholicus*
Rare but regular wanderer from w. Mexico, mostly in fall. Tropical Kingbirds are most often found in open situations close to the ocean, about an estuary, in pastures, in towns, sitting on a telephone wire or fence line, or on a bare tree branch. Fall records are from early September through early December, but 85% occur from the second wk of October through the third wk of November. Movements seem to shift from yr to yr; in some yrs the bulk of movement is in October, in other yrs November.

Outside this period, 1 was at the mouth of the Elk R., Curry Co., on 11 Jun 1982, 1 was reported from Cape Arago, Coos Co., 18 Feb 1985, and another was photographed at Cape Blanco, Curry Co., 26 Jul to 8 Aug 1998. There are few inland sightings. One was photographed at Malheur NWR HQ, Harney Co., 27 Sep 1995. Another was photographed and heard calling on Sauvie I., Multnomah Co., 1-17 Nov 1996, and 1 was there 14-26 Nov 2006 (Irons 2007a). One was observed at Grand I., Polk Co., 11 Oct 1998. A bird seen 3 Nov 1973 near Eugene was probably this species (Contreras 2006).

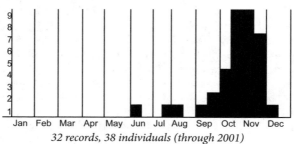

32 records, 38 individuals (through 2001)

*Cassin's Kingbird *Tyrannus vociferans*
Vagrant. Breeds from the sw. U.S. to c. Mexico.

There is 1 accepted Ore. record: an imm. was photographed near Canby, Clackamas Co., and remained from 10 Oct to mid-Dec 2001.

In addition, there is a record of an imm. female that was collected at Mercer, Lane Co., on 4 Aug 1935. The specimen has been lost, and the record has not been reviewed by the OBRC. However, Alden Miller and Ralph Browning both saw the specimen and concluded that it was correctly identified.

Western Kingbird *Tyrannus verticalis*

COOS	CLAT	LANE	BENT	PORT	CENT	MALH
1 May		21 Apr	26 Apr	26 Apr	21 Apr	23 Apr

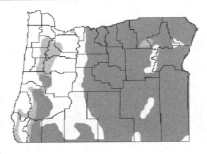

Fairly common summer resident e. of the Cascades. Range also extends westward through open valleys within the Siskiyou Mtns. and into the Rogue and Umpqua valleys, where it is also fairly common. Uncommon to rare in summer in the Willamette V. but found annually, with more birds and nesting reports from s. locales, especially sc. Lane Co, where several pairs breed annually. Nesting records exist throughout the Willamette V., but recent breeding has been confirmed only as far n. as Marion and Polk cos. Rare to very rare breeder along the s. coast n. to interior Coos Co.

Regular and rare to locally fairly common transient on the coast at least n. to Tillamook. Seen regularly in migration along Elk R. bottomlands, Curry Co. Rare spring and casual fall migrant in open areas in the w. Cascades, such as golf courses, pastures, developed (e.g., residential, industrial) areas, and reservoir edges. There have been no records for this species in winter in the state. In w. Ore., typically arrives mid- to late Apr, though there are a few reports as early as March. Transients in non-breeding areas are usually gone by the end of May. Fall migration at Malheur NWR begins in early Jul, peaking 15-25 Aug, and most have left the state by early to mid-Sep. Records of late individuals include 13 Oct 1998 near the mouth of the Elk R., Curry Co., 18 Oct 1985 at Nehalem, and 6 Nov 1982 at Barview.

> Note: Any kingbird seen after late September is more likely to
> be a Tropical Kingbird and should be carefully examined.

Eastern Kingbird *Tyrannus tyrannus*

COOS	CLAT	LANE	BENT	PORT	CENT	MALH
				28 May	13 May	19 May

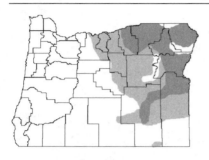

Breeds throughout open agricultural areas and moist grasslands with some tree cover in most of lowland ne. Ore., with spotty distribution in c. and se. Ore. Abundance variable from locally common to rare. Most abundant in irrigated valleys of ne. Ore.; more local in se. Ore. in Harney and s. Malheur cos.; sparsely distributed in Owyhee Uplands. The only documented nesting site in w. Ore. is the Sandy R. delta along the Columbia R. near Portland, where 1 or 2 pairs have nested each yr since 1993. Migrants may occur throughout open habitats of e. Ore.

Typically arrives in late May, with a few records for early May. Rare late spring transient in w. Ore. (0-3 birds/yr) with most sightings along the s. and c. coast. Migratory movements are much less often reported in fall than in spring. At Malheur NWR, fall migration occurs during Aug, and by Sep few birds remain. Late dates in e. Ore. include 12 Sep at Malheur NWR, and 15 Sep in Harney Co. A late date in w. Ore. is 10 Sep at Seaside.

*Scissor-tailed Flycatcher *Tyrannus forficatus*

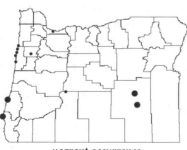

vagrant occurrence

Vagrant. Breeds in the sc. U.S., from e. New Mexico and n. Kansas to ne. Mexico.

Casual vagrant to Ore., with 17 accepted records to date. In addition, there are several unreviewed sight records. The majority of records are from early May to early Jul, mainly from coastal locations, but 1 was photographed at Davis L.,

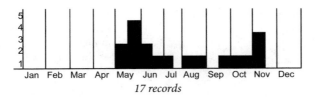

17 records

Klamath Co., on 14 Jun 1978; 1 was at Fairview, Multnomah Co., on 25 May 1992; 1 was near Burns, Harney Co., on 15 Jul 2000; and 1 was photographed at Malheur NWR, Harney Co., 21-26 May 2005. There are 2 Aug records from Dallas, Polk Co,. and Malheur NWR. Fall records have occurred at various coastal locations and near Burns, Harney Co., from late Sep to mid-Nov.

Family Laniidae

Loggerhead Shrike *Lanius ludovicianus*

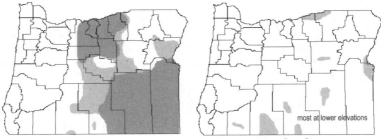

winter distribution

Breeds in open habitats e. of the Cascades where rare but regular in the winter, especially at low-elevation sites. Absent from forested landscapes and higher-elevation sites in the Blue and Wallowa mtns. Uncommon and declining in ne. Ore. where most birds are found in s. Union Co. W. of the Cascades, there are usually a few records each yr during fall, winter, and spring in open habitats of the coast and the Willamette, Umpqua, and Rogue valleys. Early migrants in e. Ore. and se. Wash. appear in Feb, with most arriving mid-Mar to 1 Apr. Migrants typically depart by mid-Sep. Later departure dates to mid-Nov known from higher-elevation sites. However, because this species winters throughout most of its lower-elevation Ore. range in low densities, extreme arrival and departure dates should be interpreted with caution.

Northern Shrike *Lanius excubitor*

winter distribution

Uncommon to locally common winter visitor in open habitats statewide. Absent some yrs along the s. coast. Rare, only in open areas (e.g., clearcuts, reservoir edges, pastures), in the Coast Range and Cascades. Commonest shrike in winter e. of the Cascades except during mild winters when Loggerhead Shrikes remain in warmer areas, e.g., Klamath and Summer L. basins, and Snake R. V. This is the only shrike that regularly occurs in nw. Ore. Less likely to be seen farther s., but a fairly regular winter visitor in the Lower Rogue R. and Bear Cr. valleys and foothills.

In the Blitzen V. of the Malheur NWR, where both shrikes sometimes winter, Loggerhead Shrikes most often frequent desert shrub habitat while Northern Shrikes spend the majority of their time along willow-bordered meadows. Usually arrives early to mid-Oct in ne. Ore., mid- to late Oct in the Willamette V., and late Oct to early Nov on the s. coast and Klamath Basin. Typically departs Malheur by mid-Mar, but has remained as late as 16 Apr. Usually absent from the c. coast and Willamette V. after Mar. One was at Warrenton, Clatsop Co., 9 Apr 1966. In e. Ore., extreme dates of 9 Sep in Crook Co. to 9 Apr in Wallowa Co.

Family Vireonidae

Bell's Vireo *Vireo bellii*

Vagrant. Breeds in the c. U.S. e. of the Rocky Mtns. Separate populations also occur in the sw. U.S. and s. Cal.

Two accepted sight records in Ore.:
1. One was observed at Fields, Harney Co., on 22 and 24 May 1980.
2. One was observed and heard singing at Fields, Harney Co., on 6 Jun 1998.

The subspecies of the Ore. records are unknown, but the 1998 bird was brightly colored and responded only to recordings of Eastern Bell's Vireo (*V. b. bellii*).

Yellow-throated Vireo *Vireo flavifrons*

Vagrant. Breeds across the entire e. U.S. to wc. Texas and c. Florida

Two accepted Ore. records:

1. One was photographed at Malheur NWR, Harney Co., on 9 Jun 2000.
2. One was at Brookings, Curry Co., on 4 Jul 2004.

*Plumbeous Vireo *Vireo plumbeus*
Vagrant. Breeds throughout the Great Basin from e. Cal., s. Idaho and sc. Montana s. through c. Colorado and New Mexico to w. Texas and nw. Mexico.

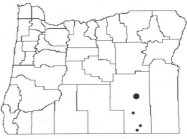

vagrant occurrence

Until 1997, this species was considered conspecific with Cassin's Vireo and Blue-headed Vireo under the name Solitary Vireo. As it can be quite difficult to separate from a drab Cassin's Vireo, the status of Plumbeous Vireo in Ore. is not fully understood, and many reports have not been sufficiently documented. This species appears to be a rare but regular migrant in se. Ore. and a vagrant farther w. A pair unsuccessfully attempted nesting near Lakeview, Lake Co., in 1996 (not reviewed by the OBRC), and the species may breed occasionally in the se. corner of the state.

There are only 5 accepted Ore. records to date:
1. One was at Malheur NWR HQ, Harney Co, 25-26 May 2002.
2. One was at Fields, Harney Co., on 13 June 2002.
3. One was at Colony Cr., Harney Co., on 23 May 2003.
4. One was photographed at Roaring Springs Ranch, Harney Co., on 26 May 1992.
5. One was photographed at Malheur NWR HQ, Harney Co., on 7 June 2005.

In addition, there are numerous unreviewed or insufficiently documented records that probably provide a reasonable sense of the species' frequency and distribution. The first Ore. report was a sighting from Plush, Lake Co., 28 May 1976. The species has been reported from Harney Co. each spring since 1992. One was photographed in Catlow V., Harney Co., on 25 May 1992. Another, photographed at Fields, Harney Co., was singing and acting territorial from 22 May to well into Jun 1994. Singles were near

5 records

Joseph, Wallowa Co., on 3 Sep 1993 and at the Enterprise Fish Hatchery, Wallowa Co., on 17 Sep 1993. Other sightings were at Indian Ford CG, Deschutes Co., on 17 Sep 1994; Klamath Marsh NWR, Klamath Co., on 19 Jun 1998; near Ironside, Malheur Co., on 5 Jun 1999; and near Sisters, Deschutes Co., on 28 May 2001. All future records should be carefully documented.

Cassin's Vireo *Vireo cassinii*

COOS	CLAT	LANE	BENT	PORT	CENT	MALH
15 Apr		7 Apr	17 Apr	12 Apr	30 Apr	30 Apr

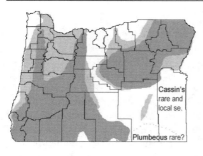

Uncommon to fairly common summer resident in forests and woodlands, except along immediate coast and rarely in n. Coast Range. Not known to breed in se. Ore. e. of Hart Mtn. Uncommon transient throughout the state. Migration taken individually or in small groups, often with flocks of other species. Main movement mid-Apr through May; earliest w. of the Cascades 19 Mar, e. Ore. 18 Apr. Some post-breeding movement to higher elevations. Fall migration not conspicuous. Most obvious during Sep with sharply reduced numbers through Oct. Latest at Tillamook, 13 Nov 1974; Bandon, 29 Nov 2008 (Rich Hoyer, ALC) and Oak Grove, Clackamas Co., 31 Dec 1997.

*Blue-headed Vireo *Vireo solitarius*
Vagrant. See taxonomic notes under Plumbeous Vireo. Breeds from nw. Canada s. across the ne. U.S. The status of this species in Ore. is not yet fully understood, as it was only recently recognized as a full species and can be difficult to distinguish from fresh fall-plumaged Cassin's Vireos.

There are only 2 accepted Ore. records to date:
1. One was at Bayocean Peninsula, Tillamook Co., on 4 Oct 1980.
2. One was photographed at Malheur NWR HQ, Harney Co., on 25 May 2003.

In addition, there are several sightings that have not been reviewed by the OBRC. Single individuals were reported on the Bayocean Peninsula, Tillamook Co., on 5 Oct 1985; at Mt. Tabor Park, Portland, Multnomah Co., on 29 Mar 1992; in the Summer L. basin, Lake Co., on 9 Sep 1992 and

13 Sep 1993; in Sawyer Park, Bend, Deschutes Co., on 3 Oct 1993; and 1 was photographed at Malheur NWR HQ, Harney Co., on 9 Sep 1998.

Hutton's Vireo *Vireo huttoni*
See *BOGR* for taxonomy. A fairly common permanent resident occurring almost exclusively w. of the Cascade crest. Most common at lower elevations, especially in the lowland forests of the Coast Range in sw. Ore.; less regular in the Cascades above the w. foothills. Also known to occur in forests 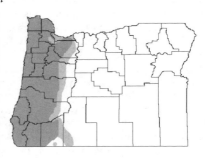 of sw. Klamath Co. in small numbers; extremely rare elsewhere in the state. Three unproven reports exist for Malheur NWR; this species has not been recorded elsewhere in e. Ore. Begins singing in late Feb or early Mar. Information on extent of dispersal and migration is vague. Most populations are considered resident but may exhibit erratic local dispersal, such that individuals may be present locally in fall, winter, and spring, but absent in summer. There is clearly substantial movement away from breeding areas, as evidenced by birds found in Sep in mountainous forest habitat in e. Douglas Co., and a noticeable influx Oct-Feb in w. valleys in winter. In winter joins mixed-species flocks that usually include other foliage gleaners such as chickadees, kinglets, bushtits, and nuthatches.

> I.D. Note: Blue-gray legs and feet (vs. orange-yellow feet in Ruby-crowned Kinglet) can sometimes be a surprisingly conspicuous feature on imperfectly seen birds. The legs are also distinctly heavier than the tiny thin legs of kinglets, a feature that makes the legs quite visible at a distance, unlike those of kinglets. This is true to a lesser extent of the bill as well.

Warbling Vireo *Vireo gilvus*

COOS	CLAT	LANE	BENT	PORT	CENT	MALH
28 Apr	11 May	21 Apr	23 Apr	26 Apr	6 May	10 May

Two subspecies groups: e. *gilvus* and w. *swainsonii* group. Only *swainsonii* is known to breed in Ore. Breeds in moderate densities in deciduous habitat throughout Ore. from sea level to montane areas. Mostly nests along river corridors and low-elevation woodlands where deciduous canopy is more common. During migration found in almost any deciduous habitat, including areas not typically used for breeding, such as riparian willows not associated with canopy trees. Begin to arrive in w. Ore. in late Apr, peak arrivals in early May. A few arrive in e. Ore. in early May (rarely late Apr), with peak arrivals in late May, and smaller numbers of birds into early Jun. Fall migration is Aug to late Sep, with several records in Oct. At Malheur NWR, peak migration 25 Aug to 7 Sep, and latest record 25 Sep 1987.

> I.D. Note: A study of molt differences between e. and w. Warbling Vireos (Voelker and Rohwer 1998) may be useful in distinguishing some birds in fall. W. (*swainsonii* group) birds do not molt flight feathers prior to fall migration, while e. birds (*gilvus* group) do. For this reason, a Warbling Vireo showing worn flight feathers or juv. buffy tips to wing coverts *in fall* is probably a *swainsonii*-group bird, while a bird with fresh wing and covert plumage is probably a *gilvus*-group bird.
>
> Because adult Warbling Vireos migrate much earlier in fall (some depart in mid-summer) than do juvs., late migrants in September are far more likely to be juvs., and a fresh-plumaged bird (that is, a bird that shows no buffy tips to coverts) among juvs. is likely to be a *gilvus*-group e. bird.
>
> E. birds are also likely to have:
>
> • a less contrasting cap (the cap that makes w. birds more often confused with a Tennessee Warbler or Philadelphia Vireo).
>
> • a slightly larger, longer bill than w. birds with a paler lower mandible and less uniformly dark upper mandible (Pyle 1997).
>
> Authorities disagree about which subspecies are "yellower" underneath in fall. In our experience, fall *swainsonii* Warbling Vireos are variable in this characteristic. In our opinion it is not likely to be helpful as a field characteristic for separating e. and w. Warbling Vireos.

*Philadelphia Vireo *Vireo philadelphicus*
Vagrant. Breeds across Canada from ne. British Columbia and Newfoundland s. to the. Great Lakes region.
   There are 2 accepted Ore. records:
1. One was photographed at Fields, Harney Co., on 3 Jun 1991.
2. One was photographed at Malheur NWR HQ, Harney Co., on 3 June 2004.
This species can be surprisingly difficult to separate from bright Warbling Vireos, and all sightings should be carefully documented.

Red-eyed Vireo *Vireo olivaceus*

COOS	CLAT	LANE	BENT	PORT	CENT	MALH
		2 Jun		31 May	8 Jun	

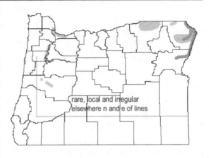

rare, local and irregular
elsewhere n and e of lines

Status in Ore. is not well known, perhaps owing to fluctuations in numbers of birds. Fairly common (Imnaha canyon) to rare summer breeder in Wallowa Co.; uncommon to rare breeder in Union Co., Baker Co., e. Grant, and e. Umatilla cos., and n. Malheur Co. Breeding has also occurred in the Owyhee V. of Malheur Co., but it does not breed there today. Elsewhere e. of the Cascades, the species' distribution is far less clear. In addition to what is noted above, the species has been reported during the breeding season at scattered locations, mainly n. of the Great Basin but occasionally to Klamath Co.

W. of the Cascades, the Red-eyed Vireo has a disjunct range and irregular status. In the n. Willamette V., found from Sauvie I. and Portland e. along the Columbia R. to the mouth of the Sandy R. and upriver to Roslyn L. Occurs locally along the Willamette R. at Luckiamute, Polk Co.; Grand I., Yamhill Co.; and near Stayton and Scio in Marion Co., as well as up the S. Santiam R. at Crabtree, Linn Co. A long-standing group up the Middle Fork of the Willamette R. from Jasper Park to Oakridge, Lane Co., has been noted annually since the late 1970s and birds have also been found at Fern Ridge Res., Lane Co. Has bred irregularly and locally s. to the Rogue V. It is casual along the coast in summer; it has been recorded in all Ore. coastal counties except Tillamook.

Found from late May increasing into Jun in migration. Peaks at Malheur (very few birds, sometimes none) during the first wk of Jun, and birds in ne. Ore. often are on territory by this time as well. Arrival dates in the Willamette V. vary from the second wk to the fourth wk of Jun. Migration seems somewhat protracted, although some late birds could be vagrants rather than part of the Northwest breeding population. Fall migration, following the opposite pattern from spring migration, starts in early Aug. and continues until mid-Sep.

Family Corvidae

Gray Jay *Perisoreus canadensis*

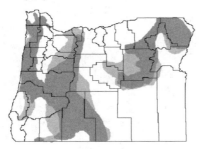

Uncommon to common throughout the Coast and Cascade ranges, but rare to uncommon in sw. Ore. and the Klamath Mtns. They occur on the immediate coast from n. Lane Co. northward, usually in older spruce/alder stands. Rare on the s. coast where they are most regular on forested inland ridges. Also found at mid- to high-elevation coniferous forests of the Blue Mtns., where it appears to be uncommon to common. Sometimes occurs at lower elevations along the fringes of the Willamette V. The brown juv. plumage is held to Jul-Sep.

Steller's Jay *Cyanocitta stelleri*

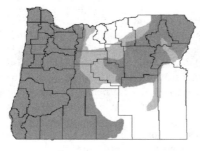

Resident in coniferous forests statewide, except for juniper, where it is present locally in winter. Jays living in lower-elevation areas likely remain on their home ranges yr-round. Upslope movements have been noted in Crater L. NP in Aug and Sep. Birds breeding at high elevations typically move downslope in winter. A few individuals may move latitudinally or longitudinally. Significant local movements are often obvious in Oct. This varies considerably from yr to yr.

Blue Jay *Cyanocitta cristata*

Rare but regular in fall and winter, especially in ne. Ore. In some yrs only 1 or 2 birds appear, in peak yrs a dozen can be scattered through the region. Most leave by Apr, but small numbers have occasionally summered. Rare irregular breeder. Nesting was verified during summer 1977 at Union, Union Co., and in 1998 at Elgin, Union Co. During the spring of 1991 a pair began nesting at Hermiston, Umatilla Co., but the attempt failed when the adults were driven off by resident Black-billed Magpies.

Western Scrub-Jay *Aphelocoma californica*

Two subspecies in Ore. *A. c. californica* breeds w. of the Cascades. *A. c. woodhouseii* is a Great Basin subspecies found in the sc. part of the state, primarily in s. Lake Co. It appears that most of the recent expansion into e. Ore. is by *californica*. *A. c. woodhouseii* has been described as shy and 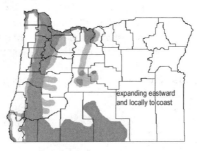 secretive, unlike the seemingly fearless *californica*. These subspecies may in fact be separate species. See *BOGR* for expanded taxonomic discussion.

Common permanent resident in w. interior valleys and foothills between the Coast Range and Cascades, especially in the Willamette, Umpqua, and Rogue valleys, and less common and more local along the s. coast and in extreme sw. Ore. In Coos Co., birds occasionally move westward in winter out of the far interior valleys (where numbers vary) as far as Coquille, rarely to the coast. Rare, but reported with increasing frequency on the c. coast. Recently, range has also expanded w. along the Columbia R. to Astoria, where it is now common, has expanded s. to Seaside and reached Manzanita in n. Tillamook Co. Western Scrub-Jays are now found in various parts of c. and e. Ore. with increasing frequency, and are rare wanderers to extreme e. sections of the state. Scrub-jays are locally common in Bend and in s. Lake and Klamath cos., especially around Adel and Lakeview.

Pinyon Jay *Gymnorhinus cyanocephalus*

Permanent uncommon to common resident in juniper and ponderosa pine woodlands of c. Ore. Ore.'s known breeding population is confined to the Metolius R. 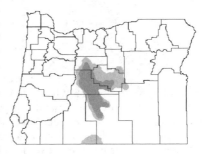 drainage eastward along the s. Ochoco Mtns., s. through Bend and e. of Newberry Crater to Silver L. basin eastward to the Lost Forest in Lake Co. Rare in the Klamath Basin during breeding season. Outside of the breeding season, range regularly expands e. to Sage Hen Ridge in

Harney Co., n. to n. foothills of the Ochocos, w. to e. Cascade foothills w. of Madras, and s. to the n. edge of the Summer L. basin and n. Klamath Co. Very rare from the Malheur-Harney Basin eastward. Occasional w. of the Cascades, mainly in fall and winter, with modern records almost all in interior sw. Ore. but historical records n. to Wash. Co.

Clark's Nutcracker *Nucifraga columbiana*

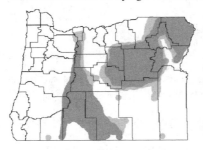

Resident along the crest of the Cascades, usually above 4,000 ft, lower on the e. slope, from the Columbia R. s. to the Cal. border, w. into the Siskiyous, and e. to the Warner Mtns., ne. throughout the Blue and Wallowa mtns. Away from the areas described above, the species is irregular (especially higher points along the Coast Range) and/or irruptive, especially in fall and winter of poor cone crop yrs, to nearly any part of the state including valleys, basins, coastal areas, and major metropolitan areas. Appears not to be resident on Steens Mtn., likely owing to the absence of pines, but has occurred there as a transient.

Black-billed Magpie *Pica hudsonia*

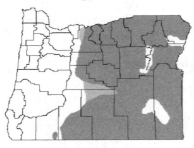

Widespread and common resident e. of the Cascades except in coniferous forests and in extreme se. Ore., where rare. Most common near agricultural, riparian and open wooded areas adjacent to open country. Very uncommon but regular visitant in the Rogue V.; rare irregular breeder. About 20 records throughout the Willamette V. since 1970. Very rare to the outer coast. The species is sometimes kept as a pet, thus some records may represent released or escaped birds. Resident throughout its range, although post-breeding and winter movements can be extensive. Spring "migration" to breeding sites is usually in progress by Feb and extends into Apr.

American Crow *Corvus brachyrhynchos*
See *BOGR* for taxonomic
discussion. Very common
resident w. of the Cascades
in interior valleys, urban
areas, and along the coast;
fairly common resident
throughout the Coast Range
lowlands and in the w.
Cascade foothills. Abundant
in the s. Willamette V.
Coastal birds are smaller

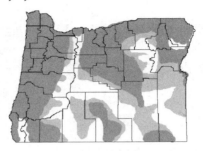

than interior birds. Occurs in the w. Cascades in areas where it was not
present 30 yrs ago, e.g., in small towns and residential clusters. E. of the
Cascades, locally common in summer in areas of human habitation or
agriculture. In winter mainly absent e. of the Cascades except in the
Klamath Basin, the Bend region, in n. Umatilla Co., and along the Snake
R. (mostly from about Brownlee Dam, Baker Co., southward), where
they are locally common to abundant. During the fall and winter, large,
communal roosts are located in foothills adjacent to valleys, or woods
in the vicinity of feeding areas, but roosting habitat has otherwise not
been studied in Ore. Winter roosts can contain as many as hundreds or
even thousands of birds, especially in colder parts of the state.

> Note: Northwestern Crow (*Corvus caurinus*) is not proven
> to have occurred in Ore. All reported specimens have been
> reidentified as American Crows.

Common Raven *Corvus corax*
Fairly common widespread resident in many habitats throughout state.
Population densities are highest e. of the Cascades and lowest in the
w. interior valleys. In the Willamette V., they are relatively rare in the
extreme n. and fairly common in the s. Locally common on the outer
coast.

Family Alandidae

Horned Lark *Eremophila alpestris*
See *BOGR* for discussion of complex taxonomy. Occurs mainly in
open, often dry, habitats with patchy herbaceous plants and grasses.
Widespread breeder in e. Ore. In w. Ore., breeds in small, scattered
populations throughout the Willamette V., with concentrations in the
c. valley on and near Baskett Slough NWR and in the Waldo Hills area
e. of Salem. Also a local and irregular breeding species on the n. coast,

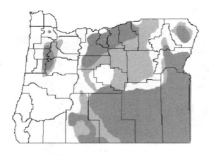

especially the s. jetty of the Columbia R. Breeds locally on some Cascade peaks.

Migrant and wintering birds are present throughout the breeding range in Ore. except not above timberline in winter. On the n. coast, an annual migrant in fall and occasional (irregular) wintering species, more rare and local on the s. coast. Occasional migrants reported in open habitats on Coast Range mountain tops. In e. Ore., post-breeding migrant flocks begin forming in Sep on Malheur NWR and reach a peak 5 Oct-5 Nov. Spring and fall migrant and wintering flocks can number in the hundreds. Flocks start to break up in Mar and by Apr most birds are paired. Influx of migrants on Malheur NWR between 10 Mar and 10 Apr, but few remain to breed.

In w. Ore., migrant and wintering flocks are usually smaller than those in e. Ore.

Family Hirundinidae
Subfamily Hirundininae

Purple Martin *Progne subis*

COOS	CLAT	LANE	BENT	PORT	CENT	MALH
1 Apr	3 May	12 Apr	28 Apr	13 Apr		

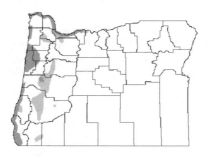

Uncommon local summer resident, principally inhabiting the Coast Range and Willamette V. Locally common at Fern Ridge Res., Lane Co., at some coastal estuaries, and at numerous colonies along the Columbia R. from Hood River to Astoria. Rarely breeds in the w. Cascades foothills and in the interior Umpqua R. basin. Transients are rare to uncommon in w. Ore., and rare to very rare e. of the Cascades. First spring migrants are sometimes seen in Mar (earliest arrival 5 Mar), but usually arrive in early Apr. In w. Ore. most young fledge in Jul and early Aug, although some nestlings are still being fed in late Aug. Martins begin departing soon after young fledge, and the last martins are typically seen in the first half of Sep.

Tree Swallow *Tachycineta bicolor*

COOS	CLAT	EUGE	CORV	PORT	CENT	MALH
15 Feb	26 Feb	4 Feb	9 Feb	9 Feb	1 Mar	2 Mar

Uncommon to locally abundant summer resident and breeding bird throughout Ore., typically near water with adjacent snags. Distribution and population levels are mainly limited by the availability of suitable nesting cavities. Widely scattered and local e. of the Cascades due to aridity. Common to 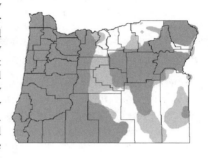 abundant migrant in all areas. Early birds arrive late Jan or early Feb with the majority moving through w. Ore. from late Feb to mid-Apr; e. of the Cascades from mid-Mar to mid-May. Flocks of many thousands regularly noted during spring migration. After fledging, young and adults gather into flocks, with most Ore. birds moving s. between mid-Jul and mid-Aug. Migrants from farther n. pass through Ore. during Aug and Sep with small groups and individuals continuing in diminishing numbers to mid-Dec. Fall flocks seldom exceed 1,000 individuals. Irregular in winter in w. interior valleys and along the coast; successful overwintering has not been demonstrated.

Violet-green Swallow *Tachycineta thalassina*

COOS	CLAT	LANE	BENT	PORT	CENT	MALH
15 Mar	10 Mar	4 Mar	2 Mar	3 Mar	12 Mar	27 Mar

Common to abundant summer resident and breeding species throughout most of Ore., although uncommon in the Klamath Basin. This swallow occurs from sea level to high peaks, and is primarily limited by availability of nesting cavities. Although a solitary nester, it will form good-sized colonies where suitable cavities are clustered. The largest colonies are found in e. Ore. on streamside rimrock and cliffs where niches and cavities are numerous. Abundant migrant in all areas. Early birds arrive in Feb, usually among migrant Tree Swallow flocks. The main movement occurs from early Mar through Apr. Timing and numbers involved are dependent on weather. Movements appear consistent on both sides of the Cascades, with larger numbers to the w. Few flocks exceed 200 birds.

Violet-green Swallows visit nest sites on arrival but it may be wks before nesting begins. After fledging (typically mid-Jul in wc. Ore.), adults and young gather into flocks, often mixed with other species, and almost immediately migrate. Urban breeders leave nest sites almost immediately when young fledge, with local gatherings along major watercourses. The peak of the fall movement e. of the Cascades occurs during Aug-Sep; in w. Ore. it extends through Oct. Fall swallow flocks are often impressive, with many thousands of birds on fence lines or on overhead wires. Occasional in winter in w. interior valleys and along the coast. Dec and Jan records are few, and it is unknown if the winter visitors are resident or transient.

Northern Rough-winged Swallow *Stelgidopteryx serripennis*

COOS	CLAT	LANE	BENT	PORT	CENT	MALH
1 Apr	17 Apr	1 Apr	1 Apr	4 Apr	7 Apr	7 Apr

Locally uncommon to common summer resident statewide, most abundant at low to moderate elevations, usually near water. Usually nests singly, but sometimes in small loose colonies, rarely more than 3 pairs. Distribution is limited in many areas by lack of suitable nest sites. Spring movement usually in small flocks with other swallow species. Main movement w. of the Cascades mid-Mar to mid-Apr, earliest 24 Feb. The main movement e. of the Cascades is early Apr to mid-May, with the earliest date of detection 6 Mar. Nesting apparently begins earlier e. of the Cascades than to the w., perhaps because water levels in w. rivers are typically high in mid-spring, covering nesting banks. Post-breeding staging in flocks at Malheur NWR is evident by mid-Jul. No such large gathering has been noted anywhere else in Ore. Southward movement begins late Jul, with most gone by late Aug, though individuals are noted through Sep. Latest Malheur NWR 4 Oct, Banks, Wash. Co., 13 Nov. Two were at Ankeny NWR 10 Dec 2000, and 1 was reported at Albany 3 Feb 2001.

> I.D. Note: Care must be taken to separate this species from Bank and imm. Tree Swallows.

Bank Swallow *Riparia riparia*

COOS	CLAT	LANE	BENT	PORT	CENT	MALH
					19 Apr	9 May

Generally uncommon, but locally common to abundant summer resident at mid- to low elevations e. of the Cascades. Numerous colonies contain 10-100 pairs; a few exceed 500 pairs. Instability of nesting sites regularly forces colonies to move to more suitable nearby locations. A few pairs occasionally nest w. of the Cascades, but most colonies are unstable and short-lived. The only currently known colonies w. of the Cascades are in Curry and Clackamas cos. At least 2 colonies were known along the Clackamas R. in the mid 2000s (Jeff Hayes p.c.).

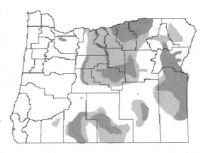

Spring migrants arrive in late Apr with most at nesting sites by mid-May. At Malheur NWR, young fledge late Jun to early Jul. Families disperse and join flocks of other swallows soon after young fledge. Pure flocks of up to 1,000 are often seen during Jul and early Aug e. of the Cascades. Individuals are occasionally observed within migrant swallow flocks in w. Ore. Rare but regular at Fern Ridge Res. in Aug; very rare there in spring. Most leave the state by mid-Aug, but migrants are noted through Sep. A late bird was at Malheur NWR 1 Oct 1993, and two were in Jackson Co., 8 Oct 1990.

Cliff Swallow *Petrochelidon pyrrhonota*

COOS	CLAT	LANE	BENT	PORT	CENT	MALH
30 Mar	18 Apr	25 Mar	31 Mar	2 Apr	5 Apr	7 Apr

Locally common to abundant breeding bird near water throughout most of Ore. Largest colonies occur on cliff faces along waterways e. of the Cascades. Much smaller colonies occur under bridges and overpasses and on other human-made structures. Abundant migrant, usually following valleys and waterways. Spring migration occurs mid-Mar to early May, with rare outriders as early as late Feb. After fledging, adults and young disperse from breeding areas almost immediately and gather into flocks, usually mixed with other swallow species. Fall flocks of Cliff Swallows seldom exceed 1,000 birds. Fall dispersal and migration occurs from late Jun to early Sep; stragglers are noted through Oct, very rarely to mid-Nov.

Barn Swallow *Hirundo rustica*

COOS	CLAT	LANE	BENT	PORT	CENT	MALH
31 Mar	9 Apr	30 Mar	31 Mar	8 Apr	8 Apr	5 Apr

Fairly common to locally abundant summer resident and breeding bird throughout Ore. Restricted primarily to human-made structures, especially farm outbuildings, bridges, and homes. Uncommon at higher elevations and in vast forested landscapes where bridges and buildings or open foraging habitats are scarce. Very common to abundant migrant, primarily over valleys and along waterways. Numbers at evening roosts often spectacular. Rare and irregular in winter to w. interior valleys and along the coast. Early individuals and small flocks arrive during Feb and Mar but remain in low numbers until main flight from late Mar through Apr.

Following independence, juvs. travel widely, often visiting other nests or colonies. By late Jul the southward movement begins with many joining other swallow species to form large conspicuous flocks. The main movement occurs from mid-Aug through Oct. There are numerous Dec and Jan records but successful overwintering has not been documented. Since the mid-1990s, small numbers have often appeared in late Dec and early Jan, mainly moving up the outer coast. It is not known where these birds are coming from or going to.

Family Paridae

Black-capped Chickadee *Poecile atricapilla*

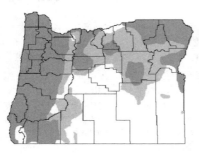

Primarily found in suburban areas and deciduous stands in w. Ore., also found, albeit sparingly, in young conifer forests (with deciduous component) of w. Cascade foothills. Common in deciduous and suburban areas of ne. Ore. They are relatively uncommon in grand fir forests of the Blue Mtns. They occur as far s. as Jordan V. in Malheur Co. Not reported from s. Harney or Lake cos. Possibly expanding in the Klamath Basin, with recent sightings along the edge of Upper Klamath L. and Link R., and rare along Lost R. Absent in the high Cascades, treeless areas in the se. quarter of the state, and deep in conifer forests or high-elevation aspen groves of e. Ore.

Mountain Chickadee *Poecile gambeli*

Resident in all types of forests from 2-10 mi w. of the Cascades summit eastward, in the Blue, Siskiyou, Wallowa, and Warner mtns., and on Hart Mtn., Steens Mtn., and other isolated mtns. e. of the Cascades. Common in pine-dominated stands at high elevations w. of the Cascade crest; this habitat is more extensive s. of Lane Co. Common in pine and mixed forests; also breeds in aspen on mtns. and in riparian zones in desert canyons. Generally sedentary species, with some irregular migratory movements downslope in winter, likely driven by the search for food. During peak movement yrs, may expand to w. Ore. and e. lowlands as

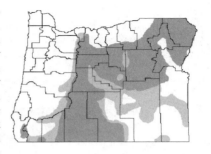

early as late summer or fall, reaching the outer coast in some yrs. Form loose non-breeding flocks in winter, often in common with other small bird species.

Chestnut-backed Chickadee *Poecile rufescens*

Permanent resident along the coast and throughout most of the Coast Range and Cascades, including foothills in forests dominated by Douglas-fir. Rare to locally uncommon at moderate elevations in the e. Blue and Wallowa mtns., locally w. to the Kamela-Meacham-Tollgate region (Trent Bray

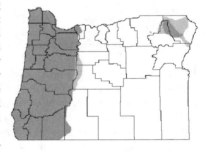

p.c.; ALC). In the Klamath Mtns., uncommon in high-elevation, true fir forests and common up to about 3,500 ft elevation in mixed-conifer forest. Abundant in winter w. of the Cascade summit. Winters sparingly in the lower Rogue R. and Bear Cr. valleys. Mostly absent from deciduous woods in the Willamette V., but flocks occur in riverine forests and in some suburban parks that have conifers or are not more than about 1 mi from conifer patches. Territorial during the breeding season but beginning in mid- to late Jul (especially in fall and winter), occurs in single- or mixed-species flocks with other small forest birds. Some short-distance movement is likely during non-breeding seasons, but remains undocumented. Chickadees are much more abundant in riparian areas of the Cascade Range during winter as compared to summer.

Oak Titmouse *Baeolophus inornatus*

See *BOGR* for taxonomy. Common permanent resident in oak woodlands of the interior Rogue V.; rare permanent resident in oak woodlands of

Illinois V.; unverified sightings only in the c. Umpqua V. Uncommon permanent resident in oak- and juniper-dominated woodlands of the Klamath Basin. Identification of Klamath Basin populations is unresolved, but thought to be Oak Titmouse. The adjacent Lava Beds National Monument area in n. Cal. (Siskiyou and Modoc Co. boundary) is the only known overlap zone of Oak and Juniper titmice.

Juniper Titmouse *Baeolophus ridgwayi*

breeding map for Oak Titmouse and Juniper Titmouse

The Juniper Titmouse occurs in scattered isolated populations e. of the s. Cascades to Idaho. It is uncommon to rare and a local permanent resident mainly in Lake Co, where it is found e. of Lakeview or Abert Rim, on Hart Mtn. Nat. Ant. Ref., in s. Warner V., w. of Adel, in Kelly Cr. Canyon and up Deep Cr. Canyon, and locally rare n. of Silver L., in the Table Rock area. A single specimen is known from Blitzen Canyon, Steens Mtn., 9 Feb 1936, with no sightings there since. Specimens exist from near Lorella, Klamath Co., and near Adel, Twentymile Cr. Canyon, and Warner V., Lake Co. Not yet reported from the Owyhee Uplands, but regularly found in Idaho 5 mi e. of Three Forks, Malheur Co. (along N. Fork Owyhee R.), and an individual was observed close to the Ore. border near McDermitt, Nevada. Reports in s. Langell V., Klamath Co., may be Oak Titmouse (see *BOGR* for further discussion). More prone than Oak Titmouse to form winter flocks. Fall dispersal is restricted to juvs. The Juniper Titmouse joins mixed-species winter flocks, especially chickadee flocks.

Family Aegithalida

Bushtit *Psaltriparus minimus*

Ore. ranges have expanded in the past 50 yrs, but with few published data and no specimens. See *BOGR* for fairly complex taxonomy. Fairly common to uncommon resident throughout Ore. except Umatilla, Union, and Wallowa cos. and at higher elevations of mountain ranges, where it is a rare fall visitant. Breeds in open woodlands and brushy places, especially deciduous bottomlands. Pairs leave flocks in Jan and Feb and begin nest building. Nesting mid-Mar to Jul, mostly May and

Jun. After fledging the family remains intact, joining other families to form a flock that remains together until the next nesting season. When not nesting, Bushtits may occur anywhere in Ore., but most move to lower elevations in winter.

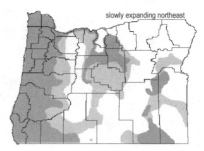
slowly expanding northeast

Family Sittidae
Subfamily Sittinae

Red-breasted Nuthatch *Sitta canadensis*
Breeds and winters throughout Ore. where conifer or mixed conifer-hardwood forests are present, including some urban areas. Winters in wooded areas from valley floors to timberline. Migratory individuals are encountered widely in areas where they do not breed, even occasionally

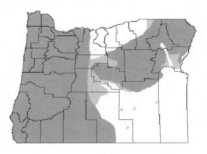

in sage desert and on rocky summits. Migration and seasonal movements within Ore. are difficult to predict. Spring migration at Malheur NWR usually between 23 Apr and 5 May. Although elevational migrations are typical, migrations within mountain ranges and to new areas are also likely as nuthatches move to areas with productive cone crops. Timing of fall migration varies. Peak periods at Malheur NWR have occurred as early as Jul and as late as Sep; variability in migration is likely related to yr-to-yr changes in populations and whether it is an irruption yr. Winter numbers in lowland w. Ore. and on the outer coast vary markedly from yr to yr. Some yrs, no birds are observed on the outer coast whereas hundreds are found in other yrs.

White-breasted Nuthatch *Sitta carolinensis*
The two Ore. subspecies differ somewhat in appearance and have very different calls and habitats. *S. c. aculeata* is a common to uncommon resident in w. Ore. lowlands; most abundant in sw. interior valleys. Common resident in oak and mixed forests, nut orchards, and suburban plantings in the Willamette V. region. Occasional summer

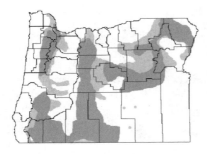

visitor in Curry Co. but no breeding records. Very rare visitor to Coos Co. in fall and winter. Essentially absent from the c. and n. coast. Largely absent from high-elevation coniferous forests. *S. c. tenuissima* common to uncommon in forested areas e. of the Cascade summit. Breeds in ponderosa pine and mixed-conifer forests in the Blue Mtns. Occasional spring and autumn visitor to Malheur NWR. March visitor to Emigrant Res., Jackson Co. Often found in mixed flocks in winter. Roosts in cavities in winter.

Pygmy Nuthatch *Sitta pygmaea*

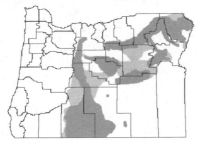

Resident of ponderosa pine-dominated forests from the e. slopes of the Cascades eastward into the Blue and Warner mtns. Abundance varies with habitat quality. Following the breeding season, occasionally found just outside edges of ponderosa pine belt. While generally considered resident, individuals occasionally range >50 mi outside breeding ranges following breeding season and on into winter. Rare at Malheur NWR and in the e. Rogue V. foothills. Rare w. to coastal Curry Co. in fall. Extremely rare to w. interior valleys. After the breeding season, typically occur as small flocks that increase in size through fall as 2 or more family groups combine.

Family Certhiidae
Subfamily Certhinae

Brown Creeper *Certhia americana*
See *BOGR* for interesting taxonomy. Uncommon to common breeder, transient and wintering bird, with some forms highly migratory and a generally poor knowledge of movements. Found in winter throughout breeding range, including high-elevation forests, but may be less abundant there in winter, and birds that are found in winter may not be

local breeders. At least partly migratory. Little information exists regarding seasonal movements, but some localized short-distance movement likely occurs between seasons. Creepers migrate through Malheur NWR: peak passage is 25 Apr to 7 May, the latest arrival 6 Jun. In fall, recorded 1 Oct-

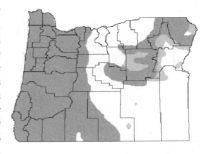

13 Nov. In some yrs a definite movement occurs in the s. Willamette V. in Oct (ALC) but this is poorly known. During winter, usually found alone, in pairs, or in flocks with chickadees, kinglets, nuthatches, woodpeckers, and other creepers.

Family Troglodytidae

Rock Wren *Salpinctes obsoletus*
The Rock Wren is a common breeder e. of the Cascade summit, rare but regular breeder at scattered rocky ridges and summits in the w. Cascades, Rogue V., and Siskiyous. Extremely rare and irregular breeder in the Willamette V. and Coast Range. In winter, very uncommon to rare resident

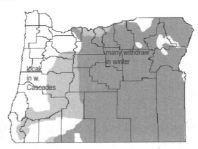

e. of the Cascades, rare in the Rogue V., and generally absent elsewhere. Spring migration extends from early Apr to mid-May, and although generally inconspicuous, peaks in early May. Post-breeding dispersal and southward migration extends from mid-Aug to late Oct and peaks in early to mid-Sep. A few birds spend at least some winters in the lower elevations e. of the Cascades (depending on severity of weather), in the Rogue V., and very rarely along the coast.

Canyon Wren *Catherpes mexicanus*
Fairly common but local breeder in Ore. e. of the Cascade summit; restricted to rocky cliffs or outcrops. Very rare, but possible breeder on the w. slope of the s. Cascades. Rare and sporadic during summer westward in the e. Rogue V. and e. Umpqua valleys. Only 1 coastal record

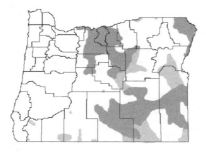

(Curry Co.). More dispersed after breeding season as evidenced by a smattering of Aug-Oct records w. of known breeding range along the Columbia Gorge, in the Willamette V., and in the Cascades. Some are resident, but there is a minor seasonal migration and dispersal. Spring migration occurs from mid-Mar through Apr without a discernible peak. Fall migration from late Aug through mid-Sep is inconspicuous and usually goes unobserved. Uncommon but regular in breeding areas during winter.

Bewick's Wren *Thryomanes bewickii*

Permanent resident w. of the Cascades, in the Klamath and Warner basins, and along the upper Columbia R. and tributaries. Locally common nester in clearcuts and along forest edges up to 2,000 ft elevation in the Coast Range and w. Cascades. Winter birds are mostly found in valley areas below 1,500 ft, with the largest number wintering w. of the Cascades.

Slowly expanding eastward. Birds have been found e. to c. Umatilla Co. and s. along the upper stretches of the Deschutes R. and White R. near White R. SP. In Umatilla Co., Bewick's Wrens are now found yr-round in the Umatilla R. and Walla Walla R. drainages, up to 2,800 ft in the Blue Mtns. Recent reports in c. Union Co (Trent Bray, p.c.) and 25 May 2002 on Cactus Mtn. above the Snake R. in e. Wallowa Co. suggest that the expansion, though slow, has not stopped. Numerous recent sightings suggest that a population may be establishing in the southeast section of Malheur NWR. Bewick's Wrens were rare in winter in the early 1990s in Union and Wallowa cos., but are becoming more regular.

House Wren *Troglodytes aedon*

COOS	CLAT	LANE	BENT	PORT	CENT	MALH
20 Apr		21 Apr	11 Apr	20 Apr	14 Apr	16 Apr

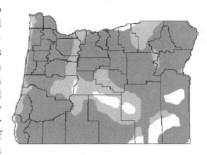

Very uncommon to common transient and summer resident in semi-open woodland habitats throughout the state. In sw. Ore., most common in oak-chaparral and mixed woodlands of valley foothills and mtns. Generally uncommon on w. slopes of the Coast Range, except in clearcuts containing snags, where it can be very common. Common in oak and mixed forests of foothills on the e. side of the Coast Range. Found in scattered locations in the Willamette V., particularly within more open brushy areas and oak woodlands. Within the w. Cascades, most often found at natural and clearcut forest openings containing suitable nesting habitat. E. of the Cascades, found in suitable wooded habitats, particularly aspen, but also found in brushy areas in late summer. Occasionally reported in winter but few well-documented records exist. Males generally arrive on nesting areas a few days prior to females (late Apr to early May). Rare as early as late Mar.

I.D. Note: During winter, Marsh Wrens are sometimes misidentified as House Wrens. Most field guides do not illustrate nw. subspecies of Marsh Wren, which have much browner caps than e. birds and often have partially obscured or limited back striping. See Unitt et al. (1996) for a discussion of the subspecies and helpful color plates.

Winter Wren *Troglodytes troglodytes*

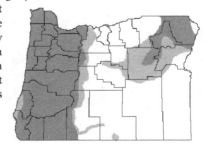

Breeds statewide in moist forested areas with dense undergrowth, primarily in areas with evergreen overstory. Absent or local in dry forests without a moist understory. Local on Steens Mtn.

Nesting activities occur Apr-Aug. Migration probably occurs throughout the state, but movements are most noticeable in spring and fall at locations such as Malheur NWR, where the species does not breed or winter. At Malheur NWR, fall migrants observed 9 Aug to 1 Nov and spring migrants during Mar and Apr. In w. Ore., increases in lowland wintering sites in late Sep-Oct and decreases Apr-May. Retreats from high altitudes in winter where snow pack is heavy; there is an obvious winter movement into lowlands.

*Sedge Wren *Cistothorus platensis*
Vagrant. Breeds in c. and s. Canada and the ne. U.S. Other subspecies occur locally in C. and S. America.

There is 1 accepted Ore. record of a territorial bird photographed at the N. Spit of Coos Bay, Coos Co., where it remained from 30 May to 12 Jun 2003.

In addition, 1 was observed at the Luckiamute R., Polk Co., on 4 Jan 2006 and stayed for about 2 wks; another was seen at E. E. Wilson WA n. of Corvallis, Benton Co., 14-15 Jan 2008. These records have not yet been reviewed by the OBRC. A report of 1 in late fall, 2008 very close to the site where the Jan 2008 bird was seen may reflect a returning individual.

Marsh Wren *Cistothorus palustris*

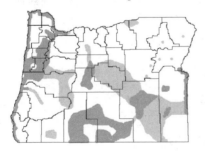

Nests statewide in appropriate wetland habitats. Particularly common during breeding season around Malheur NWR, in wetlands of Lake Co. (Summer L.), and in Klamath Basin; but also locally common in lower-elevation marshes and wet meadows of the Blue and Wallowa mtns. Less common along the Columbia R. and in the Willamette V., in coastal estuaries, and in s. Ore. coastal river valleys. Winter populations are largely restricted to wetlands on the w. side of the Cascades; common along the coast to locally fairly common to very uncommon in interior valleys. Severity of winter strongly affects wintering abundance on e. side of the Cascades. In winter, at least uncommon all yrs in Klamath Basin, Summer L., on Malheur NWR, and along the Columbia R. from Biggs eastward. Arrival dates on nesting grounds generally differ for populations e. and w. of the Cascades. At Malheur NWR, a major influx of birds occurs in early Mar, and they are abundant and widespread by Apr.

> I.D. Note: Silent skulking Marsh Wrens in coastal dune grass, especially in winter, are sometimes mistaken for Savannah or other sparrows, or House Wrens, by inexperienced observers.

Family Cinclidae

American Dipper *Cinclus mexicanus*

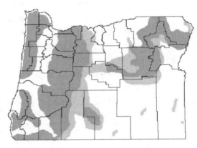

Uncommon yr-round resident in montane streams and rivers throughout Ore. Rare and local in the Coast Range of sw. Lane and nw. Douglas cos. (roughly the s. Siuslaw and Smith R. drainages). Breeds in small numbers in se. Ore., including Hart Mtn., Steens Mtn., Trout Cr. Mtns., and Mahogany Mtn. Probable breeding also occurs along the Owyhee R. Found to mouths of coastal streams where sometimes feed in salt water. Some winter movement noted, including to lower elevations from Steens Mtn., and to e. edges of Willamette V. Breeding activities can begin in Feb. Sometimes sings in midwinter.

Family Regulidae

Golden-crowned Kinglet *Regulus satrapa*

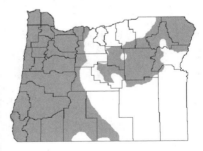

Very abundant yr-round in coniferous forests from the Cascades and w. throughout Coast Range and Willamette V. E. of the Cascades, breeds primarily in montane spruce and fir zones. In winter, common w. of the Cascade crest, and especially abundant along the coast. One of few species to be found in high Cascade forests in winter. Numbers of wintering birds vary substantially on an annual basis e. of the Cascades. In late Sep in the n.

Blue Mtns., huge numbers of these kinglets pass s. at elevations >4,000 ft. In winter, often found in pure flocks or with chickadees, Brown Creepers, and/or Red-breasted Nuthatches in mixed-species flocks. Typically appear in wintering areas in w. Ore. by late Sep to early Oct.

Ruby-crowned Kinglet *Regulus calendula*
The species breeds in high-elevation forests, primarily e. of the Cascade crest, where it is common in summer, and in the Blue, Wallowa, and locally in the Warner mtns. Frequently found late in spring in areas where they do not breed, which leads to erroneous conclusions of breeding. Found throughout in winter, mainly in lowlands. Wintering birds on n. coast mostly gone by mid-Apr, with latest birds remaining until 15 May. In Rogue V., most spring migrants move through from late Mar to late Apr, with latest spring departure 11 May.

At Malheur NWR, average date for earliest arrival is 31 Mar, with the earliest migrant recorded 2 Feb. Most migrate 10-27 Apr, with the latest spring record 20 May. Begin arriving in the Wallowas in late Apr, with peak arrival 15-25 May at 4,500 ft elevation. Common on breeding grounds in the Wallowas through Aug, after which they migrate to lower elevations, with birds leaving elevations over 5,500 ft by 10 Sep. At Malheur NWR, earliest fall arrival 3 Sep. Fall migration there peaks 24 Sep to 15 Oct, latest fall migrant recorded 13 Nov, with some winter records, almost all from s. Blitzen V. Earliest fall arrival on n. coast is 12 Sep and in Rogue V. 17 Sep.

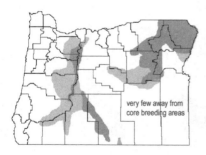

winter distribution

Family Silviidae
Subfamily Polioptilinae

Blue-gray Gnatcatcher *Polioptila caerulea*

Breeds in numerous disjunct localities and may be expanding its range in Ore. Uncommon to common summer resident in the interior Rogue V., rare summer resident in Illinois V., reported (but unverified) in the s. Umpqua V. Attempted breeding at Mt. Pisgah, c. Lane Co.

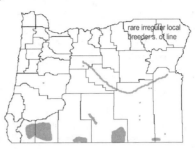

rare irregular local breeders. of line

Uncommon summer resident in the Klamath Basin; near Summer L. and at Hart Mtn. Nat. Ant. Ref., s. to Cal. Rare irregular breeder n. to c. Harney Co. (Frenchglen, Page Springs, Drewsey). Locations with late spring sightings that may indicate nesting include Cyrus Springs, Crooked R. National Grasslands; Mahogany Mtn., Battle Mtn., and Ore. Canyon Mtns., Malheur Co. Arrive early to mid-Apr in sw. Ore.; late Apr e. of the Cascades. Rare in Rogue V. in late Mar. Gnatcatchers depart breeding areas when young become independent in Aug. Some fall-winter sightings in Ore. away from breeding areas, n. to the c. coast and the Willamette V.

Family Turdidae

*Northern Wheatear *Oenanthe oenanthe*
Vagrant. Breeds in Alaska and arctic Canada, also in Greenland and widely across Eurasia to e. Siberia.

Three accepted Ore. records:
1. One was photographed at Malheur NWR, Harney Co., on 22 Jun 1977 for a highly unusual summer record.
2. An imm. bird was observed at Finley NWR, Benton Co., on 1 Oct 1988.
3. One was observed at Tillamook, Tillamook Co., on 28 Oct 1995.

Western Bluebird *Sialia mexicana*
Breeds in open habitats with suitable nest cavities and structures throughout forested mtns. and patchily in wooded lowlands; most abundant in low- to moderate-elevation foothills in w. Ore. Rare on c. and n. coast, uncommon to fairly common on s. coast. Fairly common

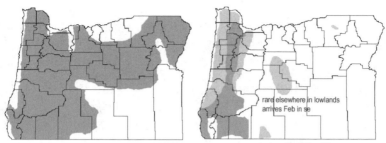

rare elsewhere in lowlands
arrives Feb in se

winter distribution

on open e. slopes of Coast Range foothills and other hills intruding into the Willamette V. In interior sw. Ore., uncommon to common in the Rogue and Umpqua valleys. Uncommon to fairly common in early seral clearcuts with snags in the w. Cascades, and rare to locally common in high Cascades. Variably rare to locally fairly common e. of the Cascades. Rare to very uncommon in Klamath Basin.

Mostly absent during breeding season from high deserts of se. Ore., and vagrant summer visitor in vast open country near Malheur NWR and Columbia Basin grasslands. In Wheeler and Grant cos. nesting in boxes in juniper savannah since 1988; otherwise uncommon in the Blue Mtns. Winters at lower elevations within breeding range, generally in greatly reduced numbers in e. Ore.; some winter birds are from more northerly populations. Spring migration is difficult to discern in w. Ore., but flocks have been observed during Apr in the w. Cascades; spring migration peaks during late Feb at Malheur NWR. Fall migration is not apparent in w. Ore. lowlands, but flocks are occasional in mountainous regions, and more common in desert and agricultural areas of e. Ore. In e. Ore., fall migration peaks at Malheur NWR late Sep-Nov.

Mountain Bluebird *Sialia currucoides*
Common breeder and transient e. of the Cascade summit except in treeless expanses. W. of the Cascade summit, breeds locally above 3,500 ft, and in higher elevations in the Siskiyou Mtns. Rare to uncommon migrant in higher w. Cascades. Uncommon in winter, mainly in sc. Ore. Occasionally stray during winter into Willamette V. and Rogue V. Rare winter visitor on coast. Spring migrants enter Ore. by late Feb; large flocks are often observed in Mar. Gather in large flocks beginning in mid-Aug; sometimes forage in association with juncos, chickadees, Yellow-rumped Warblers, and Cassin's Finches. In the Blue Mtns., Mountain Bluebirds frequent rocky meadows during late summer through Oct. They leave higher elevations in fall to move into open country. Usually migrate

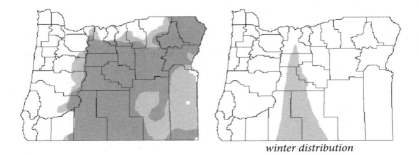

winter distribution

Sep-Oct but linger intermittently; as long as mild weather holds they often overwinter in high desert. Sometimes flock with Western Bluebirds in migration.

Townsend's Solitaire *Myadestes townsendi*

Uncommon to locally common summer resident on the w. slope of the Cascades and Klamath Mtns., generally above 1,000 ft. Uncommon to fairly common summer resident in the e. Cascades and in the Blue Mtns. from timberline down to the ponderosa pine zone. Breeds in and near open coniferous forest stands, natural forest openings, burned areas, shelterwood cuts and clearcuts to timberline. Widespread but rare migrant, summer resident and occasional breeder in the Coast Range. Fairly common to abundant migrant and winter resident in juniper woodlands e. of the Cascades. Increases rapidly following arrival in early to mid-Apr in s. Cascades. Spring influx around Malheur NWR early Mar, peak abundance 20 Mar to 7 Apr. Earliest fall transient at Malheur NWR 16 Aug, peak passage in mid-Nov. No significant influx w. of the Cascades. Rare during fall, winter, and spring w. of the Cascades in interior valleys.

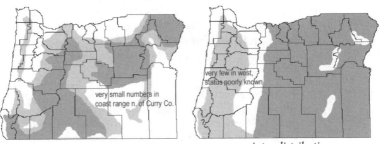

winter distribution

Veery *Catharus fuscescens*

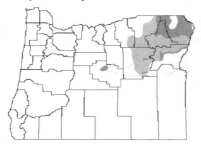

See *BOGR* for taxonomic information. Uncommon breeder in lower to middle elevations in the Blue Mtns. where sufficient riparian thickets exist for cover and forage needs. Most often found in dense riparian shrub growth, often with adjacent evergreen forest. Locally common along watercourses in Union, Wallowa, and e. Umatilla cos.; less common in n. and w. Baker Co., uncommon and local in Grant and Crook cos. The Ochoco Mtn. breeding colonies are isolated, 75 mi from the nearest known sites in c. Grant Co. Occurs irregularly in Wheeler, Morrow (possible breeder), Deschutes, Harney, and n. Malheur cos.

Casual anywhere away from breeding locations. There are reports from Deschutes, Lake (Hart Mtn.), Jackson, Josephine, Lane, and Curry cos. during migration. Rare reports of brighter birds may represent vagrant e. subspecies, but no specimens of these are known from Ore. Spring migrants are not observed on Ore. breeding grounds until late May or early Jun. In Union and Umatilla cos., they arrive by 25 May and are seldom seen after mid-Aug. They are thought to depart Ore. by early Sep, but late summer reports are essentially unknown; birds may retrace their e. migratory route.

*Gray-cheeked Thrush *Catharus minimus*
Vagrant. Breeds from se. Siberia to Alaska and across n. Canada to Newfoundland. Regular migrant through the e. U.S.

Two accepted Ore. records:
1. One was photographed at Fields, Harney Co., on 22 Sep 1984.
2. One was observed at Malheur NWR, Harney Co., on 26 Sep 1994.
While all w. U.S. and Ore. records indicate *C. minimus*, the very similar Bicknell's Thrush (*C. bicknelli*) cannot be entirely ruled out, although *bicknelli* has not been reported away from its restricted e. coast breeding and migration range.

> I.D. Note: *Catharus* thrushes pose some difficulties in identification in Ore., especially because the *salicicola* subspecies of Veery resembles the *ustulatus* subspecies group of Swainson's Thrush. Note also that several subspecies of Hermit Thrush occur in Ore., and that w. wintering forms and

Blue Mtn. breeding forms are quite different in appearance. Standard field guides are somewhat helpful in sorting out this group, but also use specialized references when available. The identification of *Catharus* thrushes is an underappreciated problem.

Swainson's Thrush *Catharus ustulatus*

COOS	CLAT	LANE	BENT	PORT	CENT	MALH
1 May	10 May	3 May	3 May	1 May	14 May	26 May

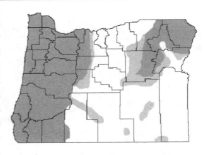

See *BOGR* for taxonomy. The "russet-backed" forms are very common summer residents in conifer forests throughout the Coast and Cascade ranges. Rare at higher elevations. Common summer resident in mixed woods and riparian areas in the Willamette V. region. Also breeds in interior sw. Ore. from Jackson Co. to w. Klamath Co. and possibly the Siskiyou Mtns. Migrates throughout w. Ore. An "olive-backed" form breeds in montane forests and aspen stands e. of the Cascades and is a common spring and fall transient in dense shrubs or woods throughout the state.

Early spring arrival reported 2 Apr 1972 in Eugene (*BOGR*) is probably erroneous; extremely rare before the last few days of Apr. Peak spring migration late May to early Jun for Willamette V. Arrival averages 26 May at Malheur NWR; earliest 30 Apr. In fall, peak migration of the Swainson's Thrush in the Willamette V. occurs during mid-Sep. In ideal conditions during mid- to late Sep, maxima of 15-20 calls/min at night over Portland, and 40+ calls/min along the immediate coast. This species is typically reported to late Oct with a few proven stragglers. There are no verified winter records of Swainson's Thrush for the state except for an injured bird photographed in Portland in mid-December 2008 (S. Finnegan).

Hermit Thrush *Catharus guttatus*

See *BOGR* for extensive taxonomic discussion. Uncommon to common summer resident of mature and old-growth forests at mid- to high elevations in the Cascade, Klamath, Blue, and Warner mtns.; uncommon to common in the s. Coast Range, and rare in the n. Coast Range;

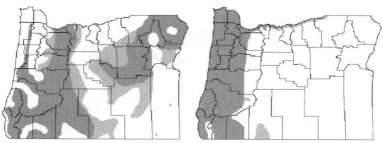

winter distribution

rare and local in se. Ore. In the Coast Range there appears to be an ongoing northward range expansion. The subspecies breeding in ne. Ore. (*auduboni*) is larger and has a grayer head than those breeding in western Ore. The n. subspecies that winter mainly in w. Ore. are quite small and dark compared to e. Ore. birds.

Wintering birds complicate understanding of early spring arrivals but clearly by mid-Apr many are moving through the state. Good numbers continue through early May in w. Ore. at which time numbers leap and birds are present in many sites. In e. Ore., the period of passage may extend longer than w. Ore., but most are gone from non-breeding areas by the end of May. The fall movement at Malheur NWR begins early in Sep (some movement in Aug) and continues to late Oct. W. of the Cascades migrants and wintering birds begin to appear in the lowlands by mid-Sep with most arriving during Oct and Nov.

Wood Thrush Hylocichla mustelina
Vagrant. Breeds from s. Ontario s. across most of the e. U.S.
　　Three accepted Ore. records:
1.　One was observed in the Mahogany Mtns., Malheur Co., on 21 May 1980.
2.　One was observed at Pike Cr., Harney Co., on 27 May 1980.
3.　One was photographed at Fields, Harney Co., on 14 Oct 1989.

American Robin *Turdus migratorius*
Common breeder and locally abundant migrant statewide. The species does not breed in open areas of se. Ore. except in canyons, riparian zones, on ranches, and occasionally near a water hole or trough. Robins can be rather scarce on relatively dry slopes and ridges away from open areas and water. Winter populations include many birds coming from breeding grounds to the n. It is also possible that some birds may travel to the lowlands from higher elevations during winter, but this has

not been verified. Migratory patterns of the robin in Ore. are poorly understood.

Varied Thrush *Ixoreus naevius*
Breeds throughout the Coast Ranges, in the Cascades and in moist montane forests e. of the Cascade crest. Rare breeder in dry pine forests e. of the Cascade crest. Fairly common breeder in low-elevation hemlock and spruce forests along n. coast, but elsewhere only rarely nests in lowland conifer forests. May breed in Wheeler, Harney, and Lake cos. in c. Ore., but no confirmed records. Common at lower elevations e. of the Cascades during winter. Transient statewide during migration. Many birds that winter in Ore. may breed farther n. Fairly common winter resident in low-elevation forests and woodlands, and regularly found in orchards and suburban backyards, especially during severe winter weather. Often common in winter in the s. Willamette V., but few are seen some yrs. Elevational migrants return to montane breeding grounds in Mar and Apr. Recorded in the Willamette V. as late as 2 May. Typically arrives on wintering grounds in valleys and foothills in late Sep, but sometimes does not appear until heavy snows blanket the Cascades in Nov-Dec. Typically in Oct, hundreds can sometimes be seen flying s. along high-elevation ridges and plateaus in the Cascades, often with American Robins.

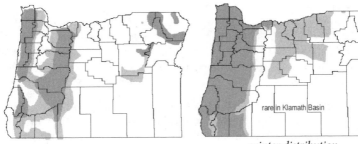

winter distribution

Family Timaliidae

Wrentit *Chamaea fasciata*
Expanding. Resident along the coastal slope; in Columbia R. lowlands upstream to Brownsmead, e. Clatsop Co., and in the s. inland to the Rogue V. of Jackson Co. and e. to near Klamath Falls. Also resident from the interior Umpqua R. V. n. in the e. Coast Range and foothills to Yamhill Co., at the s. edge of the Willamette V., and in the w. Cascades and foothills to wc. Linn Co. Cascade populations are reported as far e. as

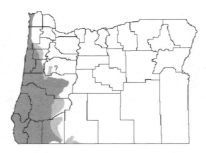

Toketee L. in the Umpqua R. basin, 10 mi ne. of Oakridge in the N. Fk. Willamette R. basin, near Vida in the McKenzie R. basin, 3 mi e. of Holley in the Calapooia R. basin, and at the valley-foothills interface in the upper reaches of the One Horse Slough drainage, 9 mi e. of Lebanon, Linn Co.

Reports from the Portland area are unconfirmed. Residents occur to 4,000 ft in the Klamath Mtns., and 4,200 ft in the w. Cascades of Douglas Co., generally at lower elevations in the n. Fall dispersants are uncommon in non-breeding locations in late summer and fall.

Family Mimidae

Gray Catbird *Dumetella carolinensis*

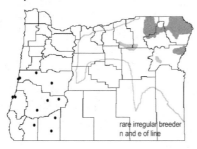

rare irregular breeder n and e of line

Fairly common breeder in dense riparian zones of the ne. Blue Mtns.; most common and regular in Wallowa and Union cos. and e. Umatilla Co. along the Umatilla R., Pine Cr., and Meacham Cr. Breeds locally in Baker Co. along the Powder R., Pine Cr., and Burnt R. There is a Jun specimen from Grant Co. Not found breeding along the lower Burnt R. in the late 1990s, although they did in the early 1980s. Rare, irregular breeder in n. Malheur Co. (Willow Cr. valley) and perhaps extreme ec. Malheur Co. Has bred rarely at Malheur NWR and in n. Harney Co., and possibly in e. and n. Grant Co., e.g., near Galena on the Middle Fork John Day R. Recently bred in s. Morrow Co. Recent reports suggest irregular breeding along the Deschutes R. in Deschutes Co. and along Simnasho Cr. and Beaver Cr. in Wasco Co. Rare elsewhere in summer.

Migratory movements are among the least known among Ore. breeders. Arrives late in spring, probably from the e. Earliest report 19 May, average about 28 May in the w. Blue Mtns. Territorial birds observed as late as 4 Jul and fledglings as late as 7 Aug. It is usually gone from the w. Blue Mtns. by the second wk of Sep. Very rare in fall at Malheur NWR (latest 10 Oct). Very rare w. of the Cascades as far as the outer coast, mainly early fall through winter (see dots on map). Casual in winter; 1 was in Corvallis 9 Jan-17 Feb 1997 and another was in La Grande in the winter of 1988-89.

Northern Mockingbird *Mimus polyglottos*
Rare permanent resident and breeder in the Rogue V., especially from Medford n. to White City. Rare but regular during all seasons elsewhere w. of the Cascades with no nesting attempts reported. Rare in spring in e. Ore. with some territorial birds remaining to summer, including occasional successful nesting in the s. half of e. Ore.; irregular in fall and winter. Migrations are individual and not conspicuous. There are noticeable increases in sightings during Apr and May with a peak period during mid- to late May. Males appeared on territory in the Rogue V. 19 May 1989 and at Fields during late May 1994. During Jun and Jul most birds reported are singing males apparently on territory. There are no noticeable fall movements but individual birds continue to be reported throughout the fall and winter. Most winter reports are from w. Ore., including the outer coast.

Sage Thrasher *Oreoscoptes montanus*

COOS	CLAT	LANE	BENT	PORT	CENT	MALH
					1 Apr	23 Mar

Breeds in shrub-steppe communities, mainly sagebrush, e. of the Cascade summit, principally in the Great Basin, and occasionally in the ne. portion of the state. Winter records are in regions where breeding birds are most numerous; all except one were of single individuals. Spring migration 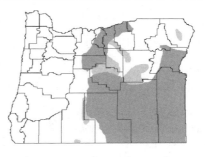 begins in mid- to late Mar and peaks in early Apr. Fall movements are mostly in Sep and early Oct. Rare at all seasons w. of the Cascade crest with about 30 records, most mid-Apr through May; however, they have been observed at least once in every month between 18 Mar and 19 Nov. About one-third of the records are coastal and the remainder are inland.

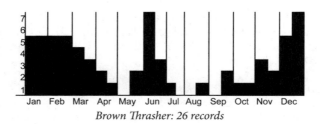

Brown Thrasher: 26 records

*Brown Thrasher *Toxostoma rufum**

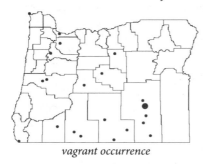

vagrant occurrence

Vagrant. Breeds from sc. Canada across the e. U.S.

Casual visitor to Ore., with 26 accepted records from many parts of the state. Most Ore. birds were found during the winter and spring. There are 11 winter records (many remained for multiple days) from late Oct to early May. Thirteen records occurred between late May and early Jul; none remained more than 2 days.

Curve-billed Thrasher *Toxostoma curvirostre*

Vagrant. Breeds from wc. Arizona and se. Colorado across c. Texas to s. Mexico. Although mostly sedentary, vagrants have strayed from s. Cal. n. to Idaho, Montana, Alberta, and Saskatchewan.

One accepted sight record for Ore. of a bird observed at Toketee L., Douglas Co., 12 Jul – 1 Aug 1995.

*California Thrasher *Toxostoma redivivum**

Vagrant. The range of this sedentary species is restricted to the chaparral-covered slopes of w. Cal. and nw. Baja Cal.

Two accepted Ore. records:
1. A singing bird was observed at O'Brien, Josephine Co., on 18 Jun 1977.
2. A dead bird was found along Table Rock Road, Jackson Co., on 21 May 1996. The specimen is at S. Ore. State U.

In addition, there is a record of a bird visiting a feeding station near Medford, Jackson Co., 24 Jul to 20 Oct 1967; it or another was at the same feeders 4-25 Feb 1968. Another was at Medford, Jackson Co., on 17 Sep 1999. These records have not been reviewed by the OBRC.

Family Sturnidae

European Starling *Sturnus vulgaris*
Common to abundant breeder in urban areas, and locally common in agricultural areas through the state where buildings and trees are present. Distribution appears highly dependent upon available cavities for nesting. Generally rare in heavily forested regions, especially the w. Cascades, and in high desert sagebrush habitat devoid of human structures, particularly in s. Malheur Co. During winter, present throughout breeding range, though often in much larger numbers in lowland valleys and absent from higher-elevation sites. During spring and fall, small flocks are regularly noted in areas where they do not breed or breed in smaller numbers. In e. Ore., many depart areas that lack winter food sources but many remain where food is present. In fall and winter, flocks build to hundreds or thousands. In prime lowland areas flocks of 5,000 to 10,000 are typical at night roosts.

Family Motacillidae

**Eastern Yellow Wagtail *Motacilla tschutschensis*
Vagrant. This species was recently split from the Yellow Wagtail (*M. flava*), which ranges widely across Eurasia. The Eastern Yellow Wagtail breeds from w. and n. Alaska to nw. Canada and from Kazakhstan and Mongolia across e. Siberia .
   There are 2 accepted sight records for Ore.:
1. A calling bird was observed in flight at the mouth of the Siltcoos R., Lane Co., on 31 Aug 1997.
2. One was seen at the n. jetty of Yaquina Bay, Lincoln Co., on 8 Sep 2002.
In addition, an imm. was photographed at the mouth of the Necanicum R., Clatsop Co., on 26 Aug 2008. This record is still under review by the OBRC.

*White Wagtail *Motacilla alba*
Vagrant. Breeds widely across Eurasia and N. Africa. A small population breeds locally in w. Alaska. The taxonomy of this species is complex; until recently, the subspecies *lugens* was considered a separate species, Black-backed Wagtail (see *BOGR* for details).
   Both *M. a. lugens* and *ocularis* have occurred as vagrants along the Pacific slope s. of Alaska, with records from British Columbia and Wash. to Cal. In addition, a third subspecies, *M. a. leucopsis*, has been reported from Ore. (2 records). These birds breed from c. and e. China and e. Russia to Korea and sw. Japan and winter in s. Asia.

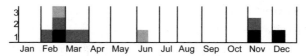

White Wagtail: 7 records
subspecies leucopsis/ocularis: 3 records
"Black-backed" Wagtail, subspecies lugens: 2 records
subspecies unknown: 2 records

Except for males in alternate plumage, all taxa can be extremely difficult to distinguish in the field, and not all records can be safely assigned to a specific subspecies. Whenever possible, future records should be carefully documented by photos or video.

There are 7 accepted Ore. records:

1. A bird of the subspecies *lugens* was photographed at Eugene, Lane Co., 3 Feb – 31 Mar 1974.
2. One bird of undetermined subspecies was observed at Umatilla NWR, Morrow Co., on 9 Feb 1975.
3. One bird of undetermined subspecies was observed at Harris Beach SP, Curry Co., on 4 Jun 1980.
4. A bird of the subspecies *lugens* was photographed at Cape Blanco, Curry Co., on 9 Nov 1996.
5. An adult male of the subspecies *leucopsis* was photographed at Gold Beach, Curry Co., on 8 Nov 1998.
6. An adult male of the subspecies *leucopsis* was photographed at North Bend, Coos Co., on 23 Feb 1999.
7. An adult, likely of the subspecies *ocularis*, was at E.E. Wilson WA n. of Corvallis, Benton Co., on 13 Dec 2002.

In addition, a bird of the subspecies *lugens* was photographed at John Day Dam, Sherman Co., on 20 Sep 1997. This record has not yet been reviewed by the OBRC.

*Red-throated Pipit *Anthus cervinus*
Vagrant. Breeds from n. Scandinavia across n. Eurasia to e. Siberia, with a small local population in w. Alaska. Rare but regular migrant in the Bering Sea and w. Aleutians.

Two accepted Ore. records:

1. A juv. was photographed at Wickiup Res., Deschutes Co., on 6 Oct 2003.
2. Two adults in breeding plumage were photographed at Cape Blanco 29-31 Apr 2004.

American Pipit *Anthus rubescens*

COOS	CLAT	LANE	BENT	PORT	CENT	MALH
					26 Mar	28 Mar

See *BOGR* for detailed discussion of taxonomy. Breeds in the Wallowa Mtns. and on Steens Mtn. Small numbers breed on high Cascade peaks, except Mt. Jefferson. Apparently absent from the Strawberry Range. Uncommon to abundant transient in open patches throughout state, from coastal beaches to alpine

winter distribution

areas. Locally common in lowlands in winter, especially in w. Ore. and on the coast. Occasional reports of pale-legged birds may be referable to *japonicus*, a rare vagrant to w. N. America, but no reports have yet been verified.

Spring movements are extended and involve both small groups and large flocks. Birds have been found in Coos Co. to 14 Apr and in Benton Co. as late as 18 May. E. of the Cascades, where few birds winter, the average arrival is 27 Mar at Malheur NWR with the earliest record (other than a rare wintering few) 13 Feb and the latest 27 May. Rare in summer away from breeding areas. Fall movements normally begin in late Aug, with peak of passage in late Sep and early Oct, somewhat variable from yr to yr. The outer coast and mountaintops typically get the first migrants. Hundreds of pipits can be found some yrs in preferred habitat in the c. Willamette V. and coastal pastures. E. of the Cascades, winter numbers are small and generally at lower elevations. Numbers in most areas vary widely from yr to yr.

*Sprague's Pipit *Anthus spragueii*

Vagrant. Breeds in short-grass prairies from nc. Alberta to sw. Manitoba and s. to Montana and S. Dakota.

There is 1 accepted Ore. record of a bird photographed near Langlois, Curry Co., on 1 Oct 2005.

Family Bombycillidae

Bohemian Waxwing *Bombycilla garrulous*

winter distribution

Fairly common winter visitor to mountain valleys in the ne. part of the state. Flocks are reported almost annually from this region, though numbers vary widely from yr to yr. During invasion yrs large flocks may move s. into se. Ore., and/or into w. interior valleys, where they are rare and erratic visitors. One breeding record, at Gearhart in 1958, is the only documented summer record. Generally begin arriving in Ore. in mid-Nov, very rare as early as mid-Sep. The majority of birds have departed the state by late Mar and Apr, with a few records extending into May.

Cedar Waxwing *Bombycilla cedrorum*

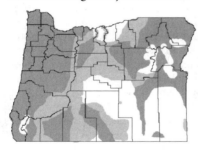

See *BOGR* for taxonomic information. Breeding range covers most of Ore., except for extensive conifer forests and expansive treeless areas, with greater breeding populations reported in lowlands. Common summer resident and migrant in open woodlands and suburban areas at low to middle elevations; uncommon and nomadic in winter. Cedar Waxwings are not territorial and have a loose migratory pattern that does not conform to regular n. and s. swings of most N. American birds, but is likely more tied to the availability of food sources. Often cluster in large flocks. They are most common in spring and summer, when they breed and feed on seasonal fruits and insects.

Numbers in Ore. increase during spring migration in late May, although in some yrs movement is noted as early as late Mar. They commonly raise two broods per yr, the first around mid-Jun and the second around mid-Jul to Aug. In mid- to late summer, often seen flycatching over ponds and rivers. Fall migration begins in late Aug, and large numbers usually move through Ore. from late Sep to late Oct; by early Nov most migrants are gone, moving s. to warmer areas.

Family Ptilogonatidae

*Phainopepla *Phainopepla nitens*
Vagrant. Breeds from interior Cal. and s. Nevada across Arizona and sw. New Mexico to w. Texas and s. to s. Baja Cal. and s. Mexico.
  Four accepted Ore. records:
1. A male was collected at Malheur NWR, Harney Co., on 17 May 1957. The specimen is now at the U.S. National Museum.
2. A young male was photographed 14 mi. e. of Gold Hill, Jackson Co., 22 Dec 1988 – Jan 1, 1989.
3. A female or imm. was at Lakeview, Lake Co., on 26 Sep 1991.
4. A male was at Bend, Deschutes Co., 23-24 May 2001.
In addition, there are sight records of single birds s. of Medford, Jackson Co., on 15 Mar 1961 and at Camp Sherman, Jackson Co., on 20 May 2001. These records have not been reviewed by the OBRC.

Family Parulidae

*Blue-winged Warbler *Vermivora pinus*
Vagrant. Breeds from se. Minnesota to Maine and s. from ne. Oklahoma to n. Alabama and n. to Maryland. In recent decades it has expanded its breeding range to the n., coinciding with decrease of the closely related Golden-winged Warbler.
  Three accepted Ore. records:
1. A male in breeding plumage was observed at Page Springs CG, Harney Co., on 20 May 1993.
2. An adult male was photographed at Indian Ford Cr., Deschutes Co., 24 Jul – 29 Sep 2000.
3. One was photographed at Malheur NWR, Harney Co., on 20 Sep 2005.
An additional record of a bird observed at the ODOT pond near Riley, Harney Co., on 9 Sep 2003 is currently under review by the OBRC.

*Golden-winged Warbler *Vermivora chrysoptera*
Vagrant. Breeds from s. Manitoba and n. Minnesota through the Great Lakes region e. to Vermont and in the Appalachians. s. to N. Carolina. It is declining in much of its range.
  Two accepted Ore. records:
1. One was observed at Indian Ford CG, Deschutes Co., on 14 Jun 1977.
2. A singing male was photographed and recorded at Malheur NWR, Harney Co., 3-4 Jun 1983.

In addition, a Blue-winged X Golden-winged Warbler hybrid (known as "Brewster's" Warbler) was at Provolt, Josephine Co., on 11 Jul 2005 for Ore.'s only record of this hybrid form.

Tennessee Warbler *Vermivora peregrina*

Very rare migrant, mostly from early May to late Jun. Ore. is off the main migration route for this species, but a few birds appear in many yrs. More unusual records include 1 near Mirror L. in the Wallowa Mtns., Wallowa Co., 9 Aug 1971; another at Indian Ford CG, Deschutes Co., 29 Jul 1976; and 1 at Lost L., Linn Co., 24 Jul 1994. Fall records are predominantly from late Aug to early Oct. There are 9 winter records for w. Ore.

> ID Note: It is similar in plumage to the w. Warbling Vireo, though its habits are more active and warbler-like. Care should also be taken to distinguish this species from gray-headed (*celata/orestera*) Orange-crowned Warblers, especially in fall. Tennessee has a short-tailed look, is brighter green on the back and whiter under the tail than an Orange-crowned, and has a very slender pointed bill.

Orange-crowned Warbler *Vermivora celata*

COOS	CLAT	LANE	BENT	PORT	CENT	MALH
30 Mar	30 Mar	19 Mar	21 Mar	19 Mar	13 Apr	25 -Apr

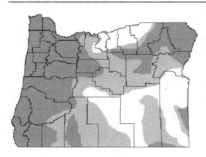

See *BOGR* for additional taxonomic information. *V. c. lutescens* (more olive-headed birds) are common to uncommon breeders from the coast to the w. slope of the Cascades, and cross the Cascades in lower densities into at least Klamath and Wasco cos. *V. c. orestera* (more grayish-headed) breeds e. of the e. base of the Cascades in mountainous regions up to near timberline; rare to very uncommon in the w. Blue Mtns. in c. Ore. and mtns. of se. Ore., and uncommon to fairly common in the Blue and Wallowa mtns. of ne. Ore. *V. c. celata* (quite gray-headed) may migrate through the state. Orange-crowned Warblers are common in migration throughout the state, even in desert regions.

Orange-crowns are uncommon to rare in winter. The classification of wintering subspecies has not been verified by specimens, thus field identifications are speculative, and generally indicate observations of birds with (*orestera* or *celata*) or without (*lutescens*) gray hoods. *V. c. lutescens* is thought to be the most common wintering subspecies along the coast and Willamette V. Both *orestera* and *celata* have been reported in winter and are very uncommon winter residents along the coast and w. Ore. inland valleys, and rare e. of the Cascades, primarily along the Columbia R.

Spring migration begins in mid-Mar along the s. Ore. coast and peaks in Apr. After nesting and prior to migration (Jul-Aug), Orange-crowned Warblers can be observed dispersing from breeding sites. Some Orange-crowned Warblers move to higher elevations, even to tree line. At high elevations in Curry Co., large numbers of juvs. move into deciduous shrub thickets in early Aug before departing on their s. migration. Fall migrants peak in early to mid-Sep, and are mostly gone by mid-Oct. Migrants are common in deciduous and brushy habitats statewide, especially at lower elevations.

Nashville Warbler *Vermivora ruficapilla*

COOS	CLAT	LANE	BENT	PORT	CENT	MALH
25 Apr		14 Apr	15 Apr	20 Apr	19 Apr	26 Apr

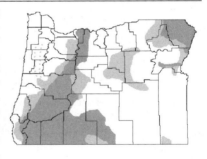

Fairly common breeding species in the interior sw. portion of the state below 4,000 ft from the Calapooya Divide s., typically in mixed conifer/hardwood forests and regenerating clearcuts. Breeds in Jackson Co., where it is common. Southward from the Illinois V. into Cal., abundance declines. Nashville Warblers also breed regularly in the Columbia Gorge and along the e. foothills of the Cascades in Wasco and Hood R. cos. below 3,000 ft. Local elsewhere, including drier foothills near the s. Willamette V. as far n. as Benton and Yamhill cos., and the w. Cascades as far n. as Santiam Pass. Also breed locally on the coastal slope, away from the outer coast, as far n. as Lincoln Co. They are very local in the Blue Mtns., occurring as far w. as Wheeler Co., but are more widespread in the foothills of the Wallowas; also breed in Baker Co. Breed sparingly in the mtns. e. of the Cascades in Klamath, Lake, and possibly Malheur cos.

Uncommon during northward migration, but common in late summer especially in thickets at higher elevations. Nashvilles typically arrive in abundance in sw. Ore. in mid-Apr, rare as early as early March. Most spring sightings for the Malheur NWR are in the first part of May. Following breeding, many move up into the mtns. Individuals and flocks frequent shrubby habitats from 3,000 to 6,000 ft beginning as early as mid-Jul. Tend to be an early fall migrant with the major movement in Aug. Scattered individuals may linger until late Sep. In recent yrs, it has become apparent that a very few Nashville Warblers linger into winter, with most reports along the coast, in the interior valley lowlands, and in towns.

*Virginia's **Warbler** *Vermivora virginiae*

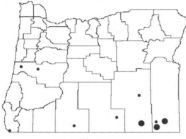

vagrant occurrence

Vagrant. Breeds in the mtns. of the s. Great Basin from s. Idaho, c. Wyoming and c. Nevada s. to se. Arizona and New Mexico, and locally in e. and s. Cal. and w. Texas.

Casual migrant and possibly a rare and irregular breeder in Ore., with 13 accepted records to date. The majority of sightings are from the se. part of the state in Harney and Malheur cos., from mid-May to mid-Jul and from late Aug to late Sep. The only sightings in w. Ore. were of individuals at Eugene, Lane Co., on 8 Nov 1979 and near Mapleton, Lane Co., on 9 Aug 1988.

In 1998, increased search efforts revealed birds in seemingly suitable breeding habitat in se. Ore., often in mountain mahogany groves. On 18 Jun 1998, 2 territorial males and 1 female were found in a remote area of Malheur Co., 10 mi. ne. of McDermitt, Nevada. Two or more pairs were near Twin Buttes in the Ore. Canyon Mtns., Malheur Co., on 19-20 Jun 1998; a male was on Battle Mt., Malheur Co., on 4 Jul 1998; and a singing territorial male was s. of Ironside, Malheur Co., on 5 Jul 1999. Subsequent searches in some of the above areas did not turn up this species, and breeding has not yet been verified in Ore.

13 records, 16+ individuals

Lucy's Warbler *Vermivora luciae*
Vagrant. Breeds in arid country from s. Cal., s. Utah, and s. Nevada s. through Arizona, New Mexico, and Texas into Mexico.
Two accepted Ore. records:
1. One was photographed along the N. Fork of the Siuslaw R., Lane Co., where it remained from 27 Dec 1986 to 24 Jan 1987.
2. One was photographed in Brookings, Curry Co., 14 Jan – 28 Mar 2004.

Northern Parula *Parula americana*

This species is a rare but regular spring migrant in Ore., with 1 to several records in most yrs. The majority of Ore. records occur from late Apr to late Jun, mostly at oasis sites e. of the Cascades. There are about 15 records from w. Ore., mainly on the outer coast in Jun or fall.

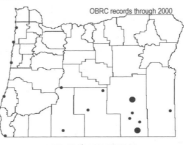

OBRC records through 2000

vagrant occurrence

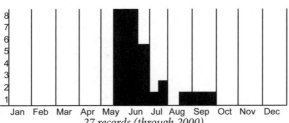

27 records (through 2000)

Yellow Warbler *Dendroica petechia*

COOS	CLAT	LANE	BENT	PORT	CENT	MALH
7 May	8 May	28 Apr	28 Apr	27 Apr	30 Apr	26 Apr

Common to abundant breeder statewide, but somewhat local, especially in w. Ore. Breeds on the e. slope of the Cascades and in the Blue and Wallowa mtns., though very local above 5,000 ft. Elsewhere e. of the Cascades, common along watercourses, or to a lesser extent, in residential areas. Rare straggler to Crater L. NP, but relatively common in the Klamath Basin. On Malheur NWR, abundant in spring, summer, and fall. Also common to locally abundant breeder in suitable habitat in extreme se. Ore. W. of the Cascades, very local and uncommon along the coast and in the Coast Range in summer. Fairly common to common in w. interior valleys, and locally in adjoining foothills. Also found regularly in small numbers along the N. Umpqua R. in the sw. Cascades in summer, though generally uncommon in this region; usually found in small "colonies" where they do occur. Common summer resident throughout Jackson Co.

Spring migrants generally arrive during late Apr, though they occasionally are seen in early or mid-Apr; very rarely the last wk of Mar. The peak of spring migration occurs mid- to late May. Average spring arrival date at Malheur NWR is 26 Apr, with the majority of transients gone by 1 Jun. Fall migration begins early, peaking from mid-Aug to early Sep, and by late Sep they are very uncommon in the state, rare but regular on the outer coast and at Malheur to early Oct. The latest fall record at Malheur NWR is 15 Oct. Several reports through Dec in w. Ore.

> I.D. Note: Possible winter sightings of Yellow Warbler should be carefully distinguished from bright *lutescens* Orange-crowned Warblers.

Chestnut-sided Warbler *Dendroica pensylvanica*

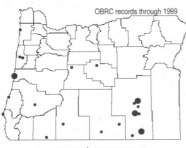

OBRC records through 1999

vagrant occurrence

Small numbers of transients are reported almost annually in Ore., with most records from the se. part of the state. The majority of spring records fall between mid-May and mid-Jul, peaking in early Jun. There are fewer fall records, mostly between mid-Aug and mid-Oct. There are also a small number of

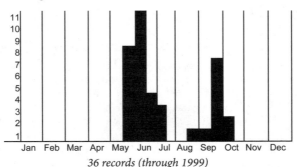

36 records (through 1999)

spring and fall records along the coast. Sightings from the w. valleys include a male at Roseburg, Douglas Co., on 19 Aug 1979; an imm. at Ashland, Jackson Co., on 30 Sep 1982; and a singing male at Corvallis, Benton Co., on 16 Jun 2005.

*Magnolia Warbler *Dendroica magnolia*

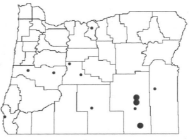
vagrant occurrence

Vagrant. Breeds from nw. Canada to Newfoundland and s. to the Great Lakes region and Pennsylvania; locally in the Appalachians.

Casual spring and fall migrant in Ore., with 29 accepted records to date. In addition, there are several unreviewed sightings. The majority of records come from e. of the Cascades. Most spring sightings occur between late Apr and mid-Jun, the majority of fall records from early Sep to late Oct. The few records in w. Ore. include a male in breeding plumage in the Coast Range, 20 mi. w. of Eugene, Lane Co., on 4 Jun 1981; an imm. female collected at Euchre Cr., Curry Co., on 8 Sep 1971; a bird at Blue River Ranger District, Lane Co., on 25 Apr 1991; and 1 mist-netted and banded at Galesville Res., Douglas Co., on 14 Jul 2000.

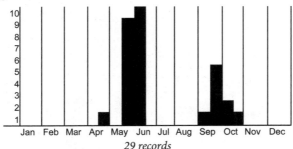
29 records

*Cape May Warbler *Dendroica tigrina*

Vagrant. Breeds in spruce forests from c. British Columbia and the s. Northwest Territories across Canada to sw. Newfoundland and s. to the Great Lakes region.

Spring and fall vagrant in Ore., with 13 accepted records and a number of unreviewed sightings. The majority of Ore. records are

13 records

vagrant occurrence

from Harney Co. Spring records occur from late May to early Jun, and fall sightings from early Sep to early Oct. Records in w. Ore. include 1 photographed at Tillamook Bay, Tillamook Co., on 19 Oct 1980; a bird at Harris Beach SP, Curry Co., on 30 May 1992; a male photographed near Gold Beach, Curry Co., 4 Feb – 4 Mar 2001; and a female at the N. Spit of Coos Bay, Coos Co., on 17 May 2004.

Black-throated Blue Warbler *Dendroica caerulescens*

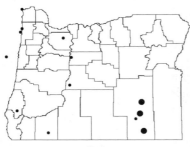

vagrant occurrence

Rare but regular in Ore. during the fall from early Sep to mid-Nov. Most records are in late Sep-early Oct. The bulk of records are at e. Ore. oasis sites. In some yrs none appear; most yrs bring 2 or 3 records.

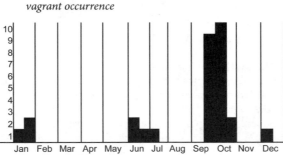

24 records (through 1991)

Very rare in winter in w. Ore.; 3 records to date. It is occasional in spring between early May and late Jun. One male was observed on territory in the Cascades of Clackamas Co. 23 Jun – 10 Jul 1979.

Yellow-rumped Warbler *Dendroica coronata*

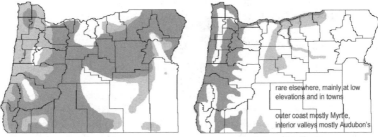

rare elsewhere, mainly at low elevations and in towns

outer coast mostly Myrtle, interior valleys mostly Audubon's

winter distribution

D. c. auduboni, the "Audubon's" Warbler, breeds from sea level to timberline in most conifer forests and aspen throughout the state; uncommon to rare at low elevations, fairly common at higher elevations and in forests with broken canopies. Rare in juniper woodland. Common to very common summer residents in the Cascades, Blues, Wallowas, and other mtn. forests e. of the Cascades. Densities are higher in the s. portion of the Cascades but then decrease into nw. Cal. Uncommon and local breeding residents at higher elevations in the Coast Range. Abundant migrant likely to occur in almost any habitat. In winter occurs regularly at lower elevations w. of the Cascades; usually the most common subspecies in the w. interior valleys in winter. Along the coast are common as far n. as Lincoln Co., becoming less common farther north E. of the Cascades a few attempt to remain during mild winters. Along the Columbia R. e. of the John Day Dam, they frequently winter in good numbers in Russian-olive stands.

  D. c. coronata, the "Myrtle" Warbler, does not breed in the state but is a common migrant and sparse winter resident in interior valleys of w. Ore.; much more common along the coast, where locally abundant, as in outer coastal wax myrtle thickets. Typically far outnumbers Audubon's on the outer coast from around the first of October through winter, more equal (in smaller numbers) in coastal river valleys. They are uncommon to rare migrants e. of the Cascades.

  Yellow-rumped Warblers tend to move n. earlier and s. later than most warblers. The northward movement occurs in w. Ore. from mid-Mar through early May. E. of the Cascades, mean arrival date is 2 Apr in the Bend area and 8 Apr at Malheur NWR. Migration peaks early Apr to early May. A post-breeding movement to higher elevations occurs in Jul and Aug. Although southward movement is observed as early as Aug, the major fall movement takes place in late Sep and Oct after most other warblers have departed. Audubon's and Myrtle Warblers tend to migrate and winter separately, but mixed flocks are occasionally encountered. Fall movements on the outer c. coast usually consist of a large influx of Audubon's during mid-Sep, with Myrtles arriving during the third wk of Sep and reaching parity during the first wk of Oct. Most Audubon's are gone by the end of the third wk of Oct.

> Note: In Ore., Myrtle Warblers forage in vegetation. They use a great array of species, but appear to prefer natives. They rarely forage on the ground (in Ore.) or on human-made substrates. Conversely, Audubon's Warblers feed in vegetation, on mown grass, in pastures, on barren earth, on manure piles, and on all manner of human structures. They associate freely, if loosely, with Western Bluebirds in winter, something not observed in Myrtle Warblers. (David Fix, p.c.)

Black-throated Gray Warbler *Dendroica nigrescens*

COOS	CLAT	LANE	BENT	PORT	CENT	MALH
15 Apr	17 Apr	6 Apr	10 Apr	5 Apr	29 Apr	12 May

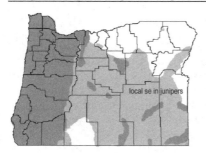

Summer resident of the foothills and valley bottoms of w. Ore. though less common in wetter areas along the coast. Extends into Cascades in fingers of riparian forests along major rivers and in young forests, especially adjacent to the riparian corridors. In se. Ore., primarily in montane juniper woodlands. Along the e. foothills of the Cascades, locally common in Hood R. and Wasco cos., uncommon to rare farther s. Also occurs very locally in the Ochoco, Blue, and Wallowa mtns.; more widespread in the mtns. and canyons of s. Lake, Harney, and Malheur cos. Common spring and fall migrant. Rare but regular in spring as early as very late Mar. The major southward movement occurs in late Aug and Sep though a few remain until late Oct; latest 15 Nov 1983 in Bend. Occasional in winter w. of the Cascades.

*Black-throated Green Warbler *Dendroica virens*

Vagrant. Breeds from nw. Canada to Newfoundland and s. from c. Minnesota to New England and in the Appalachians.

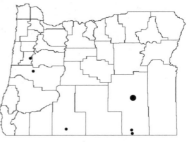

vagrant occurrence

There are 11 accepted Oregon records. The majority (7 records) are from late May to mid-Jun in se. Ore. (4 at Malheur NWR, 2 others in se. Harney Co., and 1 at Plush, Lake Co.). In addition, there is a coastal record from Cape Blanco, Curry Co. on 19 Jun 1982. The only fall record is of an imm. male at Corvallis, Benton Co., on 21 Sep 1985. There are two winter records, an imm. female at Eugene, Lane Co., 7-9 Dec 2001, and a male photographed at Klamath Falls, Klamath Co, on 9 Dec 2005.

In addition, a bird was observed at Malheur NWR, Harney Co., on 21 Sep 1987. This record has not been reviewed by the OBRC.

11 records

Townsend's Warbler *Dendroica townsendi*

COOS	CLAT	LANE	BENT	PORT	CENT	MALH
					2 May	8 May

Common breeder in the Blue and Wallowa mtns. of ne. Ore. Local summer resident in the vicinity of Mt. Hood and in the c. Cascades as far s. as Davis L., Klamath Co. Isolated territorial male Townsend's Warblers have been observed in the Coast Range and as far s. in the Cascades as Jackson Co. Also reported from the Warner Mtns. Townsend's and Hermit Warblers hybridize where ranges meet. In Ore. this is most readily observed in the Santiam Pass area. Townsend's Warblers are common spring and fall migrants throughout the state in a variety of habitats. Northward migrants are more often seen at lower elevations than Hermit Warblers. Fairly common to common migrant in w. Ore. from late Apr to early May. The major fall movement at Malheur NWR occurs 23 Aug-7 Sep. Stragglers linger until mid-Oct. Individuals and

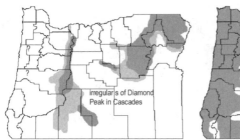

winter distribution

small flocks may be encountered through the rest of the winter among the roving bands of small forest-edge species typical of valley-edge and lower foothill situations in w. Ore., especially on the coastal slope and outer coast. Small numbers can be found throughout lower elevations in the Willamette and Umpqua and Rogue valleys.

Hermit Warbler *Dendroica occidentalis*

COOS	CLAT	LANE	BENT	PORT	CENT	MALH
27 Apr		21 Apr	28 Apr	25 Apr	10 May	

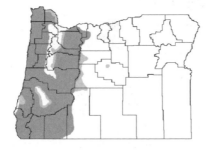

Common summer resident and migrant of coniferous forests of Coast Range, Klamath Mtns., and Cascades except pure ponderosa pine in the e. foothills of the Cascades. The possibility of scattered breeding birds in the Blue and Wallowa mtns. has been reported but not verified. Occasional in winter along the coast and in the Willamette V. Rare in e. Ore. during migration. Arrive during late Apr with peak movement in early May; early dates 7 Apr in Eugene and 17 Apr in e. Douglas Co. In se. Ore., where they do not breed, a late individual was at Fields 3 Jun 1993. The major movement s. takes place in late Aug with small numbers lingering until late Sep.

*Blackburnian Warbler *Dendroica fusca*

Vagrant. Breeds from c. Canada to Newfoundland and s. from c. Minnesota through the Great Lakes region to New England; also in the Appalachian Mts.

Six accepted Ore. records:

vagrant occurrence

1. An imm. was at Malheur NWR, Harney Co., on 18 Sep 1986.
2. An adult male was photographed e. of Nehalem, Tillamook Co.; it remained from 15 Nov 1987 to 12+ Mar 1988.
3. An adult male was observed at Benson Pond, Malheur NWR, Harney Co., on 29 May 1988.
4. An adult male was photographed at Page Springs CG, Harney Co., 1-2 Jun 1990.
5. An adult male was photographed at Fields, Harney Co., 16-17 Jun 1998.
6. One was at Page Springs CG, Harney Co., on 28 Sep 2004.

Several additional records have not been reviewed by the OBRC. An imm. was at Malheur NWR, Harney Co., on 13 Oct 1994; an adult was there on 23 May 1994 and a different bird on 24 May 1994; 1 was observed at Fields, Harney Co., on 7 Jun 1988; and 1 was observed at Salem, Marion Co., on 19 Oct 1998.

6 records

Yellow-throated Warbler Dendroica dominica

Vagrant. This species breeds from e. Nebraska and sw. Michigan to New Jersey and s. from sc. Texas to c. Florida. The Atlantic subspecies *dominica* winters locally in the se. U.S. and in the W. Indies, widespread *albilora* from s. Texas to Nicaragua. Casual (*albilora*) far n. and w. of the breeding range, mainly in fall. Vagrant to the W. Coast from s. British Columbia to Cal.

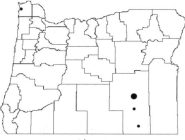

vagrant occurrence

Jan Feb Mar Apr May Jun Jul Aug Sep Oct Nov Dec

5 records

Five accepted Ore. records:

1. A singing male was photographed at Malheur NWR, Harney Co., 9-11 Jun 1985.
2. An adult male was photographed at Fields, Harney Co., on 24 Apr 1997.
3. An adult male was at Malheur NWR, Harney Co., 8-9 May 2002.
4. An adult male was photographed at Frenchglen, Harney Co., 1 Oct – 1 Nov 2003.
5. One bird was photographed at Seaside, Clatsop Co., 29 Jan – 5 Feb 2005.

In addition, 1 was observed at North Bend, Coos Co., on 27 May 1989, and 1 was photographed at Langlois, Curry Co., on 17 Jan 2009. These records have not yet been reviewed by the OBRC.

**Pine Warbler *Dendroica pinus*
Vagrant. Breeds in the e. U.S. from the Great Lakes region to Texas and Florida.

There is 1 accepted sight record for Ore. of an imm. observed at Harbor, Curry Co., on 23 Oct 1986.

In addition, a bird was photographed in La Grande, Union Co., on 20 Dec 2008 and remained into Jan 2009. This record has not yet been reviewed by the OBRC.

*Prairie Warbler *Dendroica discolor*

vagrant occurrence

Vagrant. Breeds in the e. U.S. from the s. Great Lakes region to Texas and Florida.

Casual vagrant in Ore. with 12 accepted records to date; the majority along the coast during fall (between 24 Aug and 24 Oct). A wintering male was at S. Beach, Lincoln Co., 6-26 Dec 1995. In addition, there are 3 records from e. Ore., all from Malheur NWR, Harney Co., on 10 Sep 1999, 27 Sep 2004, and 19 Sep 2005.

A number of additional reports have not yet been reviewed by the OBRC.

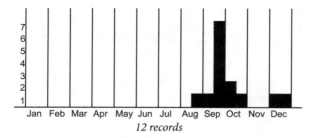

12 records

Palm Warbler *Dendroica palmarum*
Birds, presumably *D. p. palmarum* (*hypochrysea* has been reported but not proven), are regular fall transients on the outer coast and irregularly remain through the winter and spring. They are occasional spring and fall transients in the Willamette V. and have been found wintering in 1994, 1998, 1999, and 2008. They are irregular spring and fall transients e. of the Cascades. The only winter record e. of the Cascades was at the mouth of the Deschutes R., Sherman Co., on 2 Feb 1992.

The earliest fall record is from Curry Co., 9 Sep 1993. The bulk of Ore. passage occurs in late Sep through Oct, with a definite peak in early Oct. An extraordinarily heavy fall movement occurred in 1993, when about 120 were reported across the state including a total of 97 birds in Curry Co. Found annually along the coast in recent winters. Rare in spring: at least 5 records from 9 May to 7 Jun. The latest spring record is 7 Jun 1985. Two records do not fit established migratory patterns; 1 from 6 Jul 1979 near Forest Grove, Wash. Co., and the other from Salem on 1 Aug 1993.

*Bay-breasted Warbler *Dendroica castanea*
Vagrant. Breeds in the boreal forest belt across Canada and in the very ne. U.S.

Nine accepted Ore. records:

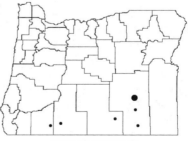

vagrant occurrence

1. A male in breeding plumage was collected at Upper Klamath Lake, Klamath Co., on 6 Jul 1963. The specimen is now in the Museum of Vertebrate Zoology, Berkeley, Cal.
2. A male was observed at Grizzly CG, Howard Prairie L., Jackson Co on 22 Jun 1976.

9 records

3. A male in breeding plumage was observed at Malheur NWR, Harney Co., on 9 Jun 1980.
4. A male in breeding plumage was photographed at Malheur NWR, Harney Co., on 25 May 1986.
5. A male was at Fields, Harney Co., on 27 May 1986.
6. An adult male was mist-netted, banded, and photographed at Hart Mountain Nat. Ant. Ref., Lake Co., on 2 Aug and recaptured on 23 Aug 1987.
7. One was photographed at Malheur NWR, Harney Co., 16-18 Sep 1988.
8. A breeding-plumaged male was photographed at Page Springs CG, Harney Co., on 27 May 1990.
9. An adult male was photographed at Malheur NWR, Harney Co., on 3 Jun 2002.

In addition, 1 was observed s. of Davis L., Klamath Co., on 13 and 22 Aug 1976. This record has not been reviewed by the OBRC.

Blackpoll Warbler *Dendroica striata*

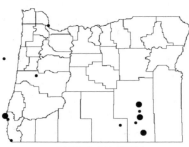

vagrant occurrence

This species is a rare but almost annual migrant in Ore., primarily in the fall. Most records are of imms. from Harney Co. and along the immediate coast. Spring records range from mid-May to early Jun, fall records from early Sep to late Oct. Two adults accompanying 2 or 3 fledged juvs. were on Sauvie I. 24-26 Jul 1969 for a possible breeding record. Other records in w. Ore. away from the coast include 1 at Fern Ridge Res., Lane Co., on 15 Sep 1988 and a bird aboard a fishing trawler 47 mi. w. off Lincoln Co, 1-3 Oct 1987.

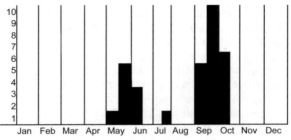

31 records, 34+ individuals (through 1996)

Black-and-white Warbler *Mniotilta varia*
This species occurs almost
annually in Ore. as a rare
but regular migrant. Spring
records range from early Apr
to mid-Jun, with a peak from
mid-Apr to May. Summer
records include a singing
male at Hilgard Junction SP,
Union Co., 11 Jun – 6 Jul
1985; 1 at Bloomberg Park
near Eugene, Lane Co., on 9
Jul 1994; a male at Malheur

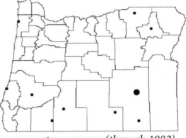

vagrant occurrence (through 1982)

NWR HQ, Harney Co., 13 Jun – 5 Jul 2000; and 1 banded near Fort
Klamath, Klamath Co., on 16 Jul 2001. Fall records occur from mid-Aug
to late Nov, with a peak during Sep. The majority of records are from e.
Ore. Very rare in winter, mostly in sw. Ore.

American Redstart *Setophaga ruticilla*
Uncommon breeder through the 1980s but now increasingly rare,
irregular, and local in ne. Ore. and rarely in the sc. Cascades. It is rare
to uncommon (in peak yrs) and local in Union and Wallowa cos., found
most often along the Grande Ronde R. upstream of La Grande. Pairs have
also been found in ne. Umatilla Co. along the Umatilla R.; most often
found from Thorn Hollow e. to the Bar M Ranch. Occasionally reported
s. to c. Baker Co. Irregular and not proven to breed elsewhere in e. Ore.
The only documented successful nesting w. of the Cascade summit was a
pair with 4 young found 2 Jul 1970 along the Rogue R. near Shady Cove,
Jackson Co.; the nest was collected. The only suggestions of nesting w. of
the Cascades since 1970 were a pair found about 15 mi ne. of Roseburg
6 Jul 1982, and a failed nesting attempt in Curry Co., Jun 2000.

Redstarts are fairly late migrants in spring, typically not appearing on their Ore. breeding grounds until late May or early Jun. Spring migration in this species is hard to describe with any accuracy, as some birds seen in se. Ore. may be en route to local breeding locales while others may be vagrants from e. populations. There are records nearly every yr from such vagrant traps as Malheur NWR HQ and Fields oasis in late May and early Jun. There are also spring records from such non-breeding locales as Cape Blanco, Summer L., Lake Co., Selmac L., Josephine Co., and the Lane Co. Coast Range. Fall movements are underway by mid-Aug and are spread across the state, but involve very few birds. Whether these represent southbound Ore. breeders or wanderers from elsewhere is not known. Most reports are from se. Ore. vagrant traps or from the outer coast through mid-Sep. Late records include 5 Oct 1993 at Gold Beach, and 11 Nov 1974 through end of month at Svenson, Clatsop Co. Occasional in winter in sw. Ore.

*Prothonotary Warbler *Protonotaria citrea*

vagrant occurrence

Vagrant. Breeds across the e. U.S. from the s. Great Lakes region to Texas and Florida.

Seven accepted Ore. records:

1. An adult female was observed at Charleston, Coos Co., on 19 Oct 1974.
2. One was mist-netted and photographed at Hart Mt., Lake Co., on 19 Aug 1976.
3. An adult in basic plumage was photographed at Malheur NWR, Harney Co., 10-11 Oct 1987.
4. A singing male was photographed at Malheur NWR, Harney Co., 30 May – 2 Jun 1993.
5. An adult male was banded and photographed at Malheur NWR, Harney Co., 19-22 Sep 1998.
6. An adult male was photographed at Halfway, Baker Co., 9-20 Nov 2001.
7. A dead female was found at Cape Meares Village, Tillamook Co., on 16 Jun 2003.

7 records

In addition, 1 was observed at Frenchglen, Harney Co, on 7 Oct 1999, and 1 was photographed and banded at Odessa Cr.., Upper Klamath L., on 2 Jul 2001. These records have not been reviewed by the OBRC.

**Worm-eating Warbler *Helmitheros vermivorus*

Vagrant. Breeds across the e. U.S. from Missouri to Massachusetts, s. to ne. Texas and nw. Florida.

Three accepted Ore. records:
1. One was observed at Malheur NWR HQ, Harney Co., on 16 Sep 1990.
2. One was observed at the mouth of the Winchuck R., Curry Co., on 1 Nov 2001.
3. A singing male was observed and its voice recorded at Malheur NWR HQ, Harney Co., 10-11 Jun 2001.

Ovenbird *Seiurus aurocapilla*

Rare but regular migrant in Ore., with 1 to several reports annually. Most records are from the se. part of the state. One was reported at Ashland, Jackson Co., on 4 Mar 1996. Spring records otherwise range from early May to mid-Jun. The only spring record away from e. Ore. was of a bird that landed on a fishing boat

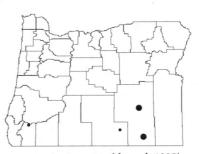

vagrant occurrence (through 1985)

5 mi. w. of Coos Bay, Coos Co., on 6 Jun 1970. There are 7 records of singing territorial males in the Cascades during Jun and Jul. No females were noted, nor was nesting suspected at any of these locations. One was singing on the Bayocean Spit, Tillamook Co., on 18 Jul 1988. A male was banded and photographed on Hart Mt., Lake Co., on 10 Jul 1979. Fall records are fewer than in spring and occur between late Aug and early Sep. One winter record, a bird photographed 7 Jan 2007 in Medford, is the only winter record for the state (Irons 2007b).

Northern Waterthrush *Seiurus noveboracensis*

An isolated population of this species has summered and presumably bred in the sc. Cascades since at least 1977. The population extends from the Little Deschutes R. n. of Gilchrist, Klamath Co., s. to the vicinity of Hwy 58, w. along Crescent Cr. and to Salt Cr. e. of the falls, Lane Co. One singing bird was in suitable habitat at Lost L., e. Linn Co., in Jun in the late 1980s, and another singing bird was in suitable habitat near the confluence of Skookum Cr. and the N. Fk. Middle Fk. of the Willamette R. in May or Jun in the early 1990s. No nest has been found in Ore., owing mainly to the impenetrable habitat. Recent reports suggest that a small population may breed in the upper Wenaha R. area of Union and Wallowa cos., not far from the Idaho colonies along the St. Joe R.

The breeding population appears to arrive during early Jun, though there is some variation in reports from yr to yr. Earliest arrival 13 May 1990 at both Gilchrist and Paulina Marsh. Birds have been reported carrying nesting material as early as 2 Jun but in most yrs are hard to find until the second wk of Jun. Generally gone by late Jul and appear to be absent in Aug. There are a number of fall records statewide from Aug through the season, including late east-side individuals on 3 Oct 1993 at Fields, Harney Co., and 28 Nov 1984 at McNary Dam 28 Nov 1984. There are 3 winter records, all on the outer coast.

*Louisiana Waterthrush *Seiurus motacilla*
Vagrant. Breeds across most of the e. U.S.

There is a single accepted Ore. record of a bird photographed and videotaped at Silver Falls SP, Marion Co., 26-30 Nov 1998.

*Kentucky Warbler *Oporornis formosus*
Vagrant. This warbler breeds across the e. U.S., from the Great Lakes region to Texas and n. Florida.

Four accepted Ore. records:
1. One was observed at Fields, Harney Co., on 16 Jun 1989.
2. A male in breeding plumage was photographed at Frenchglen, Harney Co., on 8 Jun 1990.
3. A singing male was photographed at Dead Cow Cr., Fremont NF, Lake Co., 23 Jun – 20 Jul 1996.
4. A singing male was observed at Fields, Harney Co., on 8 May 2000.

**Mourning Warbler *Oporornis philadelphia*

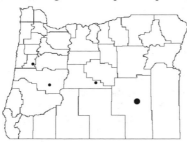

Vagrant. Breeds from ne. British Columbia across Canada and the ne. U.S. The e. counterpart of the similar MacGillivray's Warbler; especially females and imms. can be difficult to distinguish in the field.

vagrant occurrence

5 records

Five accepted sight records for Ore.:
1. An imm. was photographed at Malheur NWR, Harney Co., on 26 Sep 1982.
2. A male in breeding plumage was observed at Hills Cr. Res. w. of Oakridge, Lane Co., on 12 Jul 1984.
3. An imm. male was observed s. of Corvallis, Benton Co., on 4 Sep 1983.
4. A male was observed at Brothers, Deschutes Co., on 3 Jun 1990.
5. A singing male was observed at Malheur NWR, Harney Co., on 26 May 2001.

MacGillivray's Warbler *Oporornis tolmiei*

COOS	CLAT	LANE	BENT	PORT	CENT	MALH
28 Apr		20 Apr	23 Apr	22 Apr	2 May	5 May

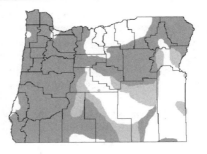

The MacGillivray's Warbler is common in the Coast Range, though rare or absent along the immediate c. and n. coast. Fairly common to abundant in the foothills of w. interior valleys and Cascades. Breed throughout Blue Mtns., locally uncommon in Union and Wallowa cos. Common to abundant in the Klamath Basin and in the Fremont NF. Breeds in se. Ore.; uncommon and local on Steens Mtn. and Mahogany Mtn. s. through the Trout Cr. Mtns., Pueblo Mtns., and Ore. Canyon Mtns. In w. Ore., spring migrants begin arriving in the latter half of Apr, rarely early Apr. Migration peaks early to mid-May. E. of the Cascades, first arrivals appear during early May (rarely late Apr), and peaks early to mid-May, with some late migrants through early Jun. Fall migration occurs statewide from mid-Aug through mid-Sep, with very few birds still present in late Oct. Fall migration at Malheur NWR begins around 7 Aug, peaks 15-25 Aug, with a late date of 10 Oct. There are at least 3 mid-winter records: 2 birds at Eugene, 31 Dec 1967; 1 bird at Astoria 2 Dec 1989; and 1 in Eugene 29 Dec 2001 – 22 Feb 2002.

Common Yellowthroat *Geothlypis trichas*

COOS	CLAT	LANE	BENT	PORT	CENT	MALH
30 Mar	5 Apr	24 Mar	4 Apr	4 Apr	20 Apr	1 May

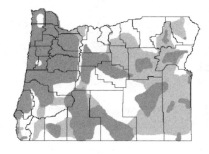

Breeds throughout Ore., including the coast and Cascades to moderate elevations. It is fairly common, but is sometimes found in very high densities, especially in coastal lowlands and w. interior valleys. Common to abundant in marshes and wetlands, especially in the Klamath Basin, Malheur NWR, and around lake and river margins and wet meadows of Malheur Co. Common summer resident and spring and fall migrant at lower elevations of Union and Wallowa cos. In w. Ore., southbound migration begins in late Aug. It peaks during the last wk of Aug and the first two wks of Sep and declines through mid-Oct. Stragglers, usually imms., may be seen well into Oct. Rare in winter in w. Ore. in interior valleys and along the coast, with fewer than 30 records prior to 1994. Winter sightings have increased since then, likely due to increased CBC coverage and observer skill. Thus far, only 1 winter record exists e. of the Cascades, from Grant Co.

*Hooded Warbler *Wilsonia citrina*

Vagrant. Breeds in the e. U.S., from the Great Lakes region s. to ne. Texas and Florida.

Ten accepted Ore. records:

1. A male was photographed and its voice recorded at Washburn Wayside, Lane Co., on 20+ Jul 1974.

vagrant occurrence

Jan Feb Mar Apr May Jun Jul Aug Sep Oct Nov Dec

10 records

2. One was observed at Malheur NWR, Harney Co., on 20 May 1977.
3. One male in breeding plumage was photographed and recorded at a rest area, along Hwy 396, 11 mi. s. of John Day, Grant Co., on 11 Jul 1982.
4. A male in breeding plumage was photographed at Wildhorse Cr., 4.5 mi. n. of Pendleton, Umatilla Co., on 21 Oct and 8 Nov 1983.
5. A male was at Harbor, Curry Co., 28 Aug – 28 Sep 1985.
6. An adult male was photographed at Malheur NWR, Harney Co., on 31 May 1992.
7. A singing male was photographed and recorded at Hart Mountain, Lake Co., 13 Aug – 8 Sep 2000.
8. A female was at Malheur NWR, Harney Co., 6-7 Oct 2000.
9. An adult male was photographed at Malheur NWR, Harney Co., 14-21 Sep 2002, and a second was present during some of that time.
10. One was photographed at Malheur NWR, Harney Co., on 1 Jun 2007.

The following additional records have not been reviewed by the OBRC: A singing male remained at Odessa CG at the s. end of Upper Klamath L., Klamath Co., through Sep 1998; a male and a female were at Hart Mt., Lake Co., 13 Aug – 8 Sep 2000; a male was at Malheur NWR HQ, Harney Co., 6-11 Oct 2000 (along with the accepted female), and 1 was photographed there on 25 May 2008.

Wilson's Warbler *Wilsonia pusilla*

COOS	CLAT	LANE	BENT	PORT	CENT	MALH
15 Apr	19 Apr	10 Apr	18 Apr	19 Apr	26 Apr	2 May

An abundant breeder in woods and tall shrubs in the Coast Range and is common in the Willamette V. and w. Cascades. Also breeds in the e. Cascades and Blue Mtns., uncommonly in scattered moist habitat patches in arid regions of Columbia Basin, High Lava Plains, and Great Basin. Occur from low elevation to treeline in appropriate habitat. Summer records exist in Malheur Co., but it is doubtful that they nest there. Abundance of the Wilson's Warbler is lower in the Cascades than in the Coast Range, and lower still e. of the Cascades. Within the Cascade Range, it is more abundant in the n. than s. Cascades.

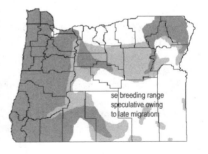

Earliest dates 22 Mar at Grants Pass, 11 Apr in Lane Co. and 15 Apr in c. Ore. Main migration early to late Apr, continuing to late May. Spring migration can involve a staggering number of birds during peaks 25 Apr to 15 May in w. Ore., and heavy migration is observed in se. Ore., sometimes through the first wk of Jun. Dispersal and migration occurs from late Jul to early Oct. The average date of latest sighting 1973-90 in the Lincoln Co. Coast Range was 16 Sep (range 2-27 Sep). Other late sightings include 25 Oct in the s. Willamette V. and 17 Nov at Summer L. At least 7 winter records (Dec) in w. Ore., mainly coastal. One winter record for e. Ore., 14 Jan 1990, near Milton-Freewater, Umatilla Co.

Canada Warbler Wilsonia canadensis

Vagrant. Breeds from ne. British Columbia across the boreal forest zone of Canada to the ne. U.S. and locally in the Appalachians.

vagrant occurrence

Seven accepted Ore. records:

1. An imm. was mist-netted and photographed at Malheur NWR, Harney Co., 25 Sep – 2 Oct 1982.
2. One was photographed at Malheur NWR, Harney Co., 2-4 Sep 1988.
3. An imm. was photographed at Seaside, Clatsop Co., 29 Oct – 1 Nov 1989.
4. A singing male was photographed at Mt. Tabor, Portland, Multnomah Co., on 24 Jun 1996.
5. One was photographed at Malheur NWR, Harney Co., on 8 Sep 2001.
6. Two birds were photographed at Malheur NWR, Harney Co., 18-29 Sep 2004.
7. An adult male was photographed at Malheur NWR, Harney Co., on 26 May 2006.

7 records

In addition, 1 was observed at Malheur NWR, Harney Co., on 9 Sep 1998, and 1 struck a window at Gold Hill, Jackson Co., on 17 Sep 1990. These records have not been reviewed by the OBRC.

Painted Redstart *Myioborus pictus*
Vagrant. Breeds from nw. Arizona, sw. New Mexico and w. Texas (locally) s. through Middle America.
    Two accepted sight records for Ore.:
1. One was observed at Tumalo, Deschutes Co., on 2 Aug 1990.
2. One was observed in Salem, Marion Co., on 5 Oct 1991.

Yellow-breasted Chat *Icteria virens*

COOS	CLAT	LANE	BENT	PORT	CENT	MALH
7 May		5 May	11 May	13 May	27 May	12 May

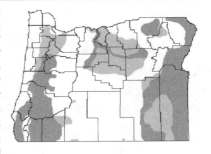

In w. Ore., the chat is an uncommon to common summer resident of interior Rogue V., occasionally to 2,100 ft elevation. It is locally uncommon summer resident in the interior Umpqua V. e. to Glide. In the Willamette V. it is a locally rare to uncommon summer resident, and rare e. to Oakridge, generally below 1,500 ft.

    Numbers decrease northward to the Columbia R. Rare to uncommon local summer resident in coastal river valleys s. of Coos R., and a rare coastal transient or visitor (possible summer resident) northward to the Columbia R. estuary. In e. Ore., the chat is a rare spring migrant in the Klamath Basin; possibly nested in 1999 along Klamath R. near the Cal. border. Rare (thought to nest) in Hart Mtn. Nat. Ant. Ref. Locally uncommon summer resident in valley riparian areas of Harney and Malheur cos., the Deschutes and John Day R. systems; ne. Ore. valleys. Rare in forested regions of Blue Mtns. Locally common in se. and ne. Ore. where habitat is excellent.

    Chats arrive in w. Ore. from late Apr to early May; e. of the Cascades, from early to mid-May. Early arrival dates include 19 Apr 1989 in the Rogue V.; 24 Mar 1990 along Bear Cr. s. of Prineville Res.; 5 Apr 1990 on Hunter Cr., s. Curry Co.; 4 Apr 1997 in the c. Willamette V.; and 21 Apr 1997 in the Applegate V. Late dates include 30 Sep 1940 in the s. Willamette V., 23 Sep 1990 at the s. jetty of the Columbia R.; 25 Sep 1990 at the mouth of the "D" R. near Lincoln City; and 22 Sep 1998 and 26 Sep 2000 in the c. Rogue V. Five verified winter records, most recently a male banded 7 Dec 2001 in Ashland, and 1 photographed in Florence 27 Dec 2001 – 4 Jan 2002.

Family Thraupidae

*Summer Tanager *Piranga rubra*

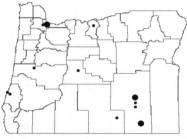

vagrant occurrence

Vagrant. Breeds from se. Cal. across the sw. states to c. Texas and widely across the se. U.S.

Casual visitor in Ore., with 16 accepted records to date. There are 9 spring records between mid-May and mid-Jun, 5 of them from Harney Co. In addition, a male was mist-netted at Hart Mt., Lake Co., on 14 June 1979; a second-yr male was at DeMoss Springs Park, Sherman Co., on 24 May 1992; a subadult male was in Portland, Multnomah Co., on 7 May 2001; and an adult male was at Millicoma Marsh, Coos Co., on 27 Jun 2001.

The remaining records occurred in the fall and winter, including a female seen at Coos Head, Coos Co., on 10 Nov 1981; a male observed at P Ranch, Harney Co., 20-24 Sep 2000; 4 records of adult and subadult males in the Portland and Beaverton area between Feb and Oct 2001, including a wintering male at Cedar Mill, Wash. Co., 10 Jan – 4 Apr 2001; a subadult male photographed at Bend, Deschutes Co., 17-25 Nov 2001; and a subadult male at Alvadore, Lane Co., on 14 Jan 2007.

There are several additional records that have not yet been reviewed by the OBRC.

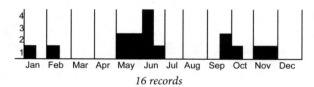

16 records

*Scarlet Tanager *Piranga olivacea*
Vagrant. Breeds from se.
Canada across much of the
e. U.S.

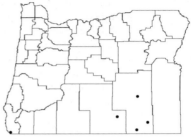

vagrant occurrence

Five accepted Ore.
records:

1. A male was
   photographed at
   Malheur NWR, Harney
   Co., on 31 May 1979.
2. A male was mist-netted
   and photographed at
   Hart Mt., Lake Co., on
   14 Jun 1979.
3. A male was photographed at Trout Cr., Harney Co., on 28 May
   1980.
4. A female was photographed at Pike Cr., Harney Co., on 31 May
   1987.
5. A female was photographed at Brookings, Curry Co., 7-10 Dec
   2001.

5 records

Western Tanager *Piranga ludoviciana*

COOS	CLAT	LANE	BENT	PORT	CENT	MALH
28 Apr	9 May	23 Apr	27 Apr	26 Apr	2 May	3 May

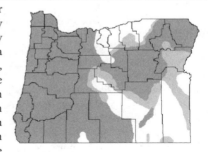

Widespread summer
resident throughout virtually
all conifer forests, especially
Douglas-fir and ponderosa
pine. In the w. Cascades,
more abundant in Rogue
and Umpqua basins than
farther n. Does not breed in
juniper woodlands. Rare in
summer in high-elevation
aspen woodlands, where
breeding has not been confirmed. Non-breeding birds often observed
outside breeding areas during mid-summer. Common to abundant

migrant that may occur anywhere in the state from alpine meadows, sagebrush flats, junipers, and lowland deciduous groves to urban and suburban neighborhoods.

Conspicuous spring migrant. Usually found singly or in small groups but occasionally performs spectacular movements. Earliest records are in mid-Mar with peak numbers w. of the Cascades late Apr through May. Peak movements e. of the Cascades early May to early Jun, stragglers to late Jun. Fall movements are inconspicuous involving individuals or small groups passing silently through the trees. Main movement takes place mid-Jul to mid-Sep with peak in late Aug and early Sep. Straggling individuals through Oct, rarely Nov. Casual in winter in w. interior valleys and on the s. coast.

Family Emberizidae

Green-tailed Towhee *Pipilo chlorurus*

COOS	CLAT	LANE	BENT	PORT	CENT	MALH
					2 May	11 May

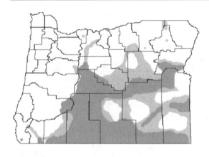

Locally fairly common e. of the Cascades in summer. Most common in n. Great Basin, where it is found in nearly all desert mtn. ranges. Particularly abundant above 6,500 ft in Pueblo Mtns. Present but more local in the Blue Mtns. Rare in nc. Ore., but known to breed in the White R. drainage, and Hood R. and Wasco cos. Locally uncommon to common on e. slope of the Cascades in c. and sc. Ore., and in the Klamath Basin. Generally absent w. of the Cascade summit, except in parts of sw. Ore. Locally uncommon on the w. slope of the Cascades in Jackson Co. Also in Douglas Co., where a small breeding population is established at Thorn Prairie; and breeding has been recorded at Reynolds Ridge. Occasionally found w. of the summit in extreme se. Lane Co. near Emigrant Pass if habitat is available owing to clearcuts, fires, or other conditions that produce local brushfields. Locally fairly common through higher elevations of the Siskiyou Mtns.

Spring migrants arrive late Apr to early May. At Malheur NWR migrants appear individually, with no apparent peak. Post-breeding dispersal to higher elevations (as high as timberline) occurs Aug-Sep. Most birds leave late Aug to early Sep; few are seen by mid-Oct. Migrants rarely reported outside of breeding range. Extremely rare in winter: only 3 records: Ashland in Dec 1977, Riverton, Coos Co., in Dec 1994 and Bend on 22 Jan 2007 (Irons 2007b).

Spotted Towhee *Pipilo maculatus*

Common statewide breeder and migrant. E. Ore. breeders (*P. m. curtatus*) are more heavily spotted than w. Ore. forms. Breeds locally on Steens Mtn. to at least 7,200 ft and elsewhere within the se. part of the state where habitat is available. Winters primarily w. of the Cascades and in small numbers in 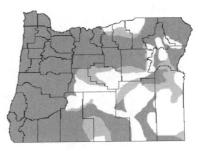 lowland areas e. of the Cascades. Some northward movement is noted in the Klamath Basin in mid-Feb, with the bulk of movement beginning in early Mar. Average spring arrival at Malheur NWR is 4 Mar, with peak of passage 15 Mar-5 Apr and stragglers through May. Fall peak of passage is from 10 Sep through 5 Oct at Malheur and most birds are gone from the Klamath Basin by late Oct.

**Eastern Towhee *Pipilo erythrophthalmus*

Vagrant. Breeds from sc. Canada across most of the e. U.S. This is the e. counterpart of the Spotted Towhee; until 1995, the two species were treated as conspecific under the name Rufous-sided Towhee.

There is 1 accepted sight record for Ore. of a female observed at West Linn, Clackamas Co., on 3 Apr 2001.

In addition, a male was photographed at Malheur NWR HQ, Harney Co., on 1 Jun 2008. This record is still under review by the OBRC.

California Towhee *Pipilo crissalis*

An uncommon to fairly common permanent resident throughout the Rogue, Applegate, and Illinois valleys. It is an uncommon and very local resident in the Umpqua V. as far n. as Myrtle Cr., and occasional sightings have occurred in and around Roseburg, where specimens

have also been collected. In the Klamath Basin it is an uncommon resident on brushy hillsides around Lower Klamath L. and s. along the Klamath R. In summers of 1984-86, 5 or more pairs were located on Short L. Mtn., just n. of Bonanza, Klamath Co., and may still be present there. Extremely sedentary and non-migratory; the origin and validity of reports n. of Sutherlin is suspect. Sight records w. to Gold Beach.

American Tree Sparrow *Spizella arborea*

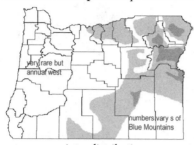

winter distribution

Winters annually in valleys within and near the Blue Mtns. from n. Morrow Co. s. and e. to n. Malheur Co. Most common in Wallowa, Union, and Baker cos. Annual s. to Malheur NWR, local w. to Summer L. W.M.A. Occasional elsewhere e. of the Cascades; rare w. of the Cascades, where single birds appear irregularly, with reports s. to Curry Co. and Ashland. Earliest arrival 6 Oct 2005 at Florence (Contreras 2006), an extraordinary date for a coastal bird, but followed 9 Oct 2005 by a bird at Gearhart, Clatsop Co. (Gross 2006). Earliest arrival in the usual winter range is 16 Oct 1993 at Umapine, Umatilla Co. and 17 Oct 1970 at Malheur NWR. Generally arrives in ne. Ore. in late Oct or early Nov and reaches Malheur NWR in Dec in yrs when they occur. Few records after mid-Feb at Malheur, with 25 Mar the latest record. The latest spring records for Ore. are 17 May 1947 and 15 May 1971 in c. Lane Co., 11 May 1985 at Bay City, and 6 May 1995 at Cape Meares.

Chipping Sparrow *Spizella passerina*

COOS	CLAT	LANE	BENT	PORT	CENT	MALH
15 Apr		1 Apr	11 Apr	18 Apr	15 Apr	

Uncommon to common summer resident in open forests and drier woodland edges throughout the state. Especially abundant in the Blue Mtns. of ne. Ore., though it is generally rare there in n.-facing wet grand fir sites >5,000 ft. It is common in sw. Ore., and locally uncommon in the n. Willamette V. and the s. Coast Range. Breeds in scattered locations in the Cascades, and throughout higher elevations of e. Ore. Rare in the high Pueblos and Ore. Canyon mtns., and on sagebrush flats. Generally absent or rare on the coast n. of Curry Co. and in densely forested areas of the n. Coast Range.

Fairly common in migration, when it can appear almost anywhere, though a genuinely rare migrant on much of the coast. This is one of Ore.'s earliest passerine migrants. They begin arriving in w. Ore. in late Mar, though they have been seen as early as 7 Feb. Peak movement occurs

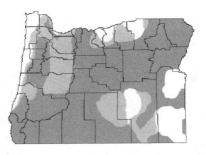

mid-Apr in w. Ore., late Apr in e. Ore. Forms flocks beginning by mid-Jul (Cascades) to early Aug (Wallowas) with other species feeding in rocky meadows. A few birds linger in w. Ore. through the winter, but most are gone by early Oct. Winter birds in the Willamette V. often use filbert orchards.

Clay-colored Sparrow *Spizella pallida*

A regular fall and winter visitant to w. Ore. in very small numbers (fewer than 10 reports per yr) and an irregular spring and occasional fall visitant to e. Ore. The majority of records are from mid-Sep through Oct with a few remaining to winter. Spring records have become annual and range from mid-May to mid-Jun.

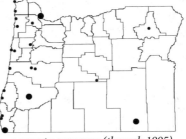

vagrant occurrence (through 1995)

The species is frequently encountered in mixed sparrow flocks, often with *Zonotrichia* species and juncos.

Brewer's Sparrow *Spizella breweri*

COOS	CLAT	LANE	BENT	PORT	CENT	MALH
					28 Apr	1 May

See *BOGR* for taxonomic information about "Timberline Sparrow." The Brewer's Sparrow is an abundant migrant and summer resident e. of the Cascades summit, particularly in the se. quarter of the state among the vast sagebrush communities of the Great Basin shrub-steppe. There is some evidence of local breeding in small numbers in the w. Cascades and in montane sw. Ore. w. to near Cave Junction. Generally a very rare migrant w. of the Cascades summit, though can be locally rare to

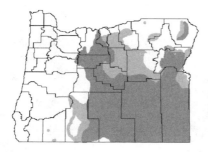

very uncommon in some yrs (e.g., Fern Ridge Res, Lane Co., where it may have bred). Casual w. of the Coast Range, where there are fewer than 10 records. In the Rogue V., many Brewer's Sparrows (males, females, juvs.) have been captured in mist-nets at The Nature Conservancy's Whetstone Preserve near Lower Table Rock during Jun and Jul. This species does not appear to nest there, but uses the area for molting prior to migration.

Spring migrants usually arrive from late Apr to early Jun, although in some yrs a few arrive as early as mid-Apr. The earliest in Ore. was a well-described bird 20 Mar 1999 at Detroit Flats in the w. Cascades in Marion Co. Within the breeding range, the earliest sighting is 2 Apr 1996 at Summer L. W.A. Significant dispersal occurs by mid-Jul and southward migration increases to peak during the last two wks of Aug. Numbers diminish rapidly during Sep and most leave by mid-Sep. Latest record is 30 Sep 1991 at Summer L., Lake Co. Reports after Sep are almost nonexistent. One well-documented bird was photographed at "D" R. in Lincoln City on 19 Oct 1999. Two undocumented records from the Umpqua V. in Douglas Co. are the only winter reports.

*Black-chinned Sparrow *Spizella atrogularis*

Vagrant. Breeds from c. Cal. across the sw. U.S. to Mexico. Casual visitor n. of its range; may have bred in Ore.

Four accepted Ore. records:
1. One was photographed at Medford, Jackson Co., on 14 Jun 1977.
2. A family group was photographed at Stukel Mtn., Klamath Co., 17-22 Jul 1990.
3. A singing male was at Stukel Mtn., Klamath Co., 22-23 Jun 1996.
4. A singing male was photographed and recorded in a clearcut near Scotts Mill, Clackamas Co., on 12 Jun 1999.

In addition, there are several records that have not been reviewed by the OBRC; most are from ceanothus- and oak-covered hillsides in sw. Ore. Two were observed on Roxy Ann Butte, Jackson Co., 7-8 Jun 1970, 3

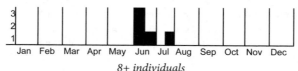

8+ individuals

were there on 2 Jul 1970; another was there on 15 May 1971; a pair was there from late May to 29 Jul 1977, and a male was there 14 Jul 1979. Two males were on a ceanothus-covered slope 10 mi. ne. of Medford on 23 May 1979, with 1 still there on 11 Jun. One was observed on Glass Butte, Lake Co., on 25 May 1996, and a male was observed at Blitzen Crossing, Steens Mt., Harney Co., on 28 Jun 1999.

Vesper Sparrow *Pooecetes gramineus*

COOS	CLAT	LANE	BENT	PORT	CENT	MALH
		5 Apr	13 Apr		8 Apr	26 Mar

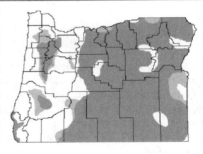

In e. Ore., the Vesper Sparrow breeds in open habitats up to 7,000 ft on desert mtns. such as Steens Mtn. and Hart Mtn. Breed irregularly below 4,000 ft, and abundance in shrub-steppe may be greater at higher elevations. Breeds w. of the Cascades in the Willamette and Umpqua valleys, in foothills and mtns. above the Rogue V., and in coastal valleys of sw. Ore. from Bandon s. in Coos and Curry cos. Abundance greatest in dry, grassy foothills of Umpqua and Rogue valleys, where it is an uncommon to locally common breeding species. In the Willamette V., rare to locally uncommon in pastures and open foothills in the s. valley, and in Christmas tree farms throughout the valley and foothills.

In the Rogue V., migrants first arrive in late Feb. In the Willamette V., early migrants may appear in mid-Mar, but most migration occurs in Apr. Early dates include individuals at Portland early Feb through 24 Mar 1979, 11 Mar in Yamhill Co., 19 Mar near Corvallis, 25 Mar at Finley NWR. Mean arrival date in Yamhill Co. 3 Apr. Rare at all seasons on the coastal slope n. of Coos Co. In e. Ore., spring migrants begin to arrive in late Mar and become abundant in early Apr. At Malheur NWR, peak spring passage 15 Apr-1 May, although most abundant after 25 Apr. An extremely early date is 28 Feb at Malheur NWR. Other early dates include 15 Mar in c. Ore. and 23 Mar in Klamath Co. Fall migration through Rogue V. mostly late Sep and early Oct. Peak fall migration at Malheur NWR early Sep. Most birds have left the state by early Oct. Late dates include 2 Nov at n. spit, Coos Bay, 1 Nov near Eugene, and in e. Ore. 23 Sep at Malheur NWR. There have been a few confirmed winter records, mainly in westside valleys and primarily near Eugene, but most reports lack verification.

Lark Sparrow *Chondestes grammacus*

COOS	CLAT	LANE	BENT	PORT	CENT	MALH
					21 Apr	25 Apr

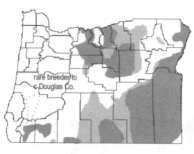

Uncommon to locally common summer resident and migrant e. of the Cascades. Rarely breeds above 6,000 ft elevation. In w. Ore., fairly common summer resident in Rogue V. and foothills. Rare and local in summer in Umpqua V. Rare but regular spring and fall migrant in c. Lane Co. Rare migrant elsewhere in the Willamette V. and along the coast and in the Cascades. Rare winter visitor in the Willamette V. Fairly common to uncommon in Rogue V. in winter, where flocks of up to 40 may be found. Very rare e. of the Cascades in winter; a Feb 1980 record at La Grande was highly unusual.

Spring migration in Ore. begins the last 10 days of Mar and peaks late Apr through mid-May. Earliest arrival date 19 Mar at Malheur NWR. Other early dates presumably representing returning birds are 31 Mar at Lower Table Rock, Jackson Co., and 16 Mar in Linn Co. Transients noted Mar-May in Lane Co. In late Jul and Aug forms foraging flocks, often with other species; often away from breeding areas. Fall migration e. of the Cascades peaks in latter half of Aug and early Sep, by mid-Sep few remain, although individuals are rarely noted into early Oct. Rare but regular migrant along coast Sep-Oct. In Lane Co., transients noted Jul-Sep; late date 26 Nov.

Black-throated Sparrow *Amphispiza bilineata*

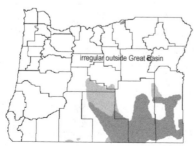

Principal breeding range is se. Ore. In many yrs apparently restricted to the arid slopes of the Alvord and Warner basins, although could have strongholds in other rarely visited basin areas in the se. corner of the state. In some yrs breeding occurs northward to the Harney, Abert, and Summer

L. basins and to the e. in Malheur Co. Breeding is rare n. and w. of the Great Basin, sometimes as far as the Painted Hills National Monument in Wheeler Co., the Boardman Army Depot in the Columbia R. basin of nc. Ore., and in the Klamath Basin. Elsewhere in the state it is an occasional vagrant with about 40 records w. of the Cascades to the outer coast (most in spring) and 2 records in ne. Ore.

Earliest spring arrival record is 28 Apr 1994 along Abert Rim. The only earlier Ore. record was away from its breeding range in Salem, 13 Mar 1987. Although a few records are from early May, most spring migrants first appear in mid-May with migration peaking by late May. Most leave on their southward migration by the end of Jul. Latest record in the breeding range was a juv. found 12 Aug 1994 at Painted Hills, Wheeler Co. The only records past this date are of 1 found on the s. Ore. coast near Brookings, 26 Sep 1985, and an extraordinary record 24 Jan 2002, also at Brookings.

Sage Sparrow *Amphispiza belli*

COOS	CLAT	LANE	BENT	PORT	CENT	MALH
					21 Mar	21 Mar

The principal breeding range of Sage Sparrow is se. and c. Ore. Found throughout the arid expanses of the Great Basin and usually associated with big sage. Common to uncommon from the alkaline basin floors to the high plateaus. Breeds to elevations of 6,800 ft. Found locally along the Columbia 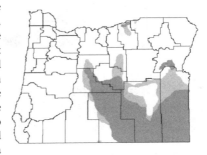 R. basin in nc. Ore., especially the Boardman Army Depot and irregularly in sagebrush-dominated valleys of the Blue Mtns. in ne. Ore. Strays are remarkably rare w. of the Cascades with only about 14 records, mostly in early spring; only 3 extralimital records are coastal. Any sw. Ore. strays should be scrutinized carefully for *A. b. belli*, likely to be split as a separate species. In some yrs a few Sage Sparrows remain throughout the winter in se. and sc. Ore., and in the lower Columbia Basin. Spring migrants begin to reach Ore. in late Feb to early Mar and numbers peak mid-Mar. Most w. Ore. records are mid-Feb through Apr, concomitant with the main passage in e. Ore. Otherwise there are single extralimital records in Jan, Jun, and Aug. Southward migration begins in late Aug and peaks in mid-Sep at Malheur NWR, with some remaining through Nov.

*Lark Bunting *Calamospiza melanocorys

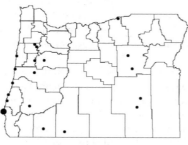

vagrant occurrence

Vagrant. Breeds in the interior prairies from sc. Canada to n. Texas.

Casual visitor to Ore., with 20 accepted and a number of additional, unreviewed records. The majority of sightings occurred from mid-May to late Sep. There appears to be no pattern or concentration of occurrences, with records scattered throughout the state. Winter records include 1 observed at White City, Jackson Co., on 13 Nov 1961; 1 at Medford, Jackson Co., on 30 Jan 1966; and 1 that was collected 5.5 mi. e. of Corvallis in Linn Co. on 3 Jan 1967. A male wintering at a Portland, Multnomah Co., feeder from early Jan to 4 May 1972 changed from full basic to full alternate plumage during its stay.

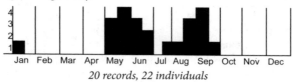

20 records, 22 individuals

Savannah Sparrow *Passerculus sandwichensis*

COOS	CLAT	LANE	BENT	PORT	CENT	MALH
					4 Apr	23 Mar

See *BOGR* for extensive discussion of subspecies. A common breeding subspecies in open grassland habitat in e. Ore., the Willamette V., and along the coast in w. Ore., and also on islands in the Columbia R. Savannah Sparrows also breed in some montane meadows (usually larger meadows) above 5,000 ft including the Warner Mtns. and Ochoco Mtns. It is a rare breeder in the Cascades. A rare breeder in the Rogue V., apparently reduced from its common resident status in the 1960s. It is an uncommon breeder in the Umpqua V. Migrants occur throughout their Ore. breeding range. Fall migrants also occur in high-elevation montane meadows of the Cascade Mtns. Winter populations throughout most of the state are reduced from that of the breeding season (except Rogue V.); uncommon to locally common in the Willamette V., and uncommon to rare in e. Ore., and along the coast. Significant winter populations can occur in the Rogue V.

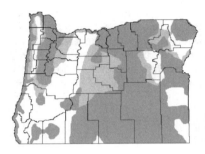
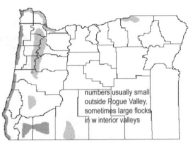

winter distribution

Early arrivals occur in the later half of Mar, but most arrive in early Apr. Migrant flocks can be large and numerous along the coastal dunes in Lane and Lincoln cos. in Apr and early May. Average arrival date 17 Apr in Yamhill Co. Peak migration in the s. Willamette V. is late Apr. Spring transients can linger into early Jun. In e. Ore., average arrival date at Malheur NWR is 22 Mar with peak of passage 5-25 Apr. Early dates in e. Ore. include 1 Mar at Malheur NWR and 6 Mar at Millican, Deschutes Co. Fall migration begins in Aug and peaks between mid-Sep and mid-Oct. Most individuals have left by late Nov with an occasional wintering bird. Occurs mostly in small to mid-sized flocks in winter (<50 birds), although occasional large flocks reported.

Grasshopper Sparrow *Ammodramus savannarum*

A widespread but very local breeder and rare migrant. It occurs in scattered "colonies" along the unforested n. slopes of the Blue Mtns. E. of the Cascades, found in the Boardman area, the Heppner area, Foster Flats in Harney Co. and locally near Vale and Jordan V., Malheur Co. W. of the Cascades, one small

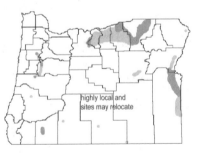

colony has persisted since 1987 in the Rogue V. (up to 6 singing males), and since 1998 the species has been observed at several additional sites. Isolated birds have been observed in the Umpqua V. Singing males have been located in the c. and s. Willamette V., including Baskett Slough NWR, near Brownsville and Lebanon, at Finley NWR, Benton Co., and Fern Ridge Res., Lane Co. (the latter since the early 1970s).

Essentially unknown in migration. Singing males have been observed beginning 23 Apr in e. Ore., 26 Apr in the Rogue V., and 5 May in the Willamette V. Once males cease singing in Jul, they are rarely observed though there are 1 Aug and 2 Sep records for the Roseburg area. At least 2 winter records exist for Fern Ridge Res. In addition, 1 found 4 Jan 1982 near Alton Baker Park, Eugene, was monitored for several days then found dead.

Le Conte's Sparrow *Ammodramus leconteii*
Vagrant. Breeds from ne. British Columbia across Canada and the ne. U.S.
   Two accepted Ore. records of this secretive species:
1. An imm. was photographed at Fields, Harney Co., on 27 Sep 1983.
2. An imm. was photographed at Fields, Harney Co., on 12 Oct 1991.

Fox Sparrow *Passerella iliaca*

COOS	CLAT	LANE	BENT	PORT	CENT	MALH
					25 Mar	10 Apr

See *BOGR* for extensive discussion of subspecies. *P. i. schistacea* (gray-headed) breeds in the Blue Mtns. and locally in Malheur Co. Darker-headed forms breed in the Cascades and se. to the Warner Mtns., Hart Mtn., and Steens Mtn. and w. in the Siskiyous to Curry Co. The breeding complex departs the state to winter in Cal. and the SW., and is replaced in Ore. during that season by dark-chocolate birds that breed in Alaska and w. Canada. These populations overlap somewhat in Ore. but there is some geographic sorting. Fox Sparrows winter abundantly on the coast and in the Coast Range. Fox Sparrows are common in winter in the w. interior valleys. A few also winter locally into the w. Cascades below the elevation of consistent snowpack, and e. of the Cascades as far n. as Umatilla Co. Bright, streaky "Red" Fox Sparrows are occasionally seen in Ore., mainly in winter w. of the Cascades, but most are not well documented and there are no specimens.

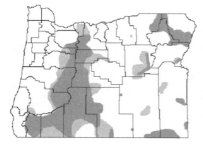 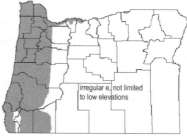

irregular e.| not limited to low elevations

winter distribution

Birds breeding in the Cascades arrive mid-Apr. At Malheur NWR the earliest record is 16 Mar; peak of passage is late Apr and early May. Studies at Hart Mtn. show that breeding birds are present by the third wk of May and that laying occurs as late as 3 Jul. Wintering birds in w. Ore. begin moving in late Mar and most are gone by late Apr. Later migrants still in "winter" habitat commonly sing, as do mid-autumn migrants. Birds breeding in the s. Cascades depart in Sep. Fall movement at Malheur NWR is extended, with birds arriving as early as Aug, peak of passage 15 Sep to 5 Oct, stragglers occurring into Nov, and only a few in winter. Migrants from the n. appear in late Sep and Oct in w. Ore., with early arrivals in the second wk of Sep, when arrivals peak in the nw. Cascades.

Song Sparrow *Melospiza melodia*

The dark reddish-brown *M. m. morphna* is a common and widespread resident of w. Ore. Post-breeding dispersal, mostly of imms., takes many to higher elevations and southward. Some movement to lower elevations in winter with transients and wintering birds from the n. increasing numbers to beyond the local breeding population. Paler forms breed in e. Ore. Most Song Sparrows move to protected riparian areas in winter with some southward movement. Wintering birds in many areas are not the local breeding birds but migrants from the n. Wintering and migrant birds include multiple forms, some of which differ markedly from local breeders.

Migratory movements can be obvious but are usually unrecorded. Permanent resident males move on territory during Jan and Feb, migrants late Feb and Mar. Nesting takes place mainly Apr to Jul, but extreme nesting dates for the s. Willamette V. are 28 Feb and 13 Aug. Fall migratory movements at Malheur NWR occur from mid-Sep to mid-Oct with most transients gone by late Nov. Peak movements in w. Ore. are in Oct. Many breeding birds remain on, or near, their territories throughout the yr while others migrate s. or move to more protected areas, often becoming locally very common.

Lincoln's Sparrow *Melospiza lincolnii*

COOS	CLAT	LANE	BENT	PORT	CENT	MALH
					6 Apr	23 Apr

Breed locally above 3,000 ft in the w. Cascades, s. at least to Howard Prairie Res., Jackson Co. A few breed at lower elevations in the w. Cascades w. to the upper Molalla R. drainage, Clackamas Co., in ec. Linn Co., and in ec. Lane Co. Breed locally in the Klamath Mtns. Lincoln's Sparrows breed in the e. Cascades and e. to the Gearhart Mtn. area, the

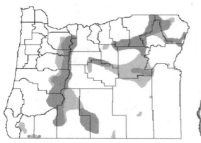

rare and irregular e,
mainly in lowlands

winter distribution

Warner Mtns., and the Blue Mtns. They also breed locally on Steens Mtn. and possibly in s. Malheur Co. The species is a rare to fairly common transient throughout the state. An obvious migrant at e. Ore. oasis sites; the earliest on record at Malheur is 22 Mar; peak of passage in the first two wks of May and stragglers seen through 21 May. In w. Ore. valleys, birds typically remain through a peak movement in late Apr, with stragglers in early May, rarely later in the month. The peak of fall passage at Malheur NWR falls between 15 Sep and 1 Oct, with the earliest on 15 Aug and the latest on 23 Oct. In the Willamette V. and c. Douglas Co., Lincoln's Sparrows begin appearing in early Sep with most movement in late Sep and Oct. Present in small numbers throughout winter, mainly in valleys w. of the Cascades, preferring wet grassy sumps.

Swamp Sparrow *Melospiza georgiana*
Rare to uncommon spring and fall transient and winter visitant in w. Ore., particularly along the coast. Local; a Nature Conservancy preserve on Tillamook Bay, Tillamook Co., Millicoma Marsh at the se. corner of Coos Bay, and the lower Coquille V., Coos Co., are well-known wintering areas. Rare and irregular e. of the Cascades; probably regular fall migrant and irregular winter visitant. There are few spring records e. of the Cascades (all in Mar) of individuals not known to have wintered. Swamp Sparrows are quite habitat-selective, using very wet sumps containing expanses of tall grass, rushes or sedges mixed with shrubs, blackberry and scattered saplings. These birds are found primarily at low elevations, but migrants have occurred in the w. Cascades in spring and fall. The earliest arrival is 16 Sep at Diamond L., Douglas Co. Usually begins arriving late Sep-Oct e. of the Cascades and during the last two wks of Oct w. of the Cascades. Usually absent after the first half of Apr. A singing bird was at Shady Cove, Jackson Co., 5 Apr 1969. Latest spring records from coastal Clatsop Co. 5 May 1990; at the upper end of Detroit Res., Marion Co., 8 May 1999; and a male singing in an alder/willow/sedge bog along Salt Cr., e. Lane Co., 17 May 1992.

White-throated Sparrow *Zonotrichia albicollis*

Rare to uncommon migrant and winter visitor, mainly in w. Ore. Rare migrant, most frequent in fall, e. of the Cascades. In winter, much rarer e. of the Cascades, where found mainly in lowland valleys with other wintering sparrows. Most e. Ore. records are from the Columbia and Klamath basins, probably reflecting

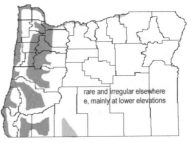

rare and irregular elsewhere e, mainly at lower elevations

winter distribution

both habitat availability and observer coverage. Occurs locally in w. Ore. as singles or small flocks along edges of wooded bottomlands and along edges of dense wooded cover, as singles or pairs commonly associating with flocks of juncos or Golden-crowned Sparrows. However, this species is at least as common, perhaps more so, in urban and suburban settings, often associating with feeder flocks of juncos. First arrives in late Sep, but most seem to arrive from late Oct through Nov, with peak numbers at wintering sites often not seen until early Dec. Spring migration is generally quiet and rarely reported. At Malheur NWR spring records fall between 25 Apr and 10 May. Late records include individuals 20 Jun 1993 at Hunter Cr., and 21 Jun 1991 at Harbor, both Curry Co.

Harris's Sparrow *Zonotrichia querula*

A very rare migrant and rare but regular winter visitor statewide. Numbers vary considerably from yr to yr but a few birds are typically found in the state every yr. They are most regular in the Columbia Basin and in valleys within the e. Blue Mtns., but also found almost annually in the Willamette V. Irregular migrant and winter visitant in the Umpqua V. Relatively late fall arrival to Ore., with birds usually first reported in late Oct (e. Ore.) or early Nov (w. Ore.); earliest 14 Sep 1983 at Mule Shoe Spring, Grant Co. Birds often remain until Apr. Several records to late May.

White-crowned Sparrow *Zonotrichia leucophrys*

Common breeder, migrant, and winter resident. Subspecies are recognizable in the field and have distinct movements. *Z. l. pugetensis* is the breeding subspecies w. of the Cascades. Migrant and winter *pugetensis* are confined to w. of the Cascades. *Z. l. oriantha* breeds in most mountain ranges throughout the e. part of the state and winters to Mexico. *Z. l. gambelii* occurs in migration statewide. Movements of different

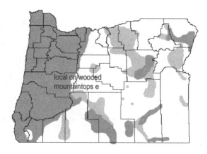

populations are not fully understood. As a breeding species, occurs across the state, but distribution is somewhat patchy. It commonly occurs in summer along the coastal strip, in the Willamette and Umpqua valleys, in the Coast Range, and at mid- to high-elevation mountain meadows of the Siskiyou Mtns., the Cascades se. to the Warner Mtns., the Blue Mtn. complex, and high ranges of se. Ore. In the w. valleys s. of c. Douglas Co., it becomes increasingly less common and is largely absent from Jackson Co.

Fall and spring see an influx of migrants throughout the state, including areas not associated with breeding. Many remain for the winter in valleys lacking snow cover. During migration *Z. l. gambelii* makes up the bulk of migrant White-crowned Sparrows e. of the Cascades, while smaller numbers move through w. Ore. Some *gambelii* stay to winter at low elevations in e. Ore., and have been observed among wintering flocks of *pugetensis* in w. Ore. Migrant *Z. l. pugetensis* stay w. of the Cascades. Migratory movement in w. Ore. begins in late Mar and is most noticeable mid-Apr to early May, when the majority of *gambelii* move through. Breeding *pugetensis* arrive on territories early to mid-Apr, and laying begins in early May. Birds depart breeding territories by mid- to late Aug, and fall migration in w. Ore. of *pugetensis* is most pronounced from late Sep to early Oct, again coinciding with the passage of *gambelii*. Breeding *oriantha* arrive mid-May and begin laying from late May to mid-Jun. Hatching begins in mid-Jun and fledging in late Jun. Birds depart the breeding grounds by mid-Sep. Migrant arrival (mostly *gambelii*) in e. Ore. begins in late Mar and peaks in mid-Apr. Autumn migration at Malheur NWR occurs from 15 Aug to 13 Nov, peaking from late Sep until early Oct.

Golden-crowned Sparrow *Zonotrichia atricapilla*
Abundant migrant in w. Ore.; less common farther e. Abundant in winter throughout the Willamette V. and locally wherever habitat permits in the Coast Range, lower elevation w. Cascades, along the outer coast, and in valleys of interior sw. Ore. Uncommon in winter (but numbers vary from yr to yr) in lowlands along the Deschutes R. drainage and in the Klamath Basin, occasional e. to Umatilla Co. and c. Lake Co., and rare to occasional in the valleys of the Blue Mtns. s. to n. Malheur Co.

Rare elsewhere in the Great Basin and Owyhee Uplands in winter.

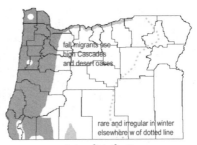

winter distribution

In fall, outriders occasionally appear in late Aug and reach even s. Ore. by mid-Sep. More typical movements bring birds to mountain ridges of w. Ore. in early Sep, and the species can be locally abundant through early Oct. The early surge of montane migrants appears to be mostly hatch-yr birds. Fewer birds move through e. Ore. The earliest fall report at Malheur NWR is 6 Sep with a peak between 20 Sept and 5 Oct. Spring movements are more extended. In the w. Cascades, earliest arrival 14 Apr and a latest departure of 17 May. Movements peak in the w. Cascades and Coast Range normally in Apr. On the e. side, the highest number recorded at Malheur NWR was 20 on 24 Apr 1940, but single birds or groups of a few are the norm. The earliest spring arrival at the refuge is 19 Mar but the average is 2 May, with a peak between 5 and 12 May. Individuals straggle into early summer fairly often. The latest date known from the state is 19 Jun 1990. There are other records of very late migrants including 13 Jun 1982 at Cape Arago.

Dark-eyed Junco *Junco hyemalis*

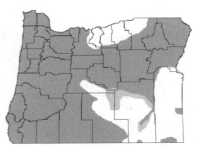

Breeds statewide (dark-hooded "Oregon Junco") except in open and very dry habitats. Winters statewide. "Gray-headed Junco," mostly pale gray with a reddish back, is a rare irregular breeder in the Trout Cr. and Ore. Canyon Mtns. The mostly gray "Slate-colored Junco" is observed regularly during winter in small numbers throughout the state; regular in ne. Ore. Individual *J. h. mearnsi* ("Pink-sided Junco") are occasionally reported, often erroneously. There is a single record of a "White-winged Junco" (*J. h. aikeni*) photographed in Bend, Deschutes Co., on Feb 26 1987. Spring movements are not conspicuous; there is a slow decline as local breeders move from farms and cities into forests and n. nesting birds begin to migrate. Spring movement begins in late Feb and reaches its peak 10 Mar to 10 Apr with stragglers through May. Post-breeding dispersals begin in Jul with large flocks often seen, most moving to higher elevations. Most birds remain at higher elevations until fall storms drive them to the lowlands. Individuals and small family groups of local breeders may appear at lowland cities and farmlands during Jul, but it is Sep before transient flocks arrive from the n. and mid-Oct before peak numbers are reached. The earliest "slate-colored" was 16 Sep near Silver L., Lake Co.

*McCown's Longspur *Calcarius mccownii*

vagrant occurrence

Vagrant. Breeds in prairies from sc. Canada, n. Colorado, and w. Nebraska. Vagrants in Ore. are often found in flocks of Lapland Longspurs and Horned Larks.

Five accepted Ore. records:

1. A male was observed along Hwy 20 e. of Burns, Harney Co., on 8 Aug 1976.
2. A male in winter plumage was among a large flock of Lapland Longspurs and Horned Larks at Lower Klamath NWR, Klamath Co., on 31 Jan 1981.
3. A male in winter plumage was at Lower Klamath NWR, Klamath Co., 13-31 Jan 1990.
4. A bird in winter plumage was photographed at North Portland, Multnomah Co., from 7 Jan into Mar 2003.
5. One bird was photographed at Lower Klamath NWR, Klamath Co., on 31 Dec 2004.

The following additional records have not been reviewed by the OBRC: 1 was at Malheur NWR, Harney Co., on 24 Nov 1956; 1 was with Lapland Longspurs at Lower Klamath NWR, Klamath Co., on 26 Nov 1986; and up to 6 were there 19 Feb – 4 Mar 2001.

5 records

Lapland Longspur *Calcarius lapponicus*

Along the outer coast, the Lapland Longspur is an uncommon but regular fall migrant, especially at the s. jetty of the Columbia R., where flocks of up to 200 occur. They are irregular on the coast in winter and spring. This longspur is regularly reported in e. Ore., but numbers vary yr to yr. Flocks of up to 500 have been reported in winter in the Klamath Basin. Casual in Umpqua and Rogue valleys, and in the Willamette V. Fall dispersal from breeding grounds begins in mid-Aug. While there are some late Aug records for Lapland Longspurs on the Ore. coast, most arrive there in mid-Sep and can be found reliably through Oct. The majority of individuals using the coastal strip leave by the end of Oct. Spring coastal records are from late Apr and early May, but are distinctly few compared to fall. Summer records include a 10 Jul 1984 report from the s. jetty of the Columbia R. and another for 1 and 8 Jul 1984 at Tillamook Bay. Wintering birds in e. Ore. are present from Nov to Mar, although there is an early fall record of 29 Aug 1996 at Harney L., Malheur NWR, and late spring sightings of 27 May 1994 along the Double O Ranch Rd., Harney Co., and 25 May 1998 at Pole Cr. Res., near Brogan, Malheur Co. In e. Ore. longspurs should be looked for in flocks of Horned Larks and Snow Buntings.

*Smith's Longspur *Calcarius pictus*

Vagrant. Breeds in the arctic tundra from c. and n. Alaska across n. Canada.

Two accepted Ore. records:

1. One was observed at the Siltcoos R. mouth, Lane Co., on 24 Sep 2000.
2. One was photographed at N. Portland, Multnomah Co., on 17 Oct 2003.

*Chestnut-collared Longspur *Calcarius ornatus*

Vagrant. Breeds in the prairies from sc. Canada to n. Colorado and nc. Nebraska.

This species occurs as a casual fall migrant and winter visitor in Ore. The OBRC has accepted 17 records to date, with a number of additional, unreviewed sightings. There are several fall records from c. and sc. Ore., including

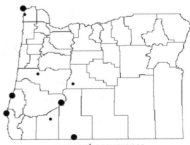

vagrant occurrence

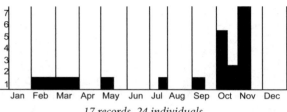

17 records, 24 individuals

birds at Lower Klamath NWR, Klamath Co., the Diamond L. sewage ponds, Douglas Co. (3 records), and Wickiup Res., Deschutes Co. (5 birds on 6 Oct 2003). Several recent fall records, mainly in sw. Ore. Single birds have also been found associated with flocks of Horned Larks in the grasslands of the Willamette V., e.g. 1 bird near the Corvallis airport, Benton Co., 11 Feb – 8 Mar 2006.

*Rustic Bunting *Emberiza rustica*

Vagrant. Breeds across n. Eurasia to ne. Siberia. Rare but regular spring vagrant in the outer Aleutians.

Two accepted Ore. records:

1. A male was observed with other sparrows in downtown Portland, Multnomah Co., on 21 Nov 1975. It was accompanied by a second bird, possibly a female.
2. One bird in winter plumage was photographed in a residential area in Eugene, Lane Co., where it remained 31 Mar – 27 Apr 1994.

Snow Bunting *Plectrophenax nivalis*

winter distribution

Irruptive. Occasional to locally common winter visitor in ne. Ore. Large flocks numbering in the hundreds can be found in Wallowa Co., e.g., 450+ seen near Enterprise in Jan 2001. Occasionally reported elsewhere in e. Ore., in much smaller numbers. Recorded several times near Vale, Malheur Co., and recorded almost annually on or near Malheur NWR. Seen as far s. as Lower Klamath NWR. Rare winter visitor along n. coast. Most often reported in small flocks of up to 30 from the s. jetty of the Columbia R. and at

Bayocean Spit, Tillamook Co. Occasionally winters at Yaquina Bay jetties. There are scattered reports along the coast s. of there, including 1 for Harbor, Curry Co., but it is generally very rare on the s. coast.

Rare and irregular in late fall and winter on bald mtn. tops and alpine meadows in the Cascades and Coast Range, e.g., Marys Peak, Benton Co. Very rare in the Willamette V.: there are several records of small numbers near Halsey and near Lebanon, both Linn Co.; and at Philomath, Benton Co. Extremely rare to interior sw. Ore.; 1 near Talent in 1994 is the only record from the Rogue V. Earliest arrival date for Malheur NWR is 29 Oct, and earliest date on the coast is 1 Oct. Generally first arrives in the state in Nov. Most records from Malheur NWR are in Dec and Mar. In ne. Ore., particularly Wallowa and Grant cos., most easily seen in Dec and Jan when it often forms huge flocks. Most leave in Mar, but seen as late as 7 Apr at Malheur NWR, and 14 Apr on the coast.

*McKay's Bunting *Plectrophenax hyperboreus*
Vagrant. Breeding restricted to a few islands in the Bering Sea. Winters mainly on the w. coast of Alaska.

Two accepted Ore. records:
1. Two birds were photographed among a Snow Bunting flock at the s. jetty of the Columbia R., 23 Feb – 9 Mar 1980.
2. A male was photographed at Depoe Bay, Lincoln Co., on 3 Jan 2004.

Family Cardinalidae

*Pyrrhuloxia *Cardinalis sinuatus*
Vagrant. Breeds from se. Arizona to Texas and Mexico.

One accepted Ore. record of a female photographed at Peoria, Linn Co., on 12 Nov 2008. It remained through Feb 2009.

Rose-breasted Grosbeak *Pheucticus ludovicianus*
Rare migrant and occasional winter visitor throughout the state. The majority of Ore. records have occurred from early Mar through Jul, mostly from mid-May to mid-Jun. Sometimes mates with Black-headed Grosbeaks. Individuals are occasionally found from mid-Sep to mid-Jan, mostly

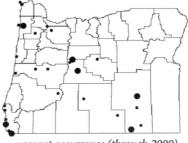

vagrant occurrence (through 2000)

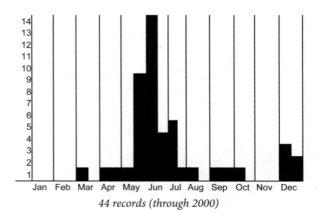

44 records (through 2000)

birds that remained less than 5 days. Casual in fall and winter. All Dec and Jan records are from w. Ore. Most w. Ore. birds have been detected at feeders.

Black-headed Grosbeak *Pheucticus melanocephalus*

COOS	CLAT	LANE	BENT	PORT	CENT	MALH
1 May	17 May	27 Apr	4 May	27 Apr	3 May	11 May

A common to fairly common breeder and common migrant in forested regions throughout the state. Areas where they are relatively scarce include the n. coast, riparian areas of nc. and extreme e. Ore., and extensive conifer forests with little deciduous canopy in the c. Cascades. Generally arrive in w. Ore. in mid- to late Apr. Early date 30 Mar 1980 at Philomath, Benton Co. Arrival e. of the Cascades peaks in mid-May, with first arrivals in early May. Fall migration typically begins in early Aug and lasts through mid-Sep, with a peak in late Aug. Males leave first, sometimes as early as late Jul. Females depart 2-4 wks later, and young of the yr are the last to go, often several wks after the last adult. Mountain-nesting grosbeaks often move to riparian areas at lower elevations in late summer and may spend several wks there before departing. A few stragglers have been recorded w. of the Cascades into mid-Oct, e.g., a bird 14 Oct 1975 at Sauvie I. Casual in winter: there are 6 w. Ore. records for Dec, with at least 2 remaining all winter. In e. Ore., 1 was at Ochoco Res. 23 Dec 1980.

*Blue Grosbeak *Passerina caerulea*

Vagrant. Breeds from c. Cal. and s. Nevada e. across the U.S., n. to S. Dakota, c. Illinois, and s. Pennsylvania. Has bred in se. Ore. at least once.

Seven accepted Ore. records:

1. A female-plumaged bird was photographed at Corvallis, Benton Co., 4-17 Jan 1975.

vagrant occurrence

2. A female-plumaged bird was observed e. of Fern Ridge Res., Lane Co., on 21 Dec 1980.
3. A pair of adults with two juvs. was photographed near Brogan, Malheur Co., from 9 Jul into Aug 1997.
4. A female was observed near Brogan, Malheur Co., on 28 Jun 1998.
5. A female was photographed at Brookings, Curry Co., 20-26 Sep 2005.
6. A female was photographed at Portland, Multnomah Co., on 17 Apr 2006.
7. A female was photographed at the Pistol R., Curry Co., on 8 Sep 2006.

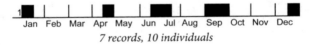

7 records, 10 individuals

Lazuli Bunting *Passerina amoena*

COOS	CLAT	LANE	BENT	PORT	CENT	MALH
1 May		30 Apr	6 May	5 May	4 May	3 May

Common breeder in the Rogue and Umpqua R. valleys and fairly common in the s. Willamette V., becoming less common n. to the Columbia R. In the n., most frequently found where there are dry, brushy, s.-facing aspects, such as in the e. Coast Range. Breed in

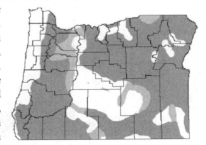

the w. Cascades with decreasing abundance northward, becoming scarce n. of Linn Co. Fairly common in low-elevation dry valleys in Curry Co., becoming uncommon n. through the interior Coquille R. valley. Rare along the immediate coast from n. Coos Co. n. to Cascade Head, Lincoln Co., occasional northward. Uncommon to fairly common along the e. slope of the Cascades through the Klamath Basin and in the mtns. of the sc. and se. portion of the state. Breed in the Blue Mtns, uncommon to locally abundant in far e. counties.

Two early spring records on 15 Mar 1947 and 25 Mar 1977. First spring arrival is usually the last wk of Apr in sw. Ore., generally appears about a wk later e. of the Cascades. Some dispersal to high-elevation meadows occurs after the breeding season. Fall passage commences in early Aug. Most birds depart the state by the end of Aug, with a late date of 9 Sep w. of the Cascades and 3 Oct 2008 (Malheur NWR, ALC) e. of the Cascades. Migrants are common to uncommon throughout the range with some irregularity of numbers noted from yr to yr. No documented winter sightings for the state, but 2 winter reports from c. Douglas Co. and a winter record from Norway Pond, Coos Co. on December 24, 2002 (Rodenkirk 2004).

Indigo Bunting *Passerina cyanea*

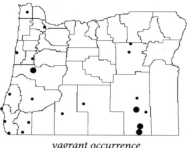

vagrant occurrence

Breeds widely across the e. U.S. and locally in the sw. U.S. in Arizona to se. Cal.

Casual visitor in Ore., with 29 accepted records to date. In addition, there are numerous unreviewed sightings. The majority of Ore. records are of males that occur from mid-Apr to mid-Jun, with territorial males remaining to early

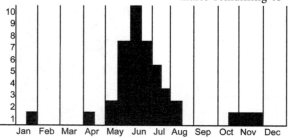

29 records

Aug. Records are scattered across e. and w. Ore. Many of these territorial birds attract female Lazuli Buntings and attempt nesting.

There appears to be no regular fall movement through Ore. Fall and winter records include birds from Eugene, Leaburg, Corvallis, Tillamook, Brookings, and Cape Blanco.

*Painted Bunting *Passerina ciris*

Vagrant. Breeds in 2 disjunct populations in the sc. U.S. (subspecies *pallidior*) and along the s. Atlantic coast (subspecies *ciris*). This colorful species is commonly kept in captivity, and some extralimital records, especially of adult males, may pertain to escaped cage birds.

Three accepted Ore. records:

1. A male in breeding plumage of the w. subspecies *P. c. pallidior* was collected at Malheur NWR, Harney Co., on 2 Jun 1963. The specimen is in the U.S. National Museum.
2. An imm. female was observed at Tumalo S.P., Deschutes Co., on 4 Oct 1981.
3. An adult male was photographed at Idleyld Park, Douglas Co., in late Dec 1999.

Two additional reports have not been reviewed by the OBRC. One bird was reported without details from Frenchglen, Harney Co., on 10 Jun 1989, and a green-plumaged bird was photographed at Harbor, Curry Co., 20-29 Nov 1992.

*Dickcissel *Spiza americana*

Vagrant. Breeds in grasslands across much of the interior e. U.S.

There are 11 accepted Ore. records, the majority between late Oct and mid-Apr in w. Ore. and from the coast. Most of these birds visited feeding stations, and many stayed for an extended period of time. Outside this time period, 1 was seen at

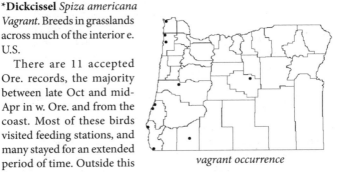

vagrant occurrence

11 records

Port Orford, Curry Co., on 19 Aug 1993; a male in breeding plumage was photographed in the Ochoco NF, Crook Co., on 26 Jul 1995; another male in breeding plumage was photographed at Harbor, Curry Co., 2-5 Jul 2000; and 1 was at Cape Blanco, Curry Co., on 20 Jun 2007.

An additional record of a bird at Malheur NWR HQ and at Malheur Field Station, Harney Co., 9-27 Jun 1996, has not yet been reviewed by the OBRC.

Family Icteridae

Bobolink *Dolichonyx oryzivorus*

Regular, locally common breeder at Malheur NWR; a few to many scattered pairs occur in ne. Ore. w. to c. Grant Co. and s. locally to Jordan V., Malheur Co. Irregular to s. Klamath Co. W. of the Cascades, some rare spring and summer records include singing males in the Willamette V. near Brooks, Marion Co., and Fern Ridge Res., Lane Co., and a pair near Ashland in Jun. Casual visitants on the coast in fall, with reports from Gold Beach, Newport, North Bend, mouth of Columbia R., and near Cape Blanco. The earliest arrival date is 30 Apr 1977 at Malheur NWR. Average arrival date at Malheur NWR is 19 May, one of the latest for any Ore. breeding species. Males arrive about 1 wk before females. All depart Malheur NWR by mid-Sep. Most coastal observations are during Sep and Oct. Late fall records include 1 on 18 Oct 1975 at Yaquina Bay, 2 on 27 Oct 1979 at North Bend, and 2 birds on 10 Dec 1979 at Myrtle Point, Coos. Co.

Red-winged Blackbird *Agelaius phoeniceus*

An abundant breeder in major wetlands and occurs in lesser numbers in small wetlands statewide. They are less common along the immediate coast, but are locally conspicuous immediately back from the coast in freshwater marshes. Redwings summer in meadows of major mtn. ranges and intervening valleys from the Cascades e., and in ne. and extreme se. Ore. The winter distribution of the redwing is reduced from summer range in areas where water freezes. Coastal sites and w. Ore. valleys support thousands in winter; as do low-elevation areas of ec. Ore., such as Boardman, Pendleton, and Hermiston areas. Limited numbers remain in major inland basins, e.g., Klamath, Summer L., and Harney. Displaying males have been observed occupying territories in early Mar. They gather in large, sexually separate flocks in agricultural fields such as cut and uncut grain, cut alfalfa, and feedlots, Jul-Sep; flocks decrease in e. Ore. late Sep and Oct, reducing to smaller numbers during winter.

Tricolored Blackbird *Agelaius tricolor*

Tricolored Blackbird breeding colonies are scattered and intermittent at specific locations, though sites used during consecutive yrs may be in the same general area. The tricolored breeds most consistently in s. Klamath Co. and c. Jackson Co. Since the 1960s, small colonies and summering  residents have been found in the Willamette V. in the Columbia R. bottomlands, n. Portland, and Ankeny NWR near Salem. Very small local colonies were discovered in the 1980s in e. Ore. near Stanfield, Umatilla Co.; Bullgate unit, Summer L., Lake Co.; Wheeler Co., where unknown prior to 1989; Wasco Co.; Crook Co.; and Deschutes Co. In the 2000s a colony appeared at Ford's Pond near Sutherlin, Douglas Co. (Ron Maertz, p.c.).

Tricoloreds disperse from breeding areas in Jul. In late summer and early fall, occasionally reported at other sites in the w. interior valleys; in Aug 2005 several were at Fern Ridge Res. (ALC). Most are thought to retreat s. to Cal. in winter, while some remain in Ore., mainly in the Rogue V. and Klamath Basin. Tricoloreds are uncommon to rare in fall and winter in e. Ore. (away from the Klamath basin, where uncommon) including Prineville, Crook Co.; Powell Butte, Deschutes Co.; Summer L. and Paisley, Lake Co.; and Jefferson Co. Winter populations of tricoloreds increase Feb-Mar in Klamath, Jackson, Deschutes, and Crook cos., with the largest concentrations noted in Apr.

Western Meadowlark *Sturnella neglecta*

The Western Meadowlark breeds in scattered locations along the coast, in w. Ore. valleys, and throughout desert shrub-steppe, grassland, and agricultural areas of e. Ore. In w. Ore., it is most common as a breeding species in the Rogue V., and common to uncommon in the Umpqua V. Now a rare breeding species in the n. Willamette V., uncommon in the c. and s. Willamette V., but locally common in the s.

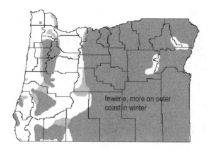

Willamette V. Small breeding populations also occur in a few s.-coastal valleys and headlands in Coos Co. They have been reported to breed in Lincoln Co. on the c. coast, but are not a breeding species on the n. coast. In e. Ore., meadowlarks enjoy a ubiquitous breeding distribution throughout unforested habitat up to 6,000 ft, and they are one of the most common breeding species in all habitat types in shrub-steppe country.

Migrants are seen both spring and fall throughout the breeding and wintering range, and a few birds stop over in open, grassy areas in the Cascades. In w. Ore. valleys and along the coast, wintering flocks increase in size and number in late Feb and throughout Mar during early northward migration. Flocks break up by late Mar, and there is a pulse of migratory movement in early Apr. In e. Ore., migrants first arrive in late Feb and most are on territories by Apr. At Malheur NWR, the earliest spring arrival has been 6 Feb, with the average arrival 27 Feb, peak of passage 10-25 Mar.

Fall migrants along the coast begin to appear in dunes and farm fields in late Aug and early Sep. In the w. valleys, flocks increase in size from Aug through Oct, probably due to arrival of n. migrants. At Malheur NWR, autumn migrants arrive in early Aug and the peak of migration is 20 Aug-20 Sep. A few linger into Oct and Nov there, with occasional wintering birds. Wintering populations in w. Ore. are generally higher than breeding populations. The highest wintering concentration in the state is in the Rogue Vy. Meadowlarks also winter in small flocks along the entire coast. Populations are reduced in winter in e. Ore., suggesting some birds migrate, but small wintering flocks at low elevations are not uncommon.

Yellow-headed Blackbird *Xanthocephalus xanthocephalus*

COOS	CLAT	LANE	BENT	PORT	CENT	MALH
		3 Apr	21 Apr	16 Apr	10 Apr	27 Mar

Abundant spring and summer resident in marshes of large alkaline lakes and wetlands in se. Ore., most notably the Klamath L. and Summer L., Malheur L., and Harney L. basins. Local and uncommon on smaller bodies of water, marshes, and flooded areas e. of the Cascade crest. Increasingly rare n. to the Columbia R., except in Morrow and Umatilla cos., where

it is locally common. Occurs
at elevations up to 5,000
ft in marshes of mountain
lakes just e. of the Cascades
crest (e.g., Davis L.). Local
and uncommon spring
and summer resident at
Fern Ridge Res., Lane Co.
(common there in some
yrs); irregular local breeder
elsewhere in the Willamette
V., at Sauvie I., and in the Rogue V.

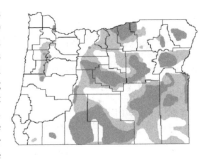

Adult males begin to arrive on breeding grounds from mid-Mar
to early Apr. In Jul, nesting areas are abandoned and they gather in
large groups in the densest stands of marsh vegetation, emerging to
forage in the morning and evening in surrounding agricultural lands.
In Aug, after completion of molt, they form large foraging flocks with
other blackbird species, roaming widely through pastures, cultivated
fields, barnyards, roadsides and even small town streets seeking food.
Southward migration may begin as early as Jul and by late Sep nearly all
have left the state, with only a few remaining to winter. Rare migrant in
the sw. Cascades and along the coast. Rare in winter in Klamath Basin,
Summer L., and other lowland areas e. of the Cascades. Irregular in
winter w. of the Cascades.

*Rusty Blackbird *Euphagus carolinus*
Vagrant. Breeds from n.
Alaska across Canada to n.
New York and Maine.
   Eight accepted Ore.
records:
1. A male was collected at
   Tillamook, Tillamook
   Co., on 20 Mar 1959.
   The specimen is in the
   Ore. State U. collection.
2. One male in fall
   plumage was observed
   along Perrydale Road, Polk Co., on 13 Nov 1977.

vagrant occurrence

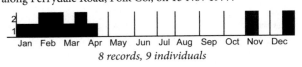

8 records, 9 individuals

3. A male was photographed at Roseburg, Douglas Co., on 24 Jan 1981.
4. A female in winter plumage was photographed at Sauvie I., Multnomah Co., 14 Feb – 3 Apr 1987.
5. Two winter-plumaged females were photographed at Sauvie I., Multnomah Co., 17-23 Dec 1987.
6. An adult male was observed on Sauvie I., Multnomah Co., 31 Dec 1993 – 11 Jan 1994.
7. A winter-plumaged female was photographed at Gold Beach, Curry Co., 2-18 Feb 2001.
8. An adult female was photographed at McNary Dam, Umatilla Co., 8-9 Nov 2003.

There are several additional records that have not been reviewed by the OBRC, including single birds near Enterprise, Wallowa Co., in Jan 2005 and Nov 2007.

Brewer's Blackbird *Euphagus cyanocephalus*

Common permanent resident along coast, concentrates in winter. W. of the Cascades, common to abundant in inland valleys. Within the Cascades, migrant and summer resident in meadows and at human settlements. E. of the Cascades, abundant summer resident and uncommon winter resident. Nests from sea level to above 6,000 ft elevation. From late summer through winter may be found in mixed flocks with starlings and other blackbirds numbering in thousands in agricultural areas w. of the Cascades and in Klamath Basin; uncommon in winter in other agricultural areas e. of the Cascades. Uncommon in winter in se. Ore. concentrates. Common spring transient throughout the state.

Common migrant throughout state late Feb to May. Breeders return to Malheur NWR around 15 Mar (earliest 3 Feb; average 10 Mar), reaching abundant numbers by 20 Mar. After breeding is complete, usually in Aug, family groups form foraging flocks with other blackbirds and starlings. Numbers most abundant in Sep, by 10 Nov only winter residents remain. Winter flocks in e. Ore. appear to be composed primarily of males.

*Common Grackle *Quiscalus quiscula*

Vagrant. Breeds widely across the e. U.S. and Canada; recently expanded its range westward and has bred in Idaho, e. Wash., and Nevada.

Casual visitor to Ore., with 27 accepted records to date. Up to 5 reports are now received annually from se. Ore., mostly from mid-Apr to late Oct. Most records involve single birds, but 4 individuals were at Colony Cr., Harney Co., on 20 May 2002. Records elsewhere in the state include a male photographed displaying unsuccessfully to female Brewer's

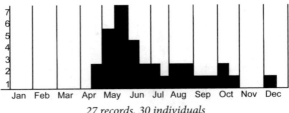

27 records, 30 individuals

Blackbirds at Veneta, Lane Co., 1 May – 19 Jun 1987; 2 individuals photographed at Port Orford, Curry Co., 6 Jun – 14 Sep 1993; 1 at Springfield, Lane Co., on 21 April 1994; a male at Brookings, Curry Co., on 17 Apr 1994; 1 at Denman Sta. W A, Jackson Co., on 3 Oct 1994; an adult male photographed at Toketee

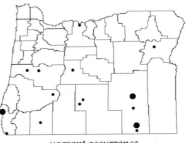

vagrant occurrence

Ranger Station, Douglas Co., 31 Jul – 18 Aug 1996; a male photographed near Tumalo, Deschutes Co., 7 Dec 1996 – late Feb 1997; and an adult male at The Dalles, Wasco Co., on 2 Jun 2000.

Great-tailed Grackle *Quiscalus mexicanus*

Rare but increasing visitor and occasional breeder in Ore. Since 1980, the species has been observed almost annually in Harney Co., usually in numbers less than 5. The first verified nesting record came in 1994 when a pair successfully fledged young near the Malheur NWR HQ. Most Harney Co. records occur from early Apr

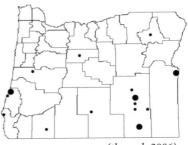

vagrant occurrence (through 2006)

to late Oct. Single birds were noted near Malheur NWR HQ on 23 Dec 1996 and 23 Feb 1997. Away from Harney Co., at least 20 individuals have appeared statewide, usually as singles but sometimes in very small flocks.

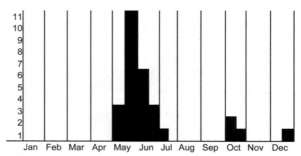

Great-tailed Grackle: 23 records, 33 individuals
(through 2006)

Brown-headed Cowbird *Molothrus ater*

COOS	CLAT	LANE	BENT	PORT	CENT	MALH
1 Apr		7 Apr		8 Apr	6 Apr	24 Apr

Common migrant and breeder in open habitats and woodland edges in all parts of the state. Most abundant in agricultural land, sagebrush and juniper steppe, coastal scrub, riparian zones, and suburban areas. Less frequently found, but present, around larger lakes, meadows, and resort areas of the Cascades. Infrequent in clearcuts among extensive conifer forests in the w. Cascades and Coast Range. Wintering cowbirds, which closely associate with other blackbirds, are now regular, but quite local in any numbers, in the w. interior valleys.

Cowbirds have a fairly conspicuous arrival in the Willamette V. in late Mar and early Apr. Numbers jump in late Apr, at which time breeding displays begin. In e. Ore., at Malheur NWR, the cowbird arrives in late Apr or early May (earliest 4 Apr 1982, average 26 Apr), and is most common mid- to late May. The top two hosts are the Yellow Warbler and Song Sparrow. Additional Ore. species among the top 17 hosts include Chipping Sparrow, Spotted Towhee, Common Yellowthroat, Yellow-breasted Chat, Red-winged Blackbird, and Willow Flycatcher.

In early Jul at Malheur NWR adults begin congregating and are moving southward by mid-Jul. In early Jul, juvs. become apparent. After leaving their foster parent, they regularly join other young cowbirds, forming small single-species flocks. Some birds remain among large flocks of blackbirds, but by Oct the majority of birds have left the state. Wintering flocks of as many as 300 have been recorded in the Willamette and Rogue valleys, but singles and smaller groups are more regular.

> I.D. Note: The identification of recently fledged birds is often problematic. Appearing alone, sometimes in unlikely locations such as coastal headlands, these tawny, streaky birds wander about on the ground behaving as if they were some misplaced vagrant sparrow or finch. Most juvs. complete a pre-basic molt by Aug and take on a more cowbird-like appearance.

*Orchard Oriole *Icterus spurius*

Vagrant. Breeds from sc. Canada across much of the e. U.S.

Seven accepted Ore. records:

1. An imm. was photographed at S. Beach, Newport, Lincoln Co., on 27 Sep 1981.

vagrant occurrence

2. A female was photographed at Toketee Ranger Station, Douglas Co., 8-10 May 1988.
3. A female was photographed at Brookings, Curry Co., 12 Nov – 12 Dec 1990.
4. A male was photographed at Fields, Harney Co., 4-7 Jun 1991.
5. A male in first spring plumage was at Brookings, Curry Co., on 7 Apr 1997.
6. An adult male was at Roseburg, Douglas Co., on 4 Apr 2001.
7. A male and female in winter plumage were photographed at Harbor, Curry Co., 15 Dec 2001 – 3 Feb 2002.

In addition, an imm. was at S. Beach, Lincoln Co., 13-16 Oct 2001. This record has not been reviewed by the OBRC.

8 records

*Hooded Oriole *Icterus cucullatus*

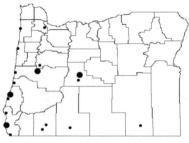

vagrant occurrence

Vagrant. Breeds in the sw. from nc. Cal. across Arizona to s. Texas.

Casual visitor to Ore., with 23 accepted and several unreviewed records. Irregular in the spring from mid-Apr to early Jun, and a rare winter visitant from late Nov to mid-Apr. All wintering records are from w. Ore. A pair remained at Hunter Cr., Curry Co., through Jun 1987, indicating a possible nesting attempt. Another was at Talent, Jackson Co., through the summer of 2001. One was observed at Coos Bay, Coos Co., 31 Aug 1991. Most Ore. records are of birds visiting hummingbird feeders. Records in c. Ore. include a male at Klamath Falls, Klamath Co., on 2-3 May 1987; an adult male at the High Desert Museum in Bend, Deschutes Co., on 17 Apr 1988; and single males in Bend on 2 May 1995 and 2 May 1996. The sole record from se. Ore. was of an adult male photographed at Fields, Harney Co., on 17 Apr 2002.

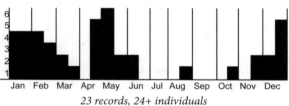

23 records, 24+ individuals

*Streak-backed Oriole *Icterus pustulatus*

Vagrant. Resident breeder in Mexico from Sonora s. to Nayarit. The species is casual n. to se. Arizona (where breeding has occurred) and a rare vagrant to se. Cal. The unprecedented Ore. record constituted by far the northernmost occurrence of this species; since then, there have been 2 other extralimital records in Wisconsin in Jan 1998 and in Colorado in Dec 2007.

One accepted Ore. record of a male photographed feeding at sapsucker wells at Malheur NWR HQ, Harney Co., 28 Sep – 1 Oct 1993.

Bullock's Oriole *Icterus bullockii*

COOS	CLAT	LANE	BENT	PORT	CENT	MALH
1 May		25 Apr	5 May	26 Apr	5 May	5 May

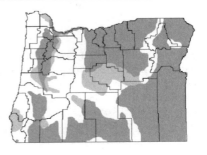

Rare to fairly common breeder, especially along major rivers and around farmsteads. Most widespread in sw. and ne. Ore. Common in Umpqua V. Uncommon in the s. Willamette V., to Linn Co.; rare but regular in Benton Co., with only 2 or 3 nests reported annually. Tendency to nest along the Ore. coast seems to vary from yr to yr; more regular on the s. coast. Generally rare or absent from higher elevations of Coast Range and Cascades. Widespread and uncommon to locally common in lowland riparian areas and in deciduous trees at farmsteads in e. Ore. In most of w. Ore., migrants or prospective breeders arrive mid- to late Apr, earliest 11 Apr in Benton Co., 9 May in Linn Co. Presumed early migrants have been seen as early as 29 Mar in Medford. In e. Ore., birds arrive about a wk later, and numbers peak around mid-May. Earliest arrival is Apr 25 and latest May 14 in vicinity of Malheur NWR. After young fledge, adult males become solitary. In the fall, migrants are most often reported during the latter half of Aug, with scattered reports until mid-Sep. As of 1994, there were 13 winter records; only 2 from e. of the Cascades.

*Baltimore Oriole *Icterus galbula*

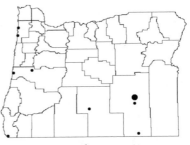

vagrant occurrence

Vagrant. Breeds from c. Alberta across se. Canada and through much of the se. U.S. away from the Gulf coast.

Casual spring migrant and very rare fall and winter visitor in Ore., with 12 accepted records to date and a number of additional unsubmitted sightings. The majority of records occur between mid-May and mid-Jun, mostly e. of the Cascades. Records from w. Ore. include single adult males photographed on the Bayocean Spit,

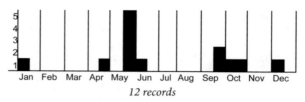

12 records

Tillamook Co., on 26 Oct 1974 and 16 Sep 1997; a singing male at Fern Ridge Res., Lane Co., 27 May – 5 Jun 1986; an imm. male photographed at Brookings, Curry Co., 29 Nov 1991 – 7 Mar 1992; an adult male at Florence, Lane Co., in Jan 2003; and a male at Tierra Del Mar, Tillamook Co., on 24 Apr 2005. Fall records in e. Ore. include an imm. that was photographed at Malheur NWR, Harney Co., on 16 Sep 1997 and a subadult male at Summer L., Lake Co., on 15 Oct 1998.

*Scott's Oriole *Icterus parisorum*
Vagrant. Breeds in arid, open country in the sw. U.S., from s. Idaho and sw Wyoming to sc. Cal. and sw. Texas.
    Two accepted Ore. records:
1. An adult female was observed at Fields, Harney Co., 4-8 Jun 1991.
2. A subadult bird was photographed at Mt. Vernon and John Day, Grant Co., 18 Apr – 18 May 1999.

Family Fringillidae
Subfamily Fringillinae

*Brambling *Fringilla montifringilla*

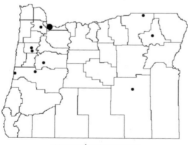

vagrant occurrence

Vagrant. Breeds across n. Eurasia to Siberia. Regular migrant in the w. Aleutians (where a pair nested on Attu in 1997), casual in the Bering Sea and farther s. in Alaska.
    There are 11 accepted Ore. records, ranging from late Oct to mid-Apr. The majority of records came from w. Ore. (Willamette V. between Portland and Eugene). In addition, there is 1 coastal record of a male photographed at Florence, Lane Co., 25-31 Oct 1990; and 3 records from e. Ore. (at La Grande, Union Co.; Umapine, Umatilla Co.; and Burns, Harney Co.).
    All Ore. records were at residential feeding stations, and several birds remained for an extended period of time.

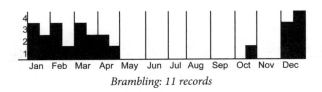

Brambling: 11 records

Subfamily Carduelinae

Gray-crowned Rosy-Finch *Leucosticte tephrocotis*
See *BOGR* for complex taxonomy. Six subspecies, 2 breed in Ore., *L. t. littoralis* and *L. t. wallowa,* the latter being considerably darker. In the Cascades, *L. t. littoralis* breeds at least occasionally on Mt. Hood, Mt. Jefferson, Three-fingered Jack, the Three Sisters, and at Crater L. It is also found but not confirmed nesting on Mt. McLoughlin, and suspected on Mt. Washington and Mt. Thielsen. It may nest occasionally on Steens Mtn., where Black Rosy Finch is the usual breeder. Rare but regular on other rocky mtn. peaks statewide. Late dates of birds in the vicinity of breeding grounds include 25 Aug at Crater L.; 30 Aug on Mt. McLoughlin; and 17 Sep in the Wallowas. In fall and winter, Gray-crowned Rosy-Finches have been found almost annually in the Coast Range on top of Marys Peak, Benton Co., since 1974. Very rare elsewhere in the Coast Range and Willamette V.

In winter, *littoralis* has been found in most of the e. third of Ore. *L. t. wallowa* irregularly winters in ne. Ore. This subspecies is often found mixed in with the more common *littoralis*. In ne. Ore., rosy-finches are a rare to locally abundant migrant and winter visitant, their status being highly irregular. Large numbers are often seen just outside Union and Enterprise, and flocks of 100+ are commonly reported near Baker. Occasional and widespread elsewhere in e. Ore. in winter. Autumn arrival on the wintering grounds is consistently in a 3-wk period in late Oct to mid-Nov, early Nov being the average. Similarly, there is a consistent departure from the wintering grounds typically in the last two wks of Mar, principally the last wk. There are very few post-Mar records at Ore. wintering grounds: e.g., 50 near Ironside, n. Malheur Co., 12 Apr 1987; 1 at Eugene 22 Apr 1974; and singles at Marys Peak, Benton Co., 16 Apr 1989 and 14 May 1995.

Black Rosy-Finch *Leucosticte atrata*
Breeds on Steens Mtn. May breed at least occasionally in the Wallowa Mtns., but not proven. Winter distribution is poorly known, but birds can be found on the lower e. side of Steens Mtn. and in the Alvord Desert in winter; rarely in c. Wallowa Co. Movements in Ore. essentially unknown; birds may not return to breeding grounds until later in spring

or early summer when snow levels allow. Birds are thought to move downslope from Steens Mtn. in fall and return in spring, but more study of this movement is needed. The species is often found in Sep along higher Steens Mtn. ridges, with flocks of 80, 50, and up to 150 the largest reported. There is a single spring record away from Steens Mtn. One was with 4 Gray-crowned Rosy-Finches along Hwy 140 west of Doherty Rim, Lake Co. on 1 Apr 1997, which is also the westernmost report for Ore.

Pine Grosbeak *Pinicola enucleator*
Uncommon to rare local breeder in the Wallowa Mtns. Irregular in the Blue Mtns in summer w. to c. Umatilla and c. Grant Cos. Rare but widespread in the high Cascades at any season. Rare to uncommon in winter, mainly in ne. Ore. but in some yrs rare as far w. as the n. coast and c. Coast Range. Rare in winter s. to Malheur NWR, Hart Mtn., and s. Deschutes Co.

Purple Finch *Carpodacus purpureus*

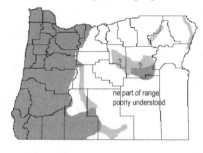

Breeds in forested areas throughout w. Ore. and locally in c. Ore.; rare breeder to ne. Ore. Nests at lower elevations of s. Cascades, rare at higher elevations; generally below 4,000 ft in Klamath Mtns. while nesting. Uncommon to locally fairly common resident in Klamath Basin. Rare to locally fairly common resident on the e. slope of the Cascades and local transient and winter visitant elsewhere in e. Ore. Rare to uncommon summer resident in ne. Ore. and Blue Mtns. above 6,000 ft. Fairly common to common transient, summer resident and winter visitant on the w. slope of the Cascades and westward. Rare transient in se. Ore.

W. of the Cascades, the Purple Finch mainly breeds in moderately moist, open or semi-open conifer forests and edge habitat at low to mid-elevations and coastal shore pine. E. of the Cascades found in ponderosa pine-aspen and mature ponderosa pine; open forests of ponderosa pine, mixed conifer (Douglas-fir, grand fir, western larch), and riparian and forest edge in the Blue Mtns. Winter numbers appear erratic; Purple Finches may be common one yr, rare the next, likely due to food availability. Spring migratory flocks frequent w. Ore. feeders from Feb into Apr (peak varies annually).

I.D. Notes: Confusion (especially of females) with Cassin's Finch is possible, especially e. of the Cascade summit. Standard field guides are sufficient, but note that both females can have some streaking on undertail coverts. The soft "vireo song" commonly causes confusion with the song of the Cassin's Vireo. The "tip" note of flyover birds can be confused with that of Red Crossbill. Red Crossbill typically issues a series of mostly grouped notes, often 2-3 "kips" separated by short gaps or stray single notes, while the finch generally issues a series of single notes separated by longer gaps.

Cassin's Finch *Carpodacus cassinii*

Fairly common to common summer resident from the Cascade summit eastward throughout all mountainous and forested regions of e. Ore. Very uncommon resident at higher elevations of Siskiyou Mtns. in Josephine Co. Breeds primarily in open, mature coniferous forests of lodgepole and ponderosa 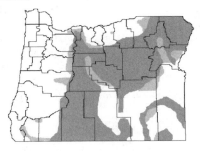 pine, but also quaking aspen, subalpine fir, grand fir, and juniper steppe or woodlands. Occupies burned forest as well. Forms small flocks in late summer and typically stays in groups nearly yr-round except for the actual nesting period. An altitudinal migrant. Most high-elevation breeders move downslope to lower elevations or into the valleys in fall, though some individuals can still be found in normal breeding areas through fall and winter. In winter, found through most of breeding range and an uncommon transient and winter visitor to lower elevations. In w. Ore., very rare winter visitor, often at feeders, w. to the e. edge of Coast Range, especially from Eugene southward.

Note: This finch of montane pine and aspen forests is a surprisingly talented mimic, often incorporating songs and calls of the Mountain Chickadee, American Robin, Western Tanager, White-breasted Nuthatch, and Townsend's Solitaire into its own song. Because first-yr males and females are identical, it is sometimes incorrectly stated that females sing.

House Finch *Carpodacus mexicanus*

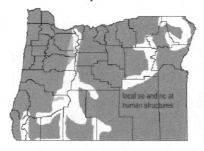

Fairly common to locally common resident in lowlands, urban, rural, and agricultural areas throughout Ore. House Finches are distinctly gregarious, especially in winter, when flocks can be >50 birds. Juvs. form large foraging flocks in late summer. Winter movement occurs at some cold locations; some individuals remain, while many may relocate to other nearby areas.

> Note: in late summer and fall, flocks of House Finches, often only those in brown plumage (perhaps mainly juvs.), occur on the outer coast swooping through dune grass as though they were longspurs or larks. This can cause temporary observer confusion.

Red Crossbill *Loxia curvirostra*

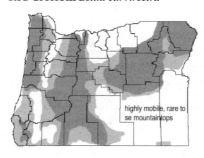

See BOGR for extensive taxonomic discussion. A nomadic and uncommon to common breeder in coastal and montane coniferous forests across Ore., but is irregularly detected wherever coniferous stands occur. Recent research indicates that populations may consist of multiple subspecies and possibly several species distinguished primarily by bill shape and calls. Of the 5 call types in Ore.:

Type 2 (=*bendirei* or *pusilla*) prefers mainly ponderosa and lodgepole pine areas of e. Ore., with vocal recordings near Burns and Bend;

Type 3 (=*minor*) prefers Sitka spruce and western hemlock of the Coast Ranges;

Type 4 (=*neogaea*) frequents Douglas-fir mainly in w. Ore., but also statewide;

Type 5 (=*bendirei* or *pusilla*) prefers lodgepole pine in higher elevation e. Ore. montane forest;

Type 7 (=*bendirei* or *pusilla*) prefers Engelmann spruce/lodgepole
pine in the same geographic range as Type 5.
Seed availability is a critical factor influencing breeding. If seed
conditions are favorable, may nest late Dec to late Aug, and may have
as many as 4 broods annually.

White-winged Crossbill *Loxia leucoptera*
Very rare and erratic visitor. Successful breeding not yet confirmed in
Ore. Only during yrs of major incursions can this species be expected
in numbers in Ore. May occur at any time of yr in ne. Ore., especially in
Wallowa Co., but also reported from John Day area, Grant Co.; Langdon
L. area, Umatilla Co.; and Anthony Ls., nw. Baker Co. Also occurs in
higher elevations in the Cascades in any season. Most reports from
Cascades come from c. portion along the crest. Seen as far s. as Mt. Bailey
area, Douglas Co., and n. to Mt. Hood (Adrian Hinkle p.c.). Throughout
range, capable of breeding at any time of yr, whenever adequate cone
crop is available. In 1977 a small flock summered near Enterprise and
attempted unsuccessfully to nest. Does not regularly migrate, though
often travels long distances in large flocks tracking cone crops. In ne. Ore.,
seen most often Oct-Mar but also recorded in summer; in c. Cascades,
most likely in summer or fall.

Common Redpoll *Carduelis flammea*
Uncommon to rare, irregular
winter visitant, mainly
in lowlands of the e. Blue
Mtn. ecoregion. In peak yrs
this species can be locally
common in Union, Wallowa,
and Baker cos. but in other
yrs it is essentially absent.
Irregular in Umatilla Co.,
rare in Grant Co. Rare and
irregular south to Malheur
NWR and vicinity. Very rare

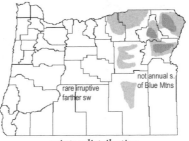

winter distribution

w. to Deschutes and Jefferson cos. Very rare to the Klamath Basin. Very
rare to w. Ore., with records as far sw. as Eugene, Florence, Coos Bay, and
Medford. Generally arrives in late Nov or early Dec (when it occurs at all)
and remains only through Feb. There are few spring records. The latest
records include 1 at Nehalem sewage ponds 12 May 1991. Even later and
remarkable because of the simultaneous occurrence were single birds
near Dallas and at Canyon Cr., Grant Co., both on 24 May 1996. One

extremely odd record was of 2 photographed on 11 Jul 2002 at a feeder near Bandon, Coos Co.; the birds were also present the following day.

**Hoary Redpoll *Carduelis hornemanni*
Vagrant. Breeds widely across n. Eurasia and from nw. Alaska to nc. Canada and Greenland. The winter range in N. America extends from s. British Columbia along the Canadian border to n. New England. Single individuals frequently stray farther s. and are usually found in flocks of Common Redpolls.
   Two accepted Ore. records:
1. Up to 3 birds were photographed among a Common Redpoll flock at Umapine, Umatilla Co., 21 Jan – 6 Feb 1986.
2. One was observed among a Common Redpoll flock 9 mi nw. of Bates, Grant Co., on 19 Jan 1990.
This species is very similar to the Common Redpoll and cannot always be safely separated in the field. Reports should be accompanied by good photographs, whenever possible.

Pine Siskin *Carduelis pinus*
Found in evergreen forests statewide; also to lowlands in winter. Gregarious throughout the yr. Often join flocks to forage even during the nesting period. Flocks may remain in lowland valleys away from nesting habitat until mid-Jun. Following breeding, adults and hatch-yr birds join into flocks and may wander widely. Flocks in fall and winter may number in the thousands in the w. Cascades. Able to withstand severe winter weather conditions. Nomadic; numbers at any given site in Ore. vary widely from yr to yr. Winter flocks can number in the hundreds in an area one yr and be absent the next.

Lesser Goldfinch *Carduelis psaltria*

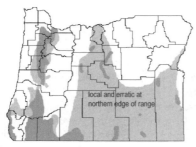

In the n. Willamette V., the Lesser Goldfinch is a fairly common breeder along the w. fringe, less common to the e. Scattered and local in the Portland area. Fairly common from the s. Willamette V. southward through the Umpqua V., reaching greatest abundance in the Rogue V. Uncommon summer resident in some interior valleys of the Coast Range n. to c. Coos Co. Local and uncommon summer resident in Lake, Harney, and Malheur cos., with nesting verified as far n. as Chukar Park CG, Malheur Co., and to Crook Co. Other summer records from Hood River, Wasco, Gilliam, Jefferson, Deschutes, Wheeler, and Grant cos. Fairly common permanent resident in s. Klamath Co., though numbers decline in winter.

Most abundant in winter in the Rogue V. They are common in the s. Willamette V., less common n. to Portland. In some winters, most birds appear to withdraw from the n. and c. Willamette V., and the species can then be hard to find. Occasional on the s. coast, usually absent n. of Coos Co. E. of the Cascades, a common permanent resident only in s. Klamath Co., where numbers decrease somewhat during winter. Winter numbers are erratic around Malheur NWR and the Blitzen V. Early spring arrival at Malheur 8 May, with peak numbers 18-22. Fall numbers peak 15-25 Aug, with a late date of 9 Sep but can be found later in fall in the Blitzen V. and at Fields.

*Lawrence's Goldfinch *Carduelis lawrencei*
Vagrant. Breeds from nc. Cal. to Baja Cal.

Four accepted Ore. records:
1. An adult male was photographed at a feeder in Florence, Lane Co., where it remained from 24 Dec 1991 to 11 Jan 1992.
2. One subadult male was observed at Lower Table Rock, Jackson Co., on 15 May 1997.
3. One was photographed at Goose L., Lake Co., 11-12 August 2007.
4. One was photographed at Winston, Douglas Co., 18-27 September 2007.

In addition, there are several reports that have not yet been reviewed by the OBRC. Single birds were in Medford, Jackson Co., on 20 Apr 1958 and 7 Jun 1967; male visited a feeder near Jacksonville, Jackson Co., from late Dec 1997 to 4 Feb 1998; and a male was photographed at Eagle Point, Jackson Co., on 8 May 2008.

American Goldfinch *Carduelis tristis*
A yr-round resident w. of the Cascades, particularly in the large interior valleys. Very small numbers in the Cascade and Coast Range mtns.; virtually absent there in winter, except at relatively low elevations. Also widespread e. of the Cascades. The species is generally common yr-round, though populations are nomadic in winter, resulting in dramatic fluctuations in local numbers. Remain in flocks longer than other passerines breeding in Ore. Huge flocks (thousands) gather in Apr and May in the Willamette V. The American Goldfinch is one of the last of Ore.'s songbirds to nest each yr. Flocks may be present into early Jun. Egg dates range from 24 May to 18 Aug. Following independence, young

birds gather into flocks, often with adult birds, which may number in the hundreds by early fall. Flocks tend to be nomadic during the winter, moving greater or lesser distances depending on food abundance.

Evening Grosbeak *Coccothraustes vespertinus*

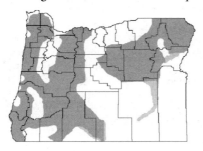

Uncommon to common yr-round resident; highly irruptive. In general, this species spends the summer in mountainous forests statewide. In spring, this grosbeak may be found in significant numbers around towns and cities during large incursions in the interior valleys of w. Ore. Here they are uncommon in fall. Lowland areas in e. Ore. may also see minor spring incursions, and birds can also be found in desert oases during fall and spring. The species is uncommon in spring and occasional in fall at Malheur NWR. Often moves into lowlands throughout the state in colder months, though numbers in the lowlands in winter vary significantly from yr to yr and decade to decade.

Spring incursions into lowlands generally occur from Mar into Jun; typically peaking late Apr and May. In some yrs, incursions in the Willamette V. are enormous, involving thousands of birds sometimes at favored foraging sites within one or two city blocks, and perhaps tens of thousands of birds in individual towns. Earliest spring arrival at Malheur NWR was 4 Apr 1971; usually arrive in May, peaking 15-30 May, and remaining well into Jun. Late migrants and/or non-breeders sometimes reported into Jun in lowlands, but rarely seen in lower elevations after mid-Jul.

Family Passeridae

House Sparrow *Passer domesticus*
Statewide around buildings at human developments of adequate size ranging from scattered farmsteads in remote and rural areas to highly populated areas, where most abundant. Absent to uncommon in the Coast Range and w. Cascades and at most mountain resort areas. Gregarious. Typically occur in small groups of 5-50+ individuals, especially during post-breeding period. Nest construction can begin in Feb.

Addendum

*White-eyed Vireo *Vireo griseus.*
Vagrant. Breeds across the e. U.S. Ore.'s first record was of a singing male photographed at Fields, Harney Co., on 9 Jun 2009. This record has not yet been reviewed by the OBRC.

Sources not included in
Birds of Oregon: A General Reference (2003, 2006)

Carlisle, J., G. Kaltenecker, and R. Brady. 2007. Status of the Broad-winged and Red-shouldered Hawks during fall migration in southwestern Idaho, 1995-2006. *Western Birds* 38(4): 251-60.

Contreras, A. 1998. Birds of Coos County, Oregon. Cape Arago Audubon Society and Oregon Field Ornithologists.

Contreras, A. 2006. Birds of Lane County, Oregon. Oregon State U. Press.

Cox, C., and J. Barry. 2005. The identification, molts and aging of American and Eurasian Wigeons in female-type plumages. *Birding* March-April 2005, 157-64.

Geier, J. 2004. Willamette basin Field Notes: Fall 2003. *Oregon Birds* 30:44-47.

Gillson, G. 2008. Field Separation of Sooty and Short-tailed Shearwaters off the West Coast of North America. Birding 40(2):34.

Gross, W. 2006. North Coast Field Notes. *Oregon Birds* 32:22-25.

Irons, D. 2007a. Field Notes: Fall 2006. *Oregon Birds* 33:18-29.

Irons, D. 2007b. Field Notes: Winter 2006-07. *Oregon Birds* 33:52-62.

Hamilton, R., M. Patten, and R. Erickson. *Rare Birds of California.* Western Field Ornithologists, 2007.

Korpi, R. 2004. Field Notes: Western Oregon, Winter 2002-2003. *Oregon Birds* 29:136-42.

Munson, D., et al. 2004. A Checklist to the Birds of Curry County, Oregon (revised). Kalmiopsis Audubon Society et al.

Unitt, P., K. Messer, and M. Théry. 1996. Taxonomy of the Marsh Wren in Southern California. Proceedings of the San Diego Society of Natural History No. 31.

Voelker, G., and S. Rohwer. 1998. Contrasts in scheduling of molt and migration in Eastern and Western Warbling Vireos. *Auk* 115:142-55.

Checklist to the Pelagic Birds of Oregon

This checklist was composed primarily to show the large potential for pelagic rarities off Oregon. Full day boat trips out 35 miles are likely to find most of the species indicated as Common and Uncommon, as well as a few of the Rare but regular seabirds, in season. The rare and irregular species as well as the very rare species are not expected. Special trips may improve the chances of seeing one of these, but these birds are not assured at any time.

This chart is reprinted here with kind permission of Greg Gillson, The Bird Guide, Inc.

	Jan	Feb	Mar	Apr	May	Jun	Jul	Aug	Sep	Oct	Nov	Dec
Wandering Albatross								●				
Shy Albatross									●●			
Laysan Albatross	━	━	━	–	–	–	–	–	━	━	━	
Black-footed Albatross	━	━	━	━	━	━	━	━	━	━		
Short-tailed Albatross			●●			●	●	–	–	–	–	–
Northern Fulmar	━						━	━	━	━	━	━
Great-winged Petrel (Hyp.)							●					
Juan Fernandez Petrel *					●							
Murphy's Petrel *			–	–	–	–			●●	●		
Mottled Petrel *	–	–	–	–	–		●			–	–	–
Hawaiian Petrel *								●●	●	●		
Cook's Petrel *								●●	●●	●●		
Parkinson's Petrel (Hyp.)										●		
Streaked Shearwater								●●				
Greater Shearwater							●					
Pink-footed Shearwater	–	–	–		━	━	━	━	━	━	–	–
Flesh-footed Shearwater		●		–	–		–	–	━	━		●●
Wedge-tailed Shearwater			●				●			●		
Buller's Shearwater							–	━	━	━		
Sooty Shearwater	–	–			━	━	━	━	━	━	━	━
Short-tailed Shearwater	━			–	–							
Manx Shearwater +												
Black-vented Shearwater +	●	●		●	●			–	–	–	–	–
Wilson's Storm-Petrel					●		●	●			●	
Fork-tailed Storm-Petrel #	–	–	–		━	━	━	━	━	━	━	━
Ringed Storm-Petrel (Hyp.)					●							
Leach's Storm-Petrel *#				–	━	━	━					
Ashy Storm-Petrel (Hyp.)					●			●				
Black Storm-Petrel					●				●			
Red-billed Tropicbird *				●	●		●		●			
Masked Booby							●					

* Found primarily in deep water more than 50 miles from shore.
+ Found primarily within 8 miles of shore.

☐ Absent

☒ Single records of very rare birds

☒ Multiple records of very rare birds

▭ Rare and irregular; single records on <15% of trips

▭ Rare but regular; expected in low numbers on 15-50% of trips

▮ Uncommon; expected in low to good numbers on 50-85% of trips

▮ Common; expected in good numbers on most trips

	Jan	Feb	Mar	Apr	May	Jun	Jul	Aug	Sep	Oct	Nov	Dec
Blue-footed Booby									●			
Brown Booby							●			●		
Red-footed Booby (Hyp.)										●		
Magnificent Frigatebird		●●	●●			●	–	–	–	–		
Red-necked Phalarope					▬	▬	▬	▬				
Red Phalarope	–	–	–				▬	▬	▬	▬		
Sabine's Gull	–	–				▬	▬	▬	▬			
Black-legged Kittiwake			▬	▬								
Red-legged Kittiwake	●●		●●					●				●
Common Tern				–				▬	▬	–		
Arctic Tern			–				▬	▬	▬			
South Polar Skua					–	–	▬	▬	▬	–	–	
Pomarine Jaeger					▬	–	–				▬	
Parasitic Jaeger				–	–		▬	▬	▬	–	–	
Long-tailed Jaeger					▬	▬	▬	▬				
Common Murre #												
Thick-billed Murre	●●		●	●	●		●		●	●		●
Pigeon Guillemot +#				▬	▬	▬	▬	▬				
Long-billed Murrelet +								●●●●	●●	●		
Marbled Murrelet +#												
Kittlitz's Murrelet (Hyp.)					●		●					
Xantus's (*hypoleucus*) Murrelet *							●		–	–		
Xantus's (*scrippsi*) Murrelet *							–	–	▬	▬	–	
Craveri's Murrelet * (Hyp.)							●		●			
Ancient Murrelet	▬			–	–			–	–		▬	
Cassin's Auklet #												
Parakeet Auklet *	–	–	–		–	–			●		●●	–	–	–
Whiskered Auklet (Hyp.)			●									
Rhinoceros Auklet #												
Horned Puffin *		–	–	–	–	–	–	●	●	●●●●●●	●		●
Tufted Puffin #				▬	▬	▬						

\# Breeds in Oregon.

Hyp. Hypothetical. Sight records only; no records yet accepted by Oregon Bird Records Committee.